W9-AJR-919

Data.
Research.
Advocacy.

Copyright ©2019 Islamophobia Studies Center
Copyright ©2019 Islamophobia Rsearch & Documentation Project

Cover Image: Kar sevaks scaling Babri Masjid on December 6, 1992, India Today.

Direct questions about this report to: Islamophobia Studies Center. To obtain copies of this report or to offer comments or feedback, please write to:

info@iphobiacenter.org and include the subject "Islamophobia in India Report."

FAIR USE NOTICE: This report may contain copyrighted material the use of which has not always been specifically authorized by the copyright owner. It is being made available in an effort to advance the understanding of political, human rights, democracy, and social justice issues. It is believed that this constitutes a "fair use" of any such copyrighted material as provided for in Section 107 of the U.S. Copyright Law. In accordance with Title 17 U.S.C. Section 107, the material in this report is distributed without profit to those who have expressed a prior interest in receiving the included information for research and educational purposes. If you wish to use copyrighted material in this report for purposes of your own that go beyond "fair use," you must obtain permission from the copyright owner. The material in this report is provided for educational and informational purposes only, and is not intended to be a substitute for an attorney's consultation. Please consult your own attorney in order to get counsel on your situation. The information in this report does not constitute legal advice.

No part of this publication may be stored in a retrieval system, transmitted or reproduced in any way, including but not limited to, photocopy, photograph and magnetic or other record, without the prior agreement and written approval of the publisher.

Design and layout by Hani David Kharufeh.

Contents

Support the work of the
Islamophobia Studies Center
by donating in one of the
following ways:

Visit: iphobiacenter.org
or
Text GIVEISC to 44321

Froward

Islamophobia in India: Modi, the BJP and the Rising Tide of Hindu Nationalism

about the rising tide of religious ultra-nationalism that utilizes violence and structural othering as a tool of gaining and expanding power.

The targets of religious ultra-nationalism in India have been Muslim, Christian, Sikh and 'lower castes' within India's society. Within the past decade, the level of targeted violence against these religious minorities has intensified, with the arrival of the BJP into national office facilitating its deployment through all structures of the state against demonized and vulnerable groups. This strategy is familiar to observers of the political dynamics in the U.S. and Europe against the backdrop of the rising tide of Islamophobia that has been stoked and deployed by extreme right-wing groups to gain legitimacy and it has been monetized into votes at the ballot box.

To date, there has been no reliable evidence, academic engagements or scholarly reports that documents this rising tide of Islamophobia in the Indian context. This lack of documentation both complicates and hinders the ability of those advocating against and countering Islamophobia. As a result, activists and advocates are often left to speak of individual incidents of violence that undermine the magnitude of the issue as seemingly isolated cases or use of "communal violence" to obfuscate the seriousness of the problem. This case-by-case approach is highly problematic, limiting the ability of advocates to assign responsibility to political elites and point to the deployment of coercive state power utilized against structurally-created marginalized and invisible populations. Ultra-nationalist political elites strategically select their targets and assess their chances of holding or expanding power on its basis. It is urgent that all cases of violence is documented, compiled and highlighted in scholarly research that is grounded in a systematic theoretical basis, ultimately allowing a critique of those responsible based on evidence rooted in a robust research methodology.

This first of its kind report on the status of Islamophobia in India is meant to provide a groundbreaking collection of evidence and provide a reference point for all future work on the subject.

The report was published through the Center for Race and Gender's Islamophobia Research and Documentation Project at the University of California, Berkeley. Our hope at IRDP is that this report will serve as a springboard for a sustained academic engagement and focus on the rise of Islamophobia in India.

The scope of the work involves the following:

1. Development of a scholarly and academic case for examining Islamophobia within the Indian context
2. Creation of a documentation strategy/method/theory for a country that lacks a centralized data collection system for religious-based hate crimes and violence
3. Extraction of a wide and diverse sample of cases to illustrate the pervasive nature of the problem
4. Documentation on political elites use of language or utilization of civil society setting to foment and stoke Islamophobia
5. Examination and documentation of participation of state agencies in systematic otherization and Islamophobia
6. Development of criteria for coding and reporting future cases into the database
7. Undertaking a cursory survey of the media and how it reflects Islamophobic discourses of political elites
8. Commencement of a literature review on existing surveys and what research and work exists presently on India and the rising tide of religious ultra-nationalism to form a bibliography and reading list.

Hatem Bazian
University of California, Berkeley & Co-Founder, Zaytuna College

Key Findings

Mus es distibu saniet as excero quiae essin conet la doluptae venim qui to occuptiatem que optaquid quo qui comnis dolleni mendia con pro temolo totatinctem resequi se essinctem que pla non ne aut es doles et ut ut hici nonsedios doluptus eost que volenet lam sum volupta sunt eostio. Mus ea di ipsam aut libearibus, consequ ibusam conecup tatur? Nequi dis et eum, nihicie ndelit dollace arciet eatem as esciet lam am, verum haria arum qui omnimodignis comnihit pro et omnit abo. Am, sed ex eos velestia cum utem invelit et aut aut volore prae eosa simus elessum qui.

India's Brand of Islamophobia

1. BJP leaders have been implicated in "communal violence" and hate. Further, the BJP has the greatest number of lawmakers in the country with declared cases of hate speech against them. The provision of tickets to those charged with hate speech has been associated with driving the conditions that lead to Islamophobia and politically-stoked violence.

2. Polarizing politics are lucrative at the ballot box where individuals affiliated with stoking 'communal' hate and violence are actually four times more likely to win than others. Our report has documented several Islamophobic statements from leading BJP members from across the political spectrum beginning with Prime Minister Narendra Modi himself.

3. It has been reported that India is experiencing and aggressive form of McCarthyism to silent dissent against the BJP. Media personnel and reporters are being tracked by BJP headed 'war rooms' that gather data on both traditional and new media, rating and categorizing it in relation to its position on the ruling BJP government, which has caused concern for many.

4. Efforts to report on forms of hate including Islamophobia in India are difficult, and have met with website closures, as well as, fostered new and creative forms of reporting such as animated videos around violence upon Muslims and the opening of websites that document hate and violence.

5. In an effort to thwart free speech, specifically speech critical of the BJP led government, journalists, students, attorneys and artists have reported an increase in online smear campaigns at the hands of Hindu nationalists, as well as threats of violence, criminal charges and the use of outdated sedition laws which can lead to life in prison.

6. A 2018 exposé revealed efforts of the BJP party to bring most main media houses in India into their folds offering to pay them to propagate their ultra-nationalist agenda.

7. In 2017 three reporters were murdered and in 2018, four journalists were murdered at the time of report compilation.

The Racialization of Demography

1. A rise in ultra-Hindu nationalism and increased emphasis on the numerical strength of a Hindu population has materialized into propaganda against 'love jihad', anti-conversion laws and the expansion of the ghar vāpasī (returning home) program. All measures restrict the ability for Hindus to convert to other religions, while simultaneously advancing and encouraging the conversion, and more than often forced conversions of other religious groups, to Hinduism.

2. This report explores the recent mobilization of rhetoric and propaganda around 'love jihad', and the impact of these exclusionary principles on Islamophobia in India. Far-right Hindu nationalists have constructed 'love jihad' as an organized conspiracy, whereby Muslim men are aggressively converting vulnerable Hindu women to Islam through trickery and marriage. As explored in this report, there is no proof pointing to the legitimacy of 'love jihad' and rather, has been exploited mere lethal mobilization strategy against love, for political gains in elections.

3. This recent mobilization around 'love jihad' over the last decade is connected to a longstanding and fruitful history of anxieties about Muslims out-growing Hindu populations, which can be traced to as early as 1909. However, the term first emerged in political and public discourse in the year of 2009.

4. Since the inception of the term 'Love jihad' has built traction by exacerbating the existing fears of 'breeding Muslims' set to overtake Hindu population in India. This is complemented by a highly patriarchal nationhood of violence against women, that simultaneously constructs reproductive women's bodies a site of communal anxiety about the future of the Hindu race, in a demographic war against other minorities.

5. The 'love Jihad' myth has been propagated through pamphlets, meetings, debates, rumors and everyday conversations, sustaining 'love jihad' as an active cultural, and ultimately a political issue that has monopolized the everyday representation of inter-religious marriages. Such propaganda around 'love jihad' was falsified through numerous investigations, including in 2009 and 2012.

6. These campaigns have intensified in recent years, whereby Hindu nationalist groups have conducted 'rescue operations' to counter 'love jihad', and reportedly deployed right-wing lawyers to identify and disclose registered cases of inter-religious marriage between Muslim men and Hindu women. Such propaganda has sparked Hindu vigilantes to not only police community members and relationships but also demand legislation to restrict inter-religious marriages altogether.

7. The year of 2014, however, saw orchestrated propaganda campaigns and popular inflammatory and demagogic appeals led by a section of Hindu publicists against 'love jihad' against the supposed 'abductions' and conversions of Hindu women by Muslim men, ranging from allegations of rape and forced marriages, to elopement, love, luring and conversion

8. Cases and events around 'love jihad' in 2017-2018 in particular, signify the shift in electoral politics to the right, reflected in the fortification of propaganda and intensified campaigns against 'love jihad'. Such rhetoric was materialized via educational awareness campaigns warning students

against 'love jihad', political commitment to forming 'Romeo Squads' that fight against 'love jihad', and various attacks against interfaith couples and any individuals suspected of facilitating interfaith marriages.

9. 'Love jihad', anti-conversion laws and ghar vāpasī have heightened Islamophobia and intensified anti-Muslim sentiment across the nation. 'Love jihad', anti-conversion laws and ghar vāpasī campaigns have not only resulted in hostile communal tensions but has also resulted in experiences of structural, as well as everyday discrimination among Muslims in their neighborhoods and daily life.

Politically-stoked Violence and the Geography of Islamophobia

1. This report contextualizes and documents politically-stoked violence against Muslim communities in India. In doing so, the negative impact of such attacks on the general security of Muslims in every day, as well as Muslim spaces is exposed. Documenting various cases of spatialized Islamophobia in 2017 onwards exposes the impacts of politically-stoked mass violence on Muslim residential patterns, internal displacement, and subsequent patterns of ghettoization and segregation. Such negative spatial outcomes are situated as a byproduct of experiences of Islamophobia, which are and sustained through discriminatory policies that further restrict the social and spatial mobility of Muslims in India.

2. Islamophobia is spatialized through 'communal violence,' attacks and contestations over the right for Muslim neighborhoods and places of worship to exist in the Indian national space. Historically, India has suffered various outbreaks of large-scale politically-stoked violence against religious minorities, particularly against Muslims that remain unresolved years later.

3. There is a pronounced geographic pattern where politically-stoked violence occurs, which can be traced in ten states. These states with the highest incidence of communal violence included Uttar Pradesh, Karnataka, Maharashtra, Madhya Pradesh, Bihar, Rajasthan, West Bengal, Jharkhand, Telangana and Assam. Collectively these ten states accounted for 1,972 cases of politically-stoked violence during the period of 2015-2017.

4. Persistent instances of politically-stoked violence against religious minorities have often been incited by politicians or religious leaders, advocating a nationalistic and exclusionary message against non-Hindu minorities. Not only have politicians propagated such violence but have failed to provide justice for the attacks against Muslim bodies and spaces over the last few decades. These instances of violence are thus more likely to occur in existing geographies of violence and potentially spread to other regions if the Modi Administration and state governments continue to fail to punish individuals who engage in violence and incitement to violence against religious minorities.

5. Statistics reveal that Muslims suffer disproportionately from communal violence given the outcomes in comparison to the population overall and in each area, further diminishing the likelihood that Muslims are enacting violence against Hindus, as some have claimed

6. Islamophobia was spatialized from 2017 onwards in a variety of ways. These included incidents of politically-stoked communal violence, the vandalism of Muslim sites, disputes and contentions over land, and the symbolic infiltration of Muslim sites, such as spying on Muslim communities, or the distributing anti-Muslim propaganda in Muslim spaces or neighborhoods to invoke fear and exclusion.

7. In documenting cases from 2017 onwards, it is exemplified that the BJP victory and subsequent implementation of ultra-right-wing nationalist discourse and policies have intensified such attacks against Muslim sites, neighborhoods and places of worship.

8. Most concerning is the direct impact of such violence on patterns of segregation and the ghettoization of Muslims. This decreased social and spatial mobility further limits the ability for Muslims to access the socio-economic opportunities required to participate in national economic growth. This also causes increased housing insecurity and an intensified geographical division of Muslims from the Hindu majority in an increasingly Islamophobic national space.

9. The spatial impacts of Islamophobia inflicted against Muslim sites, spaces and communities has restricted the residential options, choices and preferences of Muslims in India. The actual and perceived threat of violence has resulted in the exclusion of Muslim communities from the national space. This has resulted in the increased ghettoization of Muslims to limited places of security and belonging that enables the survival of these communities an increasingly hostile socio-political environment of Islamophobia.

10. Politically-stoked violence has negative impacts on the spatial and social mobility of Muslims in India. Such reduced mobility results in limited socio-economic opportunities to participate in national economic growth, housing insecurity, and an intensified geographical division of Muslims from the Hindu majority in an increasingly Islamophobic national space.

11. Rohingya refugees that have fled genocide in nearby Myanmar and sought refuge in India are an important group when assessing Islamophobia, spatialization, and mobility of Muslims in India.

12. Rohingya refugees in India encounter hate and discrimination and are vulnerable, living in makeshifts camps on the periphery of society. They are victims of surveillance, violence, razing of their camps and face threats of expulsion which will potentially be deadly.

13. Rohingya Muslims have been created as security threats by Hindu nationalists and media narrative. Descriptions of the Rohingya as "foreigners" who enter the country 'illegally" rather than as "refugees" are political and strategic. BJP leader Yogi Adityanath's vocal support of the 'Muslim ban," which acts as a barrier and virtual border wall, barring people entering the U.S. from seven Muslim predominant nations under the Trump Administration, followed by Adityanath's own election rally statement that similar action is needed to contain terror activities in India, perpetuates the nationalist narrative of Muslims as invaders of India and a threat to Hindu culture, as well as the nation.

14. Polarizing discourse attempts to solidify the link between Rohingya refugees and criminality, militancy and terrorism, potentially removing certain guaranteed protections, clearing the way for discriminatory legislation, policies, and actions toward this vulnerable population. It also makes it a possibility that 40,000 plus people may be imprisoned, deported and possibly ethnically cleansed, under the guise of security threats.

India's Beef Legislation

1. Our report demonstrates an annual increase in beef-related attacks since Prime Minister Modi took office in 2014.

2. Beef bans and cow legislation bifurcate segments of society based on religious difference and are also mobilized to divide India's Muslims and Hindus in the name of 'protecting' Mother Cow (gau mata). The bans and legislation are exclusionary and unjustly target Muslims and Dalits who tend to consume beef as either a religiously lawful meat and/or an inexpensive form of protein. They also target their livelihoods as the beef and dairy trade are mainly dominated by both groups.

3. The passage of restrictive beef legislation in various states are associated with driving the attacks upon Muslims and Dalits by emboldening people to take the law into their own hands enacting violence and death extra-judiciously upon innocent Muslims.

4. Often the beef-related attacks upon Muslims are premeditated and led by ultra-national Hindu groups wielding weapons such as knives, sticks and belts who act as judge and jury.

5. Amnesty International India has drawn a link between increasing cow legislation that predominantly targets Muslims and the growing trend of Islamophobia that must be stopped.

6. Reports and narratives indicate that many Muslims live in fear due to the increasing, volatile and unpredictable nature of beef lynching across various regions in India.

7. Officials and police are often implicated in beef related attacks, and impunity around attacks lends a sense of permissibility to an 'open hunting season' upon Muslims. Not only do attackers including those who murder, go uncharged for their crimes, in some cases they have been honored and rewarded for their crime by politicians from the BJP.

8. *Gau rakshaks* seize wealth in the form of cows from Muslims and give them to *gaushalas* (cow shelters) that have been found to pass them on to Hindus, thus redistributing the wealth of Muslims to Hindus in some cases.

9. More than half of beef related attacks were reportedly spread by rumors.

Glossary

Bajrang Dal

The Barajang Dal, classified as a "militant religious outfit" by the US' Central Intelligence Agency, forms a youth wing of the Vishva Hindu Parishad (VHP). Bajrang Dal, was founded in Uttar Pradesh in 1984 and organization is based on a Hindutva ideology (Hindu nationalism). It hosts approximately 2,500 'sites of militant training' across the country and has been demanding the construction of temples on disputed religious sites such as the Ram Temple in Ayodhya, the former site of the Babri Masjid that was destroyed by Hindu nationalists in 1992[1]. Other goals of the organization include preserving India's "Hindu" identity, stopping Muslim demographic growth, inter-faith marriage, Christian conversion, as well as the prevention of cow slaughter. This has resulted in members of the group 'moral policing' communities on issues like Love Jihad and Beef consumption.[2] This group was labeled as a Hindu extremist group as far as the year 2000 by the United States Department of State's annual report on international religious freedom as well as the World Report by the Human Rights Watch.[3]

BJP

The Bharatiya Janata Party (BJP) is one of the two major political parties in India, and the largest political party in terms of representation in the national parliament and state assemblies.[4] Since the 2014 election victory of the BJP under the leadership of Narendra Modi, there has been a climate of rising Hindu nationalism, accompanied by a rising hostility against India's religious minorities.[5] This exclusionary environment is reflected in the increased practice by the police and law enforcement of arbitrary and unlawful detention; torture, and cruel, inhuman and degrading treatment of terrorism suspects in police custody; extrajudicial killings; harassment of human rights defenders at the behest of the political executive; framing and arrests of innocents from the social and religious minorities; and fabrication as well as destruction of evidence.[6] The deterioration in conditions for religious minorities since 2014 has been attributed to the BJP's Hindu nationalistic political platform and some of its members' support of and/or membership in Hindu nationalist groups, including close ideological and organizational links to the Rashtriya Swayamsevak Sangh.[7]

Communalism

Communalism stems from a divisive politics based on communal identifications. "In India, 'communal' often refers to the politicization of religious differences, and to situations and tensions between groups structured around, and identified with, organized religion, and is

1   Please see section 4.3 for a detailed overview of the 'Case of the Babri Masjid', and the contestation over this site.
2   Rohan Dua, "VHP a militant religious organization outfit, RSS nationalist: CIA factbook". Times of India, June 15, 2018. https://timesofindia.indiatimes.com/india/vhp-a-militant-religious-outfit-rss-nationalist-cia-factbook/articleshow/64594295.cms?from=mdr
3   Barbara Larkin, Annual Report on International Religious Freedom 2000. Washington DC: Department of State, 2000, 508 https://www.gpo.gov/fdsys/pkg/CPRT-106JPRT66723/pdf/CPRT-106JPRT66723.pdf; Human Rights Watch, "World Report 2018: Rights Trends in India", Human Rights Watch, 2018. https://www.hrw.org/world-report/2018/country-chapters/india.
4   Times of India, "In Numbers: The Rise of BJP and decline of Congress", Times of India. May 19, 2016. https://timesofindia.indiatimes.com/india/In-Numbers-The-Rise-of-BJP-and-decline-of-Congress/articleshow/52341190.cms?
5   Charu Gupta, Allegories of 'love jihad' and ghar wapsi: interlocking the socio-religious with the political" In Rise of Saffron Power (India: Routledge, 2018), 104-130.
6   Aman Sethi, "'Love Jihad' in India and One Man's Quest to Prevent It", The Guardian. January 29, 2015. https://www.theguardian.com/world/2015/jan/29/love-jihad-india-one-man-quest-prevent-it
7   Kalyani D. Menon, "'Security', Home, And Belonging in Contemporary India: Old Delhi As A Muslim Place", Etnofoor, 2 (2015): 113-131. https://www.jstor.org/stable/43656022

commonly used to describe tensions between Hindus and Muslims."[8]

First Information Reports (FIR)

A First Information Report (FIR) is "a written document prepared by the police when they receive information about the commission of a cognizable offense. It is a report of information that reaches the police first in point of time".[9] Manipulation of these FIR's has been reported[10], affecting the ability of courts to provide justice and accountability to minorities under attack, such as Muslims.

Gender-based Violence

"Gender-based violence targets individuals on the basis of the person's perceived gender and gender identity. It is linked to structural violence, and in part to state violence...The scope of gender-based violence has been broadened in various parts of the world to include sexual, as well as economic and psychological violence."[11]

Ghar vāpasī

"Ghar vāpasī has been touted as the return to authentic origins, the starting point, the abode of birth. It produces and enforces notions of a primordial religious identity, whereby all and everyone are declared Hindus. The shift from the whole world to the Hindu nation is swift, as ghar vāpasī denationalizes Islam and Christianity, facilitating their "othering."[12]

Hindu Rashtra

Differentially interpreted as "Hindu Polit "Hindu Nation" or "Hindu State", Hindu

Rashtra describes the formation of a Hindu state "through cultural integration premised on Indian philosophy to position Hindus as an 'indomitable force'. This movement for Hindu cultural dominance impels Hindutva, functioning through its institutionalization in society and state, imbricating state and religion, productive of majoritarian nationalism, indissoluble from the nation."[13]

Hindutva

"Hindutva constructs an idealized Hindu as the archetypical citizen of India, and through the superiorization of the Hindu, Hindutva necessarily imagines an array of identities to be unworthy of belonging to its conception of India. Hindutva's otherization project inferiorizes a number of identities: Dalits, liberals, Christians, feminists, but most of all, Muslims. Hindutva thus envisions India to have always been a Hindu nation and perceives Islam and Muslims as an alien force which, through invasion and war, caused a seismic shift to the detriment of the natural state of Hinduness in the subcontinent"[14] Various nationalist groups in India have adopted the ideology of Hindutva, or "Hindu-ness," which has three pillars—common nation, race, and culture—and forms the basis of an exclusionary national narrative focused exclusively on the rights of Hindus. These groups' views and activities range across a spectrum from extreme activities that include means the expulsion, killing, or conversion of all non-Hindus, while more moderate forces demand greater influence of Hindu principles in the state's decision-making process.[15]

Love Jihad

The 'love jihad' conspiracy argues that Muslim

8   Angana P. Chatterji, Violent gods: Hindu nationalism in India's present: Narratives from Orissa, Gurgaon: Three Essays Collective, 2009: 12
9   Human Rights Initiative, "What is a FIR", (n.d.) July 1 2018, https://www.humanrightsinitiative.org/publications/police/fir.pdf
10   · Human Rights Watch, "Impunity in the Aftermath" 2002, July 1 2018. https://www.hrw.org/reports/2002/india/India0402-06.htm
11   Angana P. Chatterji, "Gendered and sexual violence in and beyond South Asia." Antyajaa: Indian Journal of Women and Social Change 1, 1 (2016): 19-40 https://doi.org/10.1177/2455632716646278, 23.
12   Gupta, Allegories of 'love jihad.
13   Chatterji, Violent Gods, 40
14   Prashant Waikar, "Reading Islamophobia In Hindutva: An Analysis of Narendra Modi's Political Discourse", Islamophobia Studies Journal, 2 (2018) Forthcoming.
15   United States Commission on International Religious Freedom (USCIRF), "2018 Annual Report". Washington DC: United States Commission on International Religious Freedom, 2018.

men are waging Jihad in India by luring Hindu women into marriages through trickery, in order to convert them to Islam.[16] Proponents of 'love jihad' claim that these young men are waging war by capturing innocent Hindu women's hearts, referred to as 'Love Romeos'. Right-wing nationalists in particular, construct 'love jihad' as a strategy employed by Muslim fundamentalists to boost population numbers in a supposed ongoing demographic war to outnumber Hindus in India.[17]

Mughal/Muslim invasion of India

An example of this is the Hindutva social imaginary that serves to otherize the Muslim minority in India by use of the term *Mughal* or *Mughlai* in a derogatory sense. It casts Muslims as 'outsiders' and 'invaders' of India rather than belonging to it, although their presence "is simultaneous to or predates the formation of the state."[18] Hindutva ideology works to purge the nation of all non-Hindus and in particular, Muslims, to create a pure Hindu Rashtra, or an India for only Hindus. It is argued by Hindu nationalists that Muslims from the Mughal Empire conquered India and enslaved its people, forcing a significant part of the population to become Muslim. According to this ideology, this justifies the forced conversions that ultra-nationalists are currently undertaking such as Ghar *vāpasī* to return Muslims (and others) to their natural state (Hindu), as well as the destruction of Muslim religious sites as once Hindu or on top of Hindu shrines or temples such as the claims surrounding Ayodhya.

Politically-stoked violence

This report adopts the term 'politically-stoked violence'[19] in lieu of what is commonly referred to as 'communal violence'. Communal violence, according to the Ministry of Home Affairs describes "planned and organized acts of violence by members of one community against members of another community with the intent of creating or expressing ill-will or hatred and leading to the loss of life or injuries to people".[20] 'Politically-stoked violence' critically considers the role of broader structural, political and institutional actors, such as the State and government officials in instigating such communal tensions that lead to violence against minority communities, like Muslims in India.

RSS

Rashtriya Swayamsevak Sangh (RSS), a Hindu ultra-nationalist organization set up in 1925, is the fountainhead of Hindu supremacism and anti-minority politics. Its ideologues, leaders and rank and file have openly touted their goal of creating a "Hindu" India where non-Hindus would have second-class status with fewer rights and freedoms." [21]

Saffronization

"Saffronization implies 'making saffron', the implementation and strengthening of Hindutva."[22]

Securitization

"Securitization describes the establishment of policies, discourses and practices that define the parameters of freedom, threats to national security, and mechanisms for national preservation. Securitization also

16   Saif Khalid, "The Hadiya Case and The Myth Of 'Love Jihad' In India", Aljazeera. August 24, 2017 https://www.aljazeera.com/indepth/features/2017/08/hadiya-case-myth-love-jihad-in-dia-170823181612279.html; Gupta, Allegories of 'love jihad.

17   Mohan Rao, "Love Jihad and demographic fears." Indian Journal of Gender Studies 18, 3 (2011): 425-430. https://doi.org/10.1177%2F097152151101800307

18   Sayyid wrote that Islamophobia in India operates within what he determines to be the "second theater" where "Muslims are a clear minority, marginal to the national narrative, even though their presence is simultaneous to or predates the formation of the state. See section on 'Measuring Islamophobia' for a more detailed overview on Sayyid's definition of Islamophobia.

19   This is more commonly referred to as Communal Violence. See section Politically-Stoked Violence and the Geography of Islamophobia In India of this report for a critical overview on why this report adopts the term 'politically-stoked violence' over the more commonly used 'communal violence'.

20   Ministry of Home Affairs, "Revised Guidelines of 'Central Scheme for Assistance to Civilians Victims/Family of Victims of Terrorist, Communal and Naxal Violence', (n.d), July 1, 2018 https://mha.gov.in/sites/default/files/T-Guide141008_0.pdf

21   Rao "Love Jihad and demographic fears".

22   Chatterji, Violent Gods: 125; Thomas B. Hansen, The Saffron Wave: Democracy and Hindu Nationalism in Modern India, New Delhi: Oxford University Press, 2001.

delimits the states constantly shifting relations to its internal and external Others. This process builds and fortifies the national collective and protects state sovereignty". Specific to Islamophobia in India, a legal framework of securitization empowers state-based perpetrators, such as military and paramilitary personnel and the police, to act with impunity.[23]

Sexualized Violence

"Sexual violence refers to a violence of sexual nature against an individual on the basis of the individual's perceived sex. It pertains to sexual acts committed to establishing power and control over the victim, including sexual humiliation and intimidation, sex trafficking and prostitution, abduction, sexual slavery, sexual torture, sexual mutilation, forced sterilization, rape (individual, gang and collective), forced pregnancy and coerced abortion. It is a constitutive component of gender and a form of gendered violence. It includes sexual abuse and exploitation likely intended to inflict physical, psychological and emotional harm by targeting the physical and non-corporeal body and personhood through physical and psychosocial aggression and persecution".[24] "In the contemporary era, gendered and sexualized violence continues to be a significant element of conflict and social upheaval in conflicted democracies like India."[25]

The Partition of India (1947)

What is commonly referred to as the Partition of India, describes the division of British India, whereby two self-governing countries of Pakistan and India legally came into existence at midnight on 14–15 August 1947[26]. This partition caused "one of the great human convulsions of history[27], whereby over 14 million people were displaced among religious lines, accompanied by large-scale violence, with a disputed estimated loss of up to two million lives (Talbot)[28]. The violent nature of the Partition has promoted the formation of exclusionary identities, with ongoing implications for religious minorities, particularly Muslims living in India, particularly Muslims today who are being told to "go back to Pakistan". On the flipside, the discriminatory treatment of the Hindu minority in Pakistan has also exacerbated inter-religious tensions within India. The legacy of Partition has resulted in Muslims in India being perceived as anti-India or anti-national, damaging Hindu-Muslim relationships in India.[29]

Triple Talaq

Triple talaq is the practice under which a Muslim man can divorce his wife by simply uttering "talaq" three times. It is prevalent among India's Muslim community majority of whom follow the Hanafi Islamic school of law. India's Supreme Court in August 2017 banned 'triple talaq or instant divorce, on the claims that it is unconstitutional. Debates around this practice has been highly politicized and feeds into the broader "image that Muslim women have no rights because husbands can pronounce triple talaq,". According to Flavia Flavia Agnes, a prominent women's rights lawyer, "The whole debate is skewed and political, catering to the ruling government's Muslim bashing agenda, and media is a prime player in this."[30]

23   Cited in: Angana P. Chatterji, Buluswar, Shashi and Kaur, Mallika eds. Conflicted Democracies and Gendered Violence: Internal Conflict and Social Upheaval in India. (Berkeley: Zubaan, 2016), 58

24   Chatterji, Conflicted Democracies and Gendered Violence, 22.

25   Ibid, 42.

26   Yasmin Khan, The Great Partition: The Making of India and Pakistan, North Yorkshire: Yale University Press, 2007.

27   Urvashi Butalia, The other side of silence: Voices from the partition of India, India: Duke University Press, 2000.

28   Ian Talbot & Gurharpal Singh, The Partition of India, Cambridge University Press: United Kingdom, 2009.

29   USCIRF, "2018 Annual Report."

30   Khalid Saif, "What is 'triple talaq' or instant divorce?" Al Jazeera, August 22, 2017, https://www.aljazeera.com/indepth/features/2017/05/tripple-talaq-triple-divorce-170511160557346.
html

Vishwa Hindu Parishad (VHP)

The Vishwa Hindu Parishad, abbreviated as VHP, is a right-wing Hindu nationalist organization based on the ideology of Hindutva and was classified as a "militant religious outfit" by the US' Central Intelligence Agency (CIA).[31] Founded in 1964, the VHP is a member of the Sangh Parivar group, a family of Hindu nationalist organizations led by the Rashtriya Swayamsevak Sangh (RSS). The VHP website articulates that its "objective is to Its stated objective is "to organize - consolidate the Hindu society and to serve - protect the Hindu Dharma".[32] In addition to providing a range of social services[33], it has also been involved in advancing exclusionary propaganda and policies against religious minorities, including Muslims[34]. For example, the VHP been involved in promoting religious conversion to Hinduism, particularly based on *ghar vāpasī* - the idea of reconversion to the 'authentic origins of Hinduism', circulating propaganda and opposition against alleged cases of Love Jihad[35], expanding land ownership of Hindu temples over other religious sites, and involvement in the Babri Masjid demolition.[36]

31   Dua, "VHP a militant religious organization outfit".
32   VHP, "Swagatam", 2010, 1 August 2018. http://vhp.org/swagatam/.
33   The Hindu, "VHP's social service activities", The Hindu, December 18, 2011.
https://www.thehindu.com/todays-paper/tp-national/tp-kerala/vhps-social-service-activities/article2725683.ece
34   USCIRF, "2018 Annual Report".
35   Gupta, Allegories of 'love jihad.
36   Hansen, "The saffron wave".

Introduction

India is composed of a majority Hindu population (79.8%), as well as a large Muslim minority (14.2%) and additional religious groups including Christians (2.3%), Sikhs (1.7%), Buddhists (0.7%) and Jains (0.37%) according to 2011 Census data.[47]

Country profile: Religious Diversity, and Islam in India

India is composed of a majority Hindu population (79.8%), as well as a large Muslim minority (14.2%) and additional religious groups including Christians (2.3%), Sikhs (1.7%), Buddhists (0.7%) and Jains (0.37%) according to 2011. India is the world's seventh largest country by area, and the second most populous country with over 1.2 billion people.[37] As one of the most religiously diverse countries in the world,[38] India has been characterized by rich cultural history, and economic influence.[39] According to the World Bank Group, India is in "a period of unprecedented opportunity, challenge and ambition in its development."[40] As the world's third largest economy, India has celebrated long-term GDP growth and expected to grow at over 7 percent per year.[41] Further, India's poverty levels have decreased, with extreme poverty dropping from 46 percent to an estimated 13.4 percent over the two decades before 2015, however remains home to over 176 million people living in poverty.[42] Despite this strong economic trajectory, a number of challenges remain, particularly pertaining to the uneven development and impact of such economic progress across different social groups and geographic areas.[43] Among these challenges, include human rights violations, ranging from recent violence against minorities, as well as a lack of accountability for past abuses committed by security forces.[44] Human Rights Watch in 2018, reported on a range of crucial human rights issues in question across India including violent protest and impunity from security forces, limited freedom of expression, women's, girls, children's and gender rights.[45] Among such violations has also been the mistreatment of Dalits, tribal groups and religious minorities, such as Muslims.[46] [47]

The third-largest Muslim population in the world currently lives in India, with over 120 million Muslims representing diversity in language, ethnicity and caste, culture and economic

---

37   Population Census 2011." Religion Data - Population of Hindu / Muslim / Sikh / Christian - Census 2011 India, www.census2011.co.in/.
38   Ibid
39   The World Bank Group, "The World Bank in India Overview", 2018https://www.worldbank.org/en/country/india/overview
40   Ibid
41   Ibid
42   Ibid
43   Ibid
44   Human Rights Watch, "World Report 2018"
45   Ibid
46   Ibid
47   Ministry of Home Affairs, "RGI releases Census 2011 data on population by religious communities, 2015, http://pib.nic.in/newsite/PrintRelease.aspx?relid=126326

position within and across each of India's states.[48] The great majority are Sunni Muslims, and the remainder are Shi'a as well as various other sects such as Bohras, Isma'ilis and Ahmadiyas. Muslims form a majority in the state of Kashmir, while elsewhere they are concentrated in the states of Uttar Pradesh, Bihar, West Bengal and Kerala.[49]

For example, Uttar Pradesh, India's most populous state, is home to over 22 percent of India's Muslim population, who make up over 19 percent of the overall state population. While the majority of Muslims reside in Western and Eastern Uttar Pradesh, primarily in urban areas, there remain a number of differentiating factors – for example, identification as marginalized (officially called 'Other Backward Class' or OBC) or as belonging to a specific occupational group – which have a bearing on the socio-economic and political position of Muslims.[50] Religious minorities, particularly Muslims, in India have increasingly faced a range of different forms of persecution, such as hate crimes, threats, attacks on places of worship, and forced conversion.[51]

Rise of Islamophobia in India

The persecution of religious minorities is particularly targeted towards Muslims, which has seen a steady intensification of Islamophobia over the last few decades. The creation of Pakistan as the homeland for Muslims resulted in a new minority problem for the now independent state of India and greater insecurity for Muslim inhabitants of India.[52] While the partition of India and Pakistan decreased the numerical strength of Muslims in India from over 25 percent of the population to about 10 percent, the bitter legacy of this history has been capitalized by Islamophobes to portray Indian Muslims as anti-India and anti-National, resulting in intensifying damage to Hindu-Muslim relations.[53] The Rise of Hindu fundamentalism as a political force has resulted in a rise in Islamophobia, substituting the liberal attitudes and policies that were evident in the first decades of independence with structural, institutional and everyday discrimination against Muslims in India.[54]

In the 1970s, Indian Muslims in northern India particularly becoming victims of a forced sterilization campaign. The movement to demand rights for Muslims began to grow in the period following the Emergency and has gathered fresh momentum in recent times.[55] Key points in time and events relevant to Islamophobia against Muslims in India have been: the Shah Bano case in 1985, where the demand for a uniform civil code was met with outright resistance from Muslim fundamentalist groups, polarizing views between the Hindu and Muslim communities; the destruction of the Babri Masjid (mosque) in Ayodhya in 1992, which dealt a grave blow to the secular aspirations of the Indian state; and the movement since the late 1980s for independence in Kashmir, which has had a detrimental impact for non-Kashmiri Muslims living throughout India.[56] In addition, the Gujarat riots of 2002 resulted in approximately 2,000 Muslims killed in a state-sponsored pogrom.[57] This rise in Islamophobia is closely connected with the growing influence of Rashtriya Swayamsevak Sangh (RSS) - a Hindu ultra-nationalist organization set up in 1925, which has been identified as the fountainhead of Hindu supremacism and anti-minority politics with a goal of creating a "Hindu" India. These

48   Center for the Study of Society and Secularism, "A Narrowing Space: Violence and Discrimination Against India's Religious Minorities," http://Minorityrights.org/Wp-Content/Uploads/2017/06/MRG_Rep_India_Jun17-2.Pdf, June 2017
49   Ibid
50   Ibid
51   Ibid
52   Minority Rights Group, "Muslims - India", 2018 http://minorityrights.org/minorities/muslims-2/.
53   Ibid
54   Ibid
55   Ibid
56   Ibid
57   Human Rights Watch, "World Report 2018: Rights Trends in India", Human Rights Watch, 2018. https://www.hrw.org/world-report/2018/country-chapters/india.

exclusionary politics result in the second-class status of other religious minorities, who are afforded fewer rights and freedoms. The majority of anti-minority and anti-Muslim campaigns or political groups over the decades can be directly or indirectly traced to the RSS and its various affiliates, or to a few other organizations ideologically affiliated to it.[58]

The rise of the RSS's political influence can be connected to the improved electoral performance of its political wing, the Bharatiya Janata Party (BJP), in the late 1980s. In 2014, current Prime Minister Narendra Modi led the BJP to a dramatic win in national elections, bringing it to its first-ever parliamentary majority. The BJP now also rules 13 of India's 29 states and is a partner in the governments in two more, leading to a dramatic increase and deepened Islamophobia towards Muslims in India.[59] It is this unprecedented success of the BJP that has fortified Hindu ultra-nationalist forces who form a significant portion of its base to both encourage and perpetrate attacks against religious minorities, in line with their anti-minority campaigns.

Muslim Population in India

1,210,854,977
Total Population in India

172,200,000
Muslims in India

14.2%

of India's Population
is Muslim

India's overall population is 1,210,854,977 billion people. Muslims in India number 172.2 million, or 14.2 percent of the population. Muslims are the second largest religious group after Hundus who make up 79.8 percent of the population. India is home to 11 percent of Muslims in the world.

Source: Census India, 2011.

58   Alliance for Justice & Accountability, Minority Rights Violations in India, Washington D.C, 2017, https://www.scribd.com/document/349208337/India-Minority-Rights-Violations-Report-2017#from_embed
59   Ibid.

Methodology

The purpose of this report is to highlight how the BJP is using Islamophobia to push ultra-nationalist policies and further disenfranchise Muslims as a minority group in India. Despite the importance of understanding the longstanding issue of Islamophobia in India, this report focuses on the period from January 2017 to October 2018 to capture more recent manifestations of such discrimination against Muslims.

We have utilized a mixed methods qualitative and quantitative approach. This includes literature reviews, discourse and content analysis of formal policy documents, plans and reports, the collation of official statistics, monitoring data from agencies and NGOs, records, digital fieldwork (digital ethnography) and analysis of various platforms including social media, legal documents, legislation, handbills, video, case studies, investigative reports, news articles, and key informant interviews.

Gaps and limitations of this report pertain to the availability of data, and the research consisting primarily of English language sources. In the first instance, there is limited availability of data, reports, and statistics, conflicting data, and outdated data. This is exacerbated by the difficulty for advocates and activists to speak freely without penalty and thus leads to issues of documentation. In this second instance, our research that consists of primarily English language sources has been primarily gathered from secondary media sources and literature in English. However, India has large English language penetration and the CIA Factbook reports that "English enjoys the status of subsidiary official language but is the most important language for national, political, and commercial communication."[60]

Several institutional reports that were utilized to inform this research, also rely on secondary media sources for information. Media reports are limited in their coverage of news, in that only events and issues deemed newsworthy or that make it through censorship and the editorial process are reported in some cases. To account for gaps and discrepancies, we have compared sources when possible and have also consulted experts, advocates and key informants on the ground to accompany our media-informed findings.

The Organization for Security and Co-operation in Europe (OSCE) and The Office for Democratic Institutions and Human Rights (ODIHR) have created a practical guide for documenting hate crimes in Europe that we have found useful for our purposes. The guide claimed that although some countries may not have effective data collection systems, "data from social surveys, non-governmental organizations, and other monitors can show that there is a problem that is not being detected and addressed by the existing systems."[61] Furthermore, whether or not states define, pass laws or address hate crimes, such crimes do occur and have a significant impact on the victims, community, and humanity at large.[62] This is also the case in India.

In general, information and data were extracted from the most recent information and data sets accessible. Year and date ranges are provided with the source figures, tables and maps to clarify when information and data collection

60   "The World Factbook: INDIA." Central Intelligence Agency, Central Intelligence Agency, April 09, 2018, www.cia.gov/library/publications/resources/the-world-factbook/geos/in.html
61   OSCE and ODIHR. Hate Crimes A Practical Guide. 2009, Hate Crimes A Practical Guide. https://www.osce.org/odihr/36426?download=true, 11.
62   Ibid.

occurred. In some cases, the latest source of comparable data is dated in 2017 while in others it is as recent as December 2018 when the report writing was finalized.

Data represents the particular indicator at the time of compilation and may not reflect the current situation. We acknowledge that it is not comprehensive coverage of every event, but rather it is meant to provide depth and breadth into the issues and situations at hand as much as possible. The report should energize efforts directed toward forming a dedicated academic research group focused on this subject that can address the highlighted challenges.

Report Outline

The overall structure of the report takes the form of ten sections, beginning with a short-hand summary of key terms and issues that are discussed throughout this report, accompanied by related citations for further reading.

The first major section is the introduction, which provides the country profile of religious diversity and Islam in India. Further, it introduces the issue Islamophobia in India in the context of the rise of the Hindu Right, and the BJP as the current political party in power. Specifically, it establishes the context of how the unprecedented success of the BJP that has fortified Hindu supremacist forces who form a significant portion of its base to both encourage and perpetrate attacks against religious minorities, in line with their anti-minority campaigns.

The methodology section outlines the mixed methods qualitative and quantitative approach of the study, and identifies the main sources of data and information that is analyzed throughout the remainder of the report informing the main findings and conclusions.

The next section, 'Measuring Islamophobia' establishes Salman Sayyid's 'Six clusters of Islamophobia', as the conceptual framework used throughout this report to analyze data and draw conclusions on the various dimensions of Islamophobia in India.

Section five summarizes the context required to situate Islamophobia in India today. It begins with a historical overview of rising anti-Muslim sentiment since the country's independence in 1947, and how this has manifested into anti-Muslim violence across India, particularly the states of Gujarat and Kashmir. The various dimensions of structural Islamophobia are then discussed, highlighting its negative impact on the socio-economic position of Muslims in India's growing economy. The way in which rising Hindu Nationalism and the ideology of Hindutva has further stigmatized religious minorities such as Muslims, is then discussed in relation to the current Bharatiya Janata Party (BJP)- led government, and the Hindu-majority social imaginary. This is connected to various media depictions of Hindutva and Hinduness as the favorable national identity, in contrast with negative depictions of Muslims in India.

Section six addresses the social imaginary and the creation of the Hindutva order by critically analyzing various forms of cultural production, such as top grossing Bollywood films, Hindutva hate-core music, and incendiary social media posts and fake news propagated by BJP officials that not only perpetuates Orientalist and Islamophobic imaginaries, but that also incite violence against Muslims. .

Section seven covers issues around populism and media control in India and the use of BJP war rooms to surveille and target media and reporters, the monetization and the mobilization of Islamophobia in elections. It further reveals efforts at reporting on hate and Islamophobia at present, shrinking freedoms, attempts of the BJP to institutionalize paid media to propagate BJP political positions, as well as, the manufacture of Muslims as a menace.

Section eight reports on the findings of this

research, through a detailed overview of 'significant incidents and issues' relating to Islamophobia in India from 2017 to October 2018. This section is divided by three main areas of concern throughout this time period, including attacks against bodies - beef attacks, lynching and cow vigilantism; 'Love Jihad' and conversion laws and 'Politically-stoked Violence' and the Geography of Islamophobia in India.

In relation to these significant incidents and issues, section nine notes existing initiatives and efforts undertaken to challenge anti-Muslim rhetoric, violence and discrimination in India.

Concluding with the main findings of this research report, section ten provides a range of policy recommendations for the consideration of international civil society, the international community, the government in India and social media corporations, in order to challenge Islamophobia in India.

Measuring Islamophobia

In India, "Muslims are a clear minority, marginal to the national narrative, even though their presence is simultaneous to or predates the formation of the state."

Islamophobia is often understood to be a purvey of the West. However, scholars have critiqued the presence of the phenomena in other regions, reaching from the Middle East to Asia. The causes of Islamophobia, as well as its various manifestations across these regions vary and it is thus paramount to analyze nuanced versions of Islamophobia within their specific contexts.

In the journal article entitled "A Measure of Islamophobia," Salman Sayyid laid out the multiplicity of ways Islamophobia is utilized to describe situations "conditioned by the specific cultural, socioeconomic and historical factors that have influenced the way in which Islam can be performed."[63] Sayyid wrote that Islamophobia in India operates within what he determines to be the "second theater" - when "Muslims are a clear minority, marginal to the national narrative, even though their presence is simultaneous to or predates the formation of the state."[64] Expressions of Islamophobia are often diverse and occur through a range of deployments, he emphasized.[65] Sayyid argued that "a gesture, a speech, and a police action can all be aspects of Islamophobia reflecting not an underlying unity, but a series of overlapping similarities."[66]

The purpose of drawing out the "repertoire of Islamophobia" is to "elucidate the kind of behaviors and actions that can potentially be understood through the deployment of the category," in order to facilitate a deeper understanding of the way assemblages of Islamophobia operate at different yet often intersecting levels.[67] This report examines Islamophobia in India through the gathering of otherwise disparate elements, multiple examples, evidence and measurable data into what Sayyid referred to as "recognizable formations of cruelty and injustice" that require rectification.[68] It is essential to first define a problem, in this case, Islamophobia in India utilized by the BJP to push ultra-nationalist policies, before action can be taken to solve it.

Sayyid provides a model for understanding Islamophobia, which divides Islamophobic activities into six main clusters. This model is useful in defining and interpreting data and case

---

63   S Sayyid, "A Measure of Islamophobia,"Islamophobia Studies Journal, vol. 2, no.1, 2014, 14 doi:10.18411/d-2016154.
64   Ibid.
65   Ibid.
66   Ibid.
67   Ibid,15.
68   Ibid, 22.

studies of Islamophobia in India. Throughout this report, we examine examples of the six clusters, all of which are active during our reporting period in India.

According to Sayyid, the first five clusters of Islamophobia tend to be carried out by individuals or organizations (private or public). The state may facilitate them through benign neglect or refusal to provide adequate safeguards or to challenge such actions, but it is not actively or openly involved in the perpetuation of these incidents.74 In the sixth, it is the state that plays a predominant role where Islamophobia is embedded within its structure and systems.

Sayyid's Six Clusters of Islamophobia

Shouting abuse, pushing, spitting, pulling hijabs from Muslim women, various forms of beating which can culminate in murder. What is common to all these incidents is that they target Muslims, the violence is unprovoked and they occur in public settings such as the street or the park.

Attacks on property considered to be linked to Muslims; mosques, cemeteries, business premises. These attacks may include vandalism (broken windows, hurling pig's heads into mosques, graffiti), arson, and desecration of Muslim graves.

Organized intimidation involving a number of persons acting in concert to intimidate a population that is perceived to be Muslim or friendly to Muslims. Intimidation may include marches through areas with large Muslim populations, advertising campaigns warning of the danger of Islam, as well as, Qur'an burning or demonstrations against the building of mosques or cultural centers. Distinguishes these actions is the degree of coordination requiring the expenditure of social and financial capital.

Institutionalized Islamophobia: those perceived as Muslims receive less favorable treatment than their peers in comparable positions within the same organizations. Manifestations: harassment, bullying, pointed jokes, distribution of tasks, and assessments of performance in which those considered to be Muslims are subject to adverse treatment or comment. Example: an implemented dress code placing greater burdens upon those perceived to be Muslims than other staff in the same organization. Islamophobia is not necessarily directed or coordinated by a state project, rather its occurrence is a subject of the absence of robust anti-discrimination legislation or culture, or the inclusion of Muslims within the ambit of such measures even if they exist.

Sustained and systematic elaboration of comments in the public domain that disparage Muslims and/or Islam. Disparagement could be more or less subtle.

Examples: publishing the Qur'an with Muhammad listed as the author or recycling medieval Christian polemics as the "truth" about Islam or reading specific crimes as being motivated by Islam or Muslim culture. This form of Islamophobia could be articulated on internet hate sites, newspapers, magazines, or other media. It may be in factual or fictional programs. It can also inform policy and opinion, and may be grounds for state interventions and regulations. It could also be part of the common sense of a society—the set of unexamined assumptions and beliefs that circulate in any society.

The state plays an active role including intensification of surveillance of Muslim populations using technology, agent provocateurs, and paid informers. Surveillance may be carried out by a form of secret police (that is, state agencies tasked with clandestine operating procedures). In addition, there is Islamophobia of the criminal justice system in which those deemed to be Muslims are perceived to be treated less favorably than others. This can be the result of differential sentencing, difference in the frequency of being stopped and searched by police officers. State policies could also be used to restrict expression of Muslimness—for example, limiting the building of mosques, regulating Muslim dress (bans on the burqa). What makes these activities appear Islamophobic is the degree to which they place extra burdens on sections of the population which are mostly Muslim.[69]

In the case of India, Islamophobic activities are at times undertaken by individuals, semi-organized or organized groups and more importantly by the state. By providing what Sayyid refers to as a "multiplicity of examples and contexts," a spectrum of experiences "can be marshaled by the category of Islamophobia."[70] Collectively, they form what can be considered an 'ecosystem of Islamophobia' with multiple constituents and layers that interact, coalesce and create synergy within an interconnected system.

Islamophobia in India has manifested into hate speech by elected officials leading to incitement, harassment, mob violence, and lynching, vandalism to mosques, as well as the razing of Muslim owned businesses, and refugee camps that house Rohingya refugees. It includes increased surveillance of Muslims, restrictions on their places of residence, clothing, where they pray, who they love ('love jihad'), what they eat and how they earn a living (prohibitive cow legislation). Further, Islamophobia has become more firmly grounded systematically through the legal system and state structures.

Sayyid stated that Islamophobia will come to an end only when the "hierarchy that makes it possible dissolves."[71] Therefore countering Islamophobia, stressed "requires the dismantling of the assemblages that make it possible."[72]

69   Ibid, 15-16.
70   Ibid, 20.
71   Ibid, 22.
72   Ibid.

Sayyid's Six Clusters of Islamophobia

1 Shouting abuse, pushing, spitting, pulling hijabs from Muslim women, various forms of beating which can culminate in murder. What is common to all these incidents is that they target Muslims, the violence is unprovoked and they occur in public settings such as the street or the park.

2 Attacks on property considered to be linked to Muslimsmosques, cemeteries, business premises. These attacks may include vandalism (broken windows, hurling pig's heads into mosques, graffiti), arson, and desecration of Muslim graves.

3 Organized intimidation involving a number of persons acting in concert to intimidate a population that is perceived to be Muslim or friendly to Muslims. Intimidation may include marches through areas with large Muslim populations, advertising campaigns warning of the danger of Islam, as well as, Qur'an burning or demonstrations against the building of mosques or cultural centers. Distinguishes these actions is the degree of coordination requiring the expenditure of social and financial capital.

4 Institutionalized Islamophobia: those perceived as Muslimsreceive less favorable treatment than their peers in comparable positions within the same organizations. Manifestations: harassment, bullying, pointed jokes, distribution of tasks, and assessments of performance in which those considered to be Muslims are subject to adverse treatment or comment.

Example: an implemented dress code placing greater burdens upon those perceived to be Muslims than other staff in the same organization. Islamophobia is not necessarily directed or coordinated by a state project, rather its occurrence is a subject of the absence of robust antidiscrimination legislation or culture, or the inclusion of Muslims within the ambit of such measures even if they exist.

5 Sustained and systematic elaboration of comments in the public domain that disparage Muslims and/or Islam. Disparagement could be more or less subtle.

Examples: publishing the Qur'an with Muhammad listed as the author or recycling medieval Christian polemics as the "truth" about Islam or reading specific crimes as being motivated by Islam or Muslim culture. This form of Islamophobia could be articulated on internet hate sites, newspapers, magazines, or other media. It may be in factual or fictional programs. It can also inform policy and opinion, and may be grounds for state interventions and regulations. It could also be part of the common sense of a society—the set of unexamined assumptions and beliefs that circulate in any society.

6 The state plays an active role including intensification of surveillance of Muslim populations using technology, agent provocateurs, and paid informers. Surveillance may be carried out by a form of secret police (that is, state agencies tasked with clandestine operating procedures). In addition, there is Islamophobia of the criminal justice system in which those deemed to be Muslims are perceived to be treated less favorably than others. This can be the result of differential sentencing, difference in the frequency of being stopped and searched by police officers. State policies could also be used to restrict expression of Muslimness—for example, limiting the building of mosques, regulating Muslim dress (bans on the burqa). What makes these activities appear Islamophobic is the degree to which they place extra burdens on sections of the population which are mostly Muslim.

Contextualizing Islamophobia In India

According to 2015 statistics from the NCRB, more than 67% of those in India's jails are defendants under trials, and 55% of this population is made up of Muslims, Dalits and adivasis – together constituting only a combined 39% of the country's total population.

Since the country's independence in 1947, the Muslim community in various parts of India has been subjected to hundreds of violent, sectarian attacks. The state of Gujarat in particular, is characterized by a long long history of religionized violence, with ongoing political, economic and political tensions between Hindu and Muslim communities residing in this state since 1947.[73] The overwhelming presence of a Hindu Right in Gujarat resulted in 1993 with the demolition of the Babri Masjid in Ayodhya, the systematic destruction of Muslim property in 2000,[74] and most importantly, the devastating Gujarat riots of 2002. These riots resulted in the death of approximately 2,000 Muslims in a state-sponsored pogrom under the leadership of the BJP.[75] Most importantly, in a large number of cases reported relating to the riots, the evidence was destroyed, following the incidents. The police and courts rejected more than half or the five thousand proposed cases around various forms of violence that were put forward by victims.[76]

The region of Kashmir is also fundamental to the contextualization of Islamophobia in India. The crisis in Kashmir pre-dates the emergence of India and Pakistan as nation-states post 1947 division. British colonization has always utilized a divide and rule strategy and in the context of India, this meant exploiting existing religious, cultural, linguistic, class and regional differences to maximize control over vast populations and territories. Kashmir is representative of British colonial legacy, which is similarly evidenced in the crisis around Palestine that gets projected into societal interaction in post British control. Currently, Kashmir is one of the most intensely militarized zones in the world with an estimated 500,000 Indian troops stationed in the region and

---

73   Angana P. Chatterji, Buluswar, Shashi and Kaur, Mallika eds. Conflicted Democracies and Gendered Violence: Internal Conflict and Social Upheaval in India. (Zubaan: University of California Berkeley, 2016, 133.
74   People's Union for Democratic Rights (PUDR) "Maaro! Kaapo! Baalo!' State,
Society and Communalism in Gujarat", 2002 http://www.onlinevolunteers.org/gujarat/reports/pudr/
75   Human Rights Watch, "World Report 2018"; Chatterji et al., "Conflicted Democracies".
76   Chatterji et al., "Conflicted Democracies," 135.

a constant use of state of emergency to punish the population for demanding basic human rights and freedom. In the larger context, the crisis in Kashmir allows Hindu Nationalists and the BJP leadership to project a territorial threat to the Indian homeland from a supposed internal Muslim threat that constantly is contesting India's sovereignty. Here, Islamophobia becomes intertwined with the supposed war on terrorism that feeds into the nationalist agenda that etherize and externalize the Muslim subject in the country.

In response to the weakened state of the Muslim community following the loss of life and assets in the Gujarat riots, the new national government in India, led by the Congress party, created a committee, termed the "Prime Ministers' High-Level Committee on the Social, Economic and Educational Status of the Muslim Community in India," to study the status of the Muslim community to enable the state to identify areas of intervention. Commonly referred to as the Sachar Committee, named after the Chairperson, Rajendra Sachar, the Committee submitted a report in 2006.[77] The Sachar Report found country-wide and long-term marginalization and socio-economic decline of India's Muslims, near the bottom of the national ladder, since the country's independence in 1947. More recently, the post-Sachar Evaluation Committee in 2014 similarly found that Muslims continued to suffer disproportionately from lack of access to health care, low educational attainment, and economic deprivation, particularly in urban areas[78] which can be attributed to the rise of Hindu religious parties such as the BJP.

Muslims in India are subjected to structural Islamophobia in accessing political, legal, educational and employment spaces. Indeed, a range of academics and civil rights organizations have highlighted the problematic way in which Indian Muslims are not granted the same constitutional safeguards as the scheduled castes and scheduled tribes and they are not entitled to reservations in employment and education.[79] Muslims are not entitled to reserved constituencies in central or state government assemblies, although all have Muslim parliamentary representatives. There have been several Muslim chief ministers and two Presidents have been Muslim, although the latter is a ceremonial position having little real power despite high visibility.[80] In addition, the political power of Muslims is further undermined with the striking under-representation in the civil service, military, and institutions of higher education.[81] Muslims and other minorities in India also face institutional discrimination, including in relation to law enforcement. According to 2015 statistics from the NCRB, more than 67 percent of those in India's jails are defendants under trials, and 55 percent of this population is made up of Muslims, Dalits and *adivasis* – together constituting only a combined 39 percent of the country's total population.[82] In the wake of terrorist attacks by Islamist extremists, in particular, the 2008 attacks in Mumbai, Muslims have increasingly been targeted by police through profiling, staged encounters and incarceration on false accusations of terrorism under the cover of anti-terror laws, such as the Unlawful Activities Prevention Act (UAPA). Muslims have also been the target of state violence, in particular in Jammu and Kashmir, where civil society groups have documented systematic and widespread human rights abuses by police, including arbitrary arrests, torture and extrajudicial killings[83]. Further, Muslims are provided with limited and unequal access to

77   Rajindar Sachar, "Report on Social, Economic and Educational Status of The Muslim Community Of India", Ministry of Minority Affairs, 2006. http://minorityaffairs.gov.in/reports/sachar-committee-report.
78   Post-Sachar Evaluation Committee, "Post-Sachar Evaluation Committee Report", 2014 http://iosworld.org/download/Post_Sachar_Evaluation_Committee.pdf
79   Minority Rights Group, "Muslims - India"
80   Ibid.
81   Ibid.
82   Anmol Saxena, "India: more than half of undertrials are Dalits, Muslims and Tribals", Al-Jazeera, 1 November 2016, https://www.aljazeera.com/blogs/asia/2016/11/trial-india-dalits-muslims-tribals-161101150136542.html
83   CSSS, "A Narrowing Space".

education, exacerbating the general problem of Muslims being inadequately trained or equipped to compete on equal terms at the market-place.[84] For example, the Sachar report found that Muslim identity comes in the way of admitting children to good educational institution, explaining that while Muslims apparently prefer to send their children to 'regular mainstream' schools," as a result of discrimination, Muslim children must be enrolled in religious schools (*madarsas*).[85] This occurs alongside ongoing social and cultural discrimination, such as obstacles to buying or renting property, or representations of Muslims as 'terrorists' or unpatriotic in the media or educational materials.[86] It is within this broader context of political and socio-economic hostility, that Muslims in India have been subjected to the most serious manifestations of communal riots since Partition: in many cases, violence has been actively enabled by the failure (such as lack of protection or access to justice) or even complicity (for example, through hate speech) of public officials.[87]

Hindu Nationalism and Islamophobia in India

The ideology of Hindutva – Hindu nation, is an ideology based on otherization that has been capitalized for repeated attacks against minority communities across India. Various nationalist groups in India have adopted the ideology of Hindutva, or "Hindu-ness," which has three pillars—common nation, race, and culture—and forms the basis of an exclusionary national narrative focused exclusively on the rights of Hindus.[88] Hindutva's otherization inferiorizes a number of identities: Dalits, liberals, Christians, feminists, but most of all, Muslims.[89] These groups' views and activities range across a spectrum. Yet,

both moderate and extreme forces within the Hindutva movement point to the fact that the Muslim percentage of the total population rose from 10 percent in 1950 to 14 percent in 2011, which in their view necessitates their actions that discriminate against the Muslim community. For the more extreme Hindutva groups, this means the expulsion, killing, or conversion of all non-Hindus, while more moderate forces merely want greater influence of Hindu principles in the state's decision-making process. Members of the BJP have affiliations with Hindu extremist groups, and many have used discriminatory language about religious minorities. For example, in early 2018, just after the reporting period, BJP parliamentarian Vinay Katiyar stated that "Muslims have been given their share (of land). They should go to Bangladesh or Pakistan.[90]

The unprecedented victory of the Bharatiya Janata Party in 2014 has had detrimental and multifaceted impacts on fortifying the ideology of Hindutva, and thus further discriminating against Muslims. Indeed, Gupta brings our attention to the way in which one of the critical aspects of the 2014 elections was "that for the very first time in the history of our Republic, a political party explicitly based on religious identity... secured more than 50 percent of the seats in our Parliament."[91]

Muslims, Christians, Sikhs, other minority communities, and Hindu Dalits recognize that religious freedom issues in India predate the current BJP- led government. However, the deterioration in conditions since 2014 is widely attributed to the BJP's Hindu nationalistic political platform and some of its members' support of and/or membership in Hindu nationalist groups.[92] Under the ruling Bharatiya Janata Party

---

84   Minority Rights Group, "Muslims - India"
85   Sachar, "Report on...Status of The Muslim"
86   CSSS, "A Narrowing Space", 6.
87   Ibid.
88   USCIRF, "2018 Annual Report", 164.
89   Sharma, Jyotirmaya, Hindutva: exploring the idea of Hindu nationalism (New Delhi: Penguin Books India, 2011); Waikar, "Reading Islamophobia In Hindutva"
90   USCIRF, "2018 Annual Report".
91   Gupta, "Allegories of love Jihad", 219.
92   United States Commission on International Religious Freedom, "2017 Annual Report", Washington DC: United States Commission on International Religious Freedom, 2017. http://www.

government, pro-BJP vigilantes have committed violence against religious minorities, marginalized communities, and critics of the government. The failure of authorities to investigate attacks, while promoting Hindu supremacy and ultra-nationalism, has further encouraged violence against minorities, particularly Muslims.[93] "In July, even after Prime Minister Narendra Modi finally condemned such violence [mob attacks against minority communities, especially Muslims], an affiliate organization of the BJP, the RSS, announced plans to recruit 5,000 "religious soldiers" to "control cow smuggling and 'love jihad'."[94] Indeed, the victory of the BJP has resulted in the decline of religious tolerance and religious freedom in India, whereby Hindu nationalist groups— such as the Rashtriya Swayamsevak Sangh (RSS), Sangh Parivar, and Vishva Hindu Parishad (VHP)—and their sympathizers perpetrated numerous incidents of intimidation, harassment, and violence against religious minority communities and Hindu Dalits,[95] attributed to the BJP government promotion of Hindu nationalism at the national level after its election in May 2014.[96]

> The Hindu nationalist quest for power can only succeed in a context where there exists a perceived threat - real or imagined - to the majority community of Hindus."

- Christophe Jaffrelot

uscirf.gov/sites/default/files/2017.USCIRFAnnualReport.pdf
93   Human Rights Watch, "World Report 2018".
94   Human Rights Watch, "World Report 2018".
95   United States Commission on International Religious Freedom, "2017 Annual Report".
96   CSSS, "A Narrowing Space", 4.

Social Imaginary and the Creation of the Hindutva Social Order

The ORF offered a definition of hate speech for the purposes of their report as: 'expressions that advocate incitement to harm—discrimination, hostility, violence—based upon the targets being identified with a certain social or demographic group. It includes speech that advocates, threatens or encourages violent acts.' [159]

Globalization has played an important role in the recent emergence of right-wing nationalism. To elaborate further, right-wing nationalism in India though distinct, is following the trend of similar movements across several nation states and into political offices via the election of individuals such as America's Donald Trump, France's Marine Le Pen, and Austria's Sebastian Kurz. Muslims and Islam have been at the center of many of the global right-nationalist movements that mobilize Islamophobia, whether Muslims have been constructed as a demographic, economic, spatial, cultural, political, religious or physical threat. This is also the case in India where right-wing nationalism is driven by the ideology of Hindutva and its quest for "sociocultural homogenization."[97]

Christophe Jaffrelot explains that in India "the strategy of stigmatisation and emulation of 'threatening Others' is based on a feeling of vulnerability born of a largely imaginary threat posed by 'aliens,' principally Muslims and Christians."[98] However, "within Hindu nationalist discourse, the 'threatening Other' has historically been the Muslim community...[and] protecting the 'Hindu nation' against conversion to Islam has, in turn, been of central concern to leading Hindu nationalist organizations."[99] In the Hindutva social imaginary, Muslim dogmatism is juxtaposed against what Hindutva scholar Jyotirmaya Sharma refers to as the "assimilative and tolerant Hindu civilization."[100] Thus, India has its own imagined 'clash of civilizations.' It is here that he says "a continuous struggle in which the Hindus are perennial victims and Muslims the archetypal aggressors" is perpetuated, although Hindus constitute a large majority in India. Tolerance is also perceived as an innate quality assigned to Hinduism, therefore any conflict

97   Nagothu Naresh Kumar, "Dissecting Hindutva: A Conversation with Jyotirmaya Sharma," Toynbee Prize Foundation, June 30, 2017, http://toynbeeprize.org/interviews/jyotirmaya-sharma/.

98   Christophe Jaffrelot, The Hindu Nationalist Movement and Indian Politics: 1925 to the 1990s: Strategies of Identity-Building, Implantation and Mobilisation (Delhi:Viking Penguin in Association with C. Hurst & Co.,1996), 522.

99   Peggy Froerer, "Emphasizing 'Others': the emergence of Hindu nationalism in a central Indian tribal community," 2006. Journal of the Royal Anthropological Institute, vol 12, issue 1, 40.

100   Kumar, "Dissecting Hindutva: A Conversation with Jyotirmaya Sharma," 2017.

must logically come from outside of its folds.[101]

The strategy of stigmatisation, Jaffrelot claims, is the "cornerstone of the Hindu nationalist movement."[102] Thus, Muslims are both imagined and created as the distinct threatening Other, "those whose origins and allegiances apparently lie outside of this community," and therefore beyond the dominant cultural cartography, defined as the Hindu society.[103] Sanjeev H.M Kumar claims that "the term 'Hindu society' itself here becomes a synecdoche to indicate the notion of the Hindu nation (a geopolitical space marked only for the Hindus)."[104]

According to Jaffrelot, the strategy of stigmatisation has led the Bharatiya Janata Party (BJP) to power and it continues to contribute "to the political success of the movement in recent years."[105] In fact, it has been argued that the "Hindu nationalist quest for power can only succeed in a context where there exists a perceived threat – real or imagined – to the majority community of Hindus."[106]

Such social imaginaries are made visible and brought into conscience through both verbal and non-verbal practices of learned dispositions. Within this imaginary, the Muslim subject has been and continues to be constructed through a dynamic process of making and remaking. Cultural production such as films, movies, music, news, and social media all serve as possible sites for political and communal mobilization through the creation of a common 'enemy Other.'

Film

When considering the concept of social imaginary "cinema has assumed a crucial role by virtue of its pervasive mass appeal and its ability to deeply push itself into the popular psyche and create a penetrative impact upon the thinking and imagination of people."[107] This is especially concerning when considering the work of Jack Shaheen, who revealed Hollywood's century long use of distorted lenses portraying Arabs and Muslims as "heartless, brutal, uncivilized, religious fanatics through common depictions of Arabs kidnapping or raping a fair maiden; expressing hatred against the Jews and Christians; and demonstrating a love for wealth and power."[108] He warned that these stereotypes become deeply ingrained through continuous repetition and reproduction. Kumar claims that Bollywood deploys metonymies of fear and Islamophobic narratives in its representations of Muslims through "its reductionist employment of Muslims as a synecdoche to signify a terrorist, religious extremist, Pakistan loyalist, anti-Hindu and a traitor."[109]

By critically examining two of the top-grossing Bollywood films entitled *Raees* (2017) and *Padmaavat* (2018), those familiar with both Shaheen's *Reel Bad Arabs* and Edward Said's *Orientalism* and *Covering Islam*, can immediately recognize the epistemic otherization structures at work in India and how they manifest through various mediums and forms of cultural production.

101   Ibid.
102   Jaffrelot, "The Hindu Nationalist Movement," 522.
103   Ibid. and Sanjeev H.M Kumar, Metonymies of Fear: Islamophobia and the Making of Muslim Identity in Hindi Cinema, Society and Culture in South Asia, vol 2, issue: 2, July 1, 2016, 235.
104   Sanjeev H.M Kumar, Constructing the Nation's Enemy: Hindutva, Popular Culture and the Muslim 'Other' in Bollywood Cinema, Third World Quarterly, 2013, vol, 34, issue 3, 458.
105   Jaffrelot, "The Hindu Nationalist Movement," 522.
106   Hansen, The Saffron Wave, 208.
107   Kumar, "Constructing the Nation's Enemy," 458.
108   Jack G. Shaheen, "Reel Bad Arabs: How Hollywood Vilifies a People," The Annals of the American Academy of Political and Social Science, vol 588, 2003: 171, http://www.jstor.org.libproxy.berkeley.edu/stable/1049860.
109   Kumar, "Metonymies of Fear," 235.

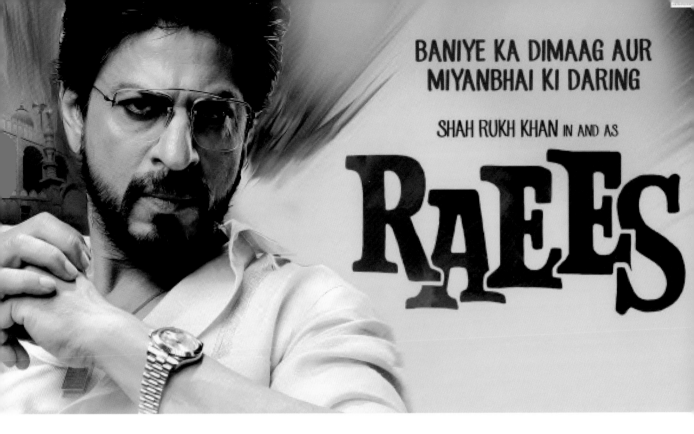

BANIYE KA DIMAAG AUR
MIYANBHAI KI DARING

SHAH RUKH KHAN IN AND AS

RAEES

Raees

Raees is a crime thriller directed by Rahul Dholakia in 2017. The film earned five nominations at the 63rd Filmfare Awards, including Best Actor for Shah Rukh Khan. It held the position as highest grossing Bollywood film of 2017 for several months.[110] Coming from a life of poverty, bootlegging is a source of survival for Raees Alam, a young Muslim, who takes it up as a child in the film. Filling his elementary school backpack with liquor and signalling others when the police raid his town, creates Raees as a character in opposition to the state which is viewed as the upholders of laws and prohibitions. Thus, Raees is criminalized and can be viewed as 'anti-national' or in opposition to the state even as a child, simply because he was born a Muslim. His impoverished community that struggles to eat and make ends meet, is collectively under constant state surveillance, police presence, and subject to raids throughout the film. His section of town in the film appears to be the equivalent of an open air prison.

As Raees ages, he and his partners are represented as the leaders of the bootlegging mafia, in spite of the fact that alcohol and crime are forbidden and immoral in Islam. Thus Muslims in the film not only go against Islamic tenets, and take part in criminal activities and the seedy underworld in India, they are actually constructed as the leaders of it. In one particular action scene that is set in a souk filled with animal carcasses, full of bearded Muslim butchers wearing kufis (signifiers of Muslim identity that have become risky), Muslim characters weaponize the halal meat around them slaughtered for the Muslim holiday Eid Ul Adha (a time of growing tension and restrictions in India). The main character Raees gets in a bloody fight with several local butchers. The men pummel each other with bloody pieces of meat and one falls unconscious in a puddle of animal blood on the ground. The scene has been described by one critic of the film as "a perfect gift for the RSS, who label Muslims as beef-eating savages and are advocating a ban on cow

---

110   TNN, "'Raees' Worldwide Box-office Collection: Shah Rukh Khan's Film Powers past 250-crore Mark - Times of India," The Times of India, February 20, 2017, https://timesofindia.india-times.com/entertainment/hindi/bollywood/box-office/raees-worldwide-box-office-collection-shah-rukh-khans-film-powers-past-250-crore-mark/articleshow/56970149.cms.

slaughter!"[111]

In another scene, Raees takes part in the Shia Muslim practice of self-flagellation drawing blood from his body, which plays to familiar Orientalist tropes of savagery, violence and the backwardness of Islam. In one shot he also jumps over a Shia religious shrine. The scene has compelled members from the Shia community in India to lodge a complaint with police for its use of symbols.[112] Later in the film, Raees stopped a communal procession from coming through his part neighborhood, although he issued warnings ahead of time. He and his supporters are represented as the cause of the violent riots that ensue because of it, and the other religious community is shown to only fight back in self defense. However as demonstrated in our report, Muslims as a minority are overwhelmingly the victims in such violence, which is often incited by communal processions and their participants.

At the end of the movie, Raees is taken by police out into a remote area and extra-judiciously shot dead by the officer who has hunted him for most of his life. This scene is eerily reminiscent of the fake encounter killings that target Muslim men in India today, particularly in Uttar Pradesh which is led by BJP's Yogi Adityanath.[113] It also calls to mind the landmark Supreme Court decision Om Prakash v. State of Jharkhand, (2012) 12 SCC 72 against such state sponsored terrorism. The ruling held that, "It is not the duty of police officers to kill [the] accused merely because they are dreaded criminals - Police have to arrest [the] accused and put them up for trial - Killings by trigger happy police personnel, who liquidate criminals and project the incident as an encounter, stringently deprecated - Such killings are illegal and amount to State-sponsored terrorism."[114]

Cluster six of Sayyid's 'Theaters of Islamophobia' actualized throughout the film in many scenes,

such as the embeddedness of Islamophobia and corruption in the criminal justice system in which those deemed to be Muslims were discriminated against via on screen police raids, stop and search protocol, police intensification of surveillance of the Muslim population, the use of clandestine operating procedures, secret police operations, and differential sentencing towards Muslims as reflected in the in the form of extrajudicial murder of Raees by an officer vested with state power, rather than a trial.

111   Milia Ali, "'Raees' Worldwide Box-office Collection: Shah Rukh Khan's Film Powers past 250-crore Mark," The Times of India, February 20, 2017, https://timesofindia.indiatimes.com/entertainment/hindi/bollywood/box-office/raees-worldwide-box-office-collection-shah-rukh-khans-film-powers-past-250-crore-mark/articleshow/56970149.cms.

112   Chandna Kumar, "More Trouble for Shah Rukh Khan: Shia Community Offended by Raees Scene," Hindustan Times, https://www.hindustantimes.com/, December 15, 2016, https://www.hindustantimes.com/bollywood/more-Trouble-for-shah-rukh-khan-shia-community-offended-by-raees-scene/story-noJIL997hd4udticwqCrnM.html

113   see Neha Dixit, "A Chronicle of the Crime Fiction That Is Adityanath's Encounter Raj," The Wire, February 24, 2018, https://thewire.in/rights/chronicle-crime-fiction-adityanaths-encounter-raj for encounter killings, also note that several profiles of those killed in staged/fake encounter killings are Muslim men although such murders by police include others.

114   Om Prakash v. State of Jharkhand (2012) 12 SCC 72, http://www.supremecourtcases.com/index2.php?option=com_content&itemid=99999999&do_pdf=1&id=43052.

Padmaavat

Padmaavat is an Indian epic period drama directed by Sanjay Leela Bhansali that was released in 2018. In her review of the film, Aparita Bhandari explained that the story of Padmavati is legendary across much of India and even revered in some parts.[115] Legend has it that Padmavati was "so beautiful that her mere description inspired Alauddin Khilji, ruler of Delhi Sultanate, to capture the queen and Chittor."[116] When he succeeded and Padmavati's husband Maharawal Ratan Singh was killed in battle, legend narrates that Padmavati's and the women of Chittor "committed jauhar – throwing themselves in fire rather than being captured by Khilji and having their honour besmirched." [117] The legend upholds stereotypes of the pure, beautiful Indian woman, faithful to her husband even in death, who would choose self immolation rather than submit to a Muslim conqueror—juxtaposed against the over-sexed, barbarian Muslim male who would travel to fight a war just to possess such a woman. It is reminiscent of tropes around "love jihad," specifically the innocent Hindu girl desired by the deviant Muslim male and lured into romantic relationships, mirrored in intimate scenes between Khilji and Padmaavat in the film. It also appeals to BJP/RSS propaganda that imagines Muslims as foreign invaders who allegedly conquered India and subjugated Hindus.

The film opens with the expected Orientalist sets, designs, and costumes. The protagonist Khilji is seen ripping his teeth into a big chunk of meat he holds with his hand. Furthering the barbarian trope, his hair is matted, and his eyes are lined with kohl as he and his men maraud around the desert under a collection of green flags with a white crescent to symbolize Islam. Khilji also engages in non-marital relations with a girl prior to his marriage and "treats his wife like a slave

115   Aparita Bhandari, "Review: Padmaavat Perpetuates Stereotypes and Carries a Dangerous Message," The Globe and Mail, January 30, 2018, https://www.theglobeandmail.com/arts/film/film-reviews/review-padmaavat-perpetuates-stereotypes-and-carries-a-dangerous-message/article37787050/.
116   Ibid.
117   Ibid.

on their wedding night."[118] The construction of the character Khilji is the antithesis of a Muslim. He appears to be a dirty, savage and not representative of the cleanliness, manners or behaviors required by Islam.

In her critique of Padmaavat, Indian journalist Rana Ayyub wrote that "beneath the grandiosity and stunning frames of "Padmaavat" lies a disturbing attempt at selling dangerous stereotypes that might yield immediate favors for Bhansali but leaves a disturbing impression of a community on a generation that seeks great inspiration from popular cinema."[119] Ayyub also claimed:

In India, as in democracies around the globe, mainstream cinema has been a powerful tool that shapes public opinion and narrative. In a communally sensitive atmosphere in the country where lynchings and murders in the name of religion are becoming a norm, Bhansali [film Director] has strengthened the stereotype of the evil, diabolic, murderous Muslim, a trope that forms the basis of right-wing hate of minorities. The calls for demolition of the Taj Mahal or disparaging comments about the iconic monument by leaders of the BJP has been an extension of this narrative that chooses to see the Taj Mahal as a Muslim monument built by the Mughals.[120]

From its inception, the film has been shrouded in controversy:

- **Jan 2017:** Production is halted after Hindu extremist group Karni Sena vandalises the set in Rajasthan state. Director Sanjay Leela Bhansali is slapped by a member of the group

- **March 2017:** The crew moves filming to Maharashtra state but protests continue. Bhansali denies claims that the film depicts a "romantic dream sequence" between Padmavati and Alauddin Khilji

- **Aug 2017:** Many Bollywood celebrities voice their support for the film

- **Sept 2017:** Two posters of the film are released, prompting further outrage from Karni Sena and other right-wing groups. Protesters burn the posters

- **Nov 2017:** Karni Sena continues its protests in Rajasthan, demanding a nationwide ban on the film. The group also threatens to chop off the nose of lead actress Deepika Padukone. The film's 1 December release date is delayed

- **Dec 2017:** Indian censors clear the film but suggest changing the name to "Padmaavat"

- **Jan 2018:** The Supreme Court orders the film to be released nationwide and tells four states which banned it - Haryana, Rajasthan, Gujarat and Madhya Pradesh - to ensure law and order is maintained.

(Timeline courtesy of BBC, 2017).[121]

118   Rana Ayyub,"Opinion: Bigotry And Islamophobia In Bhansali's "Padmaavat," NDTV.com, February 06, 2018, https://www.ndtv.com/opinion/bigotry-and-islamophobia-in-bhansalis-Padmaavat-by-Rana-ayyub-1808938.
119   Ibid.
120   Ibid.
121   "Padmaavat: Why a Bollywood Epic Has Sparked Fierce Protests," BBC News, January 25, 2018, https://www.bbc.com/news/world-asia-india-42048512.

Music

Cultural production in the form of music "plays an important role in propagating and reinforcing racist ideology and recruiting new members into racist groups, particularly for young people."[122] Further, in Europe and the U.S, it has been mobilized by racists to promote white nationalism through a genre of music referred to as "white power" and hate core music. Infused within the hate music are lyrics that "demonize variously conceived non-whites and advocate racial pride and solidarity... with pounding rhythms and a charging punk or metal-based accompaniment."[123] An article by *The Print* entitled "The Rise of the Communal Hate Soundtrack in India," has revealed a similar growing trend in India of Islamophobic music promoting 'Hindutva power' that is played at political and religious gatherings, as well as processions. Similar to white power music, the songs consist of a mix of electric beats and are infused with hate and incendiary speech. They include Islamophobic clips made by leading BJP members, including excerpts from Prime Minister Modi and Chief Minister of Uttar Pradesh Yogi Adityanath.[124] This vitriolic works as an "ideological propagation tool" garnering thousands of likes and subscribers on social media platforms, as well as millions of views for various YouTubers.[125]

These Islamophobic incitement pieces are also played by DJs outside of mosques in Muslim areas. Further, police have been critical of the March 2018 festival processions in the areas of Bihar and West Bengal blaming these types of songs for "contributing to the communal violence witnessed around Ram Navami."[126] Although some in the government have framed this and other acts of "communal violence" as isolated

122   Australian Human Rights Commission, "Examples of Racist Material on the Internet," December 14, 2012, https://www.humanrights.gov.au/publications/examples-racist-material-internet.

123   Benjamin R. Teitelbaum, "Saga's Sorrow: Femininities in Despair in the Music of Radical Nationalism," Ethnomusicology, vol. 58, no. 3, Fall 2014, 405-406.

124   Kumar Anshuman, "The Rise of the Communal Hate Soundtrack in India," The Print, April 6, 2018, theprint.in/politics/the-rise-of-the-communal-hate-soundtrack-in-india/47672/.

125   Ibid.

126   Ibid.

cases, others have claimed that there were three month long formulated plans "to play these songs during the processions ...with the sole purpose of spreading communal hatred" through intentional and organized acts of intimidation.[127] The following are samples of the Islamophobic lyrics making their rounds online and on the ground at rallies and processions provided by Kumar Anshuman at *The Print*:

Ram ji ke kaam mein taang jo adaayega, maa ki kasam jinda nahi jayega (The one who impedes the work of Ram will not go alive, I swear on my mother's life).

Laxmi Dubey

Ram Lalla hum jayenge, mandir wahin banayenge, door hato Allah walon, janmabhoomi ko ghera hai, masjid kahin aur banao tum, ye Ram Lalla ka dera hai (Child Ram, we'll go and build the temple there itself... Scram, men of Allah! The birthplace has been surrounded. Make your mosque somewhere else, this is Ram Lalla's establishment).

Lucky DJ

Jis din jaag utha Hindutva, anjam bolega, topi wala bhi sar jhukae Hindustan bolega, topi wala bhi bolega, jai shree Ram, jai shree ram (The day Hindutva awakes, the end result will speak. The man in the cap will say 'Hindustan' with a bowed head. The man in the cap will also say 'jai shree Ram, jai shree Ram').

Pakistan mein bhi bhagwa lehrayega, tu kya tera baap bhi Ram naam chillayega (The saffron flag will fly in Pakistan too, you and your father will scream the name of Ram).[128]

Vivek Pandey

The lyrics appeal to national Hindu sentiments and focus on contentious issues as segues into Islamophobic speech including the Babri Masjid demolition by Hindu nationalists in Ayodhya and the calls to build a Hindu temple in its place, Partition in India resulting in Muslims being told leave and go to Pakistan as a Muslim home rather than staying in India, as well as, the threat that India ("Ram Lalla's establishment") will take over Pakistan where the "saffron flag will fly," and the resistant Muslim will finally submit to the Hindu Rashtra by declaring their loyalty to Hinduism and recite/scream "jai shree Ram."[129] The lyrics clarify that anyone who does not submit to the Hindu Rashtra project is impeding the work of Lord Ram and therefore they "will not go alive."[130]

Of particular concern is a report by *Citizens for Justice and Peace,* which reveals that prior to the ethnic-religious cleansing of Muslims in Modi led Gujarat in 2002, *kar sevaks* (religious volunteers) armed with weapons attacked Muslims and forced them to shout "Jai Shri Ram!" (a chant of loyalty to the Hindu God Rama) while "pulling the beards of some of them" and stabbing them with "trishuls" (a sharp, bladed trident like weapon).[131] The report also claims that *kar sevaks* shouted Islamophobic slogans similar to some of the lyrics and incendiary speeches by ultra-nationalist politicians in Hindutva power music, such as:

"Jai Shriram!," "Muslim Bharat Chodo, Pakistan Jao," (Muslims quit India!, go to Pakistan), "Mandir Vahin Banayenge," and "Dudh mango tho Kheer denge, Kashmir mango tho Kheer denge" ("Ask for milk and we'll give you kheer (pudding), But ask for Kashmir and we'll cut you up")."[132]

127   Ibid.
128   Ibid.
129   Ibid.
130   Ibid.
131   Citizens for Justice and Peace, Crime Against Humanity-An Inquiry into the Carnage in Gujarat Findings and Recommendations, report, vol. II (Mumbai: Anil Dharkar, 2002), 12 .
132   Ibid.

Social Media

When it comes to social media, Prime Minister Narendra Modi seems to have adopted a strategic "silence is golden" stance, or at least it is "golden" regarding certain issues plaguing the nation. He has been accused of 'selectively tweeting' which has been viewed by some as curious given his "very active Twitter presence," his ability to connect with audiences and his fiery oratory past.[133] This includes the "responsibility for some of the worst religious violence ever seen in independent India" when he served as Chief Minister of Gujarat during the 2002 massacre of thousands of Muslims.[134] Interestingly during his 2014 election campaign to become Prime Minister, Modi sought to be heard even by the remotest corners of India so much that he rallied via 3D hologram.[135] The first candidate to use a hologram technology during an election, Modi beamed himself into rallies in 90 of India's most remote villages. Overall "Magic Modi" was able to address "more than 800 rallies in a hologram" reaching millions with his words.[136] In comparison, U.S President-elect Donald Trump reportedly held a total of 307 speeches and rallies during his 2016 campaign.[137]

Other than the official Modi smartphone app, the social media platform Twitter is a key mode of communication utilized by Modi to communicate with the public. At the time of writing, @narendramodi had posted 22.4K tweets total and had a large following numbering 46 million. However, his feed is strategically utopian, cleansed from violence and several political, economic and domestic issues facing the country. A May 2018 *India Today* article recently paralleled a side by side of breaking news on the ground in India and Modi's politically orchestrated tweets. It revealed that Modi posted photo ops at the Kremlin while state violence was unleashed upon the citizens of Tamil Nadu. As masses filled the street following the "brutal rape and murder of an eight-year-old in Kashmir's Kathua and the rape of a 17-year-old allegedly by a BJP MLA in Unnao," Modi tweeted holiday wishes for Puthandu.[138] Some have attributed Modi's social media feed to his overall image making that is controlled and strategic down to whether he wears a kurta or Nehru jacket or is recorded practicing yoga in his yard.[139] Still others find his silence on issues such as the rape of young girls, lynching and murder, as approval for vigilantism executed against Muslim and Dalits.[140]

Some members of the BJP have followed suit selectively posting on social media, but their posts have been more revealing. For example, demonstrating outrage on social media on behalf of cow protection and condemning violence and death against animals, while remaining silent regarding cow-related lynching of Muslims. To better gauge selective outrage on the part of members of the BJP, *Alt News* analyzed 100 Twitter timelines of the most active BJP MPs/MLAs/Spokespersons regarding a particular case of cow slaughter in Kerala to see if the members also tweeted condemnations regarding the cow-related lynching of impoverished, Muslim, dairy farmer Pehlu Khan. Their analysis found that the BJP members who condemned the slaughter of a cow "never tweeted about the lynching of Pehlu Khan."[141]

133   Nishtha Gupta, "The Curious Case of Modi and His Selective Tweets," India Today, May 25, 2018, www.indiatoday.in/india/story/the-curious-case-of-modi-and-his-selective-tweets-1241826-2018-05-25

134   Aditya Chakrabortty, "Narendra Modi, a Man with a Massacre on His Hands, Is Not the Reasonable Choice for India | Aditya Chakrabortty," The Guardian, April 07, 2014, https://www.theguardian.com/commentisfree/2014/apr/07/narendra-modi-massacre-next-prime-minister-india.

135   NDTV, "3D Avatar of Modi to Campaign in Delhi's Streets," YouTube, November 14, 2013, https://www.youtube.com/watch?v=6cSREmEMOX0.

136   Dean Nelson, "'Magic' Modi Uses Hologram to Address Dozens of Rallies at Once," The Telegraph, May 02 2014, https://www.telegraph.co.uk/news/worldnews/asia/india/10803961/Magic-Modi-uses-hologram-to-address-dozens-of-rallies-at-once.html.

137   Candace Smith and Liz Kreutz, "Hillary Clinton's and Donald Trump's Campaigns by the Numbers," ABC News, November 07, 2016, https://abcnews.go.com/Politics/hillary-clinton-donald-trumps-campaigns-numbers/story?id=43356783.

138   Gupta, "The Curious Case of Modi and His Selective Tweets," 2018.

139   "Narendra Modi's Image Factory." The Economist, August 9, 2018, www.economist.com/asia/2018/08/09/narendra-modis-image-factory.

140   Jug Suraiya,"The Meaning of the Silence of Prime Minister Modi," Times of India Blog, April 14, 2018, blogs.timesofindia.indiatimes.com/jugglebandhi/the-meaning-of-the-silence-of-prime-minister-modi/

141   "Outrage over Slaughter of a Cow vs a Human – an Analysis of 100 BJP Leaders Active on Social Media," Alt News, May 31, 2017, https://www.altnews.in/outrage-slaughter-cow-vs-human

However, while silence and selective outrage is one tactic strategically mobilized, BJP members, ultra-nationalists and their allies have weaponized the internet to disseminate their own version of reality through propaganda, stoking Islamophobia and inciting violence. For instance, in July of 2017 after an Islamophobic meme of the Prophet Muhammad was posted on social media by Souvik Sarkar, some BJP leaders attempted to capitalize on the tensions it caused in Bengal. The BJP's Asansol district IT in-charge Tarun Sengupta was arrested on charges for "spreading fake news and creating communal disharmony" and for "posting fake images and videos on social media to stir communal trouble."[142] He posted a polarizing image, that after fact checking demonstrated it was not related to the current events, but was "taken from a Bhojpuri movie called *Aurat Khilona Nahi* released in 2014."[143] In the image, a male is seen pulling the saree of a woman in distress with a look of fear on her face, which can be understood as Muslim aggression in several ways depending on the imagination (violence/rape/public disrobing), toward Hindu women. It also evokes the need to '*save Hindu women from Muslim men*,' a common Islamophobic trope. Other members of the BJP shared the same photo including Vijeta Malik, an official of the BJP's Haryana unit.[144] Then BJP spokesperson Nupur Sharma followed by circulating a second image alleging that it was also from the incident unfolding in Bengal.[145] It was actually a photo of a toppled and burning vehicle from the 2002 Gujarat riot. Even after Twitterati proved that the photos and film clips were fake, Sharma still insisted that they were representative of the way Hindus are treated by Muslims.[146] Thus even when presented with reality, the BJP spokesperson continued to propagate the Hindutva imaginary over the truth, stoking Islamophobia and inciting violence.

In addition, Islamophobia is often mobilized around election cycles in several countries across the globe and the same is true for India. Political parties including the BJP have cyber war rooms and troll armies ready to engage in propaganda and fake news. A piece by *The Quint* entitled, "Beware: Fake News Fever in Karnataka as Assembly Polls Approach" revealed how members of the BJP stoke Islamophobia to polarize communities and incite violence against Muslims.[147] Among the examples was the case of Paresh Mesta. Following a period of violence in Uttara Kannada, where Hindus constitute 82.61 percent of the population and Muslims only 13.8 percent, the BJP took to social media claiming that the young man found dead in a local pond was a BJP member who had been tortured to death by Muslims.[148]

In fact, Mesta's father clarified that his son was not been a member of the BJP and to rebuke the false claims, police released forensic results proving that the young man had not been tortured.[149] Yet during this time of heightened tension, BJP MP Shobha Karandlaje mobilized Islamophobia on Twitter stoking the smouldering tension to "provoke Hindus against Muslims and disturb the peace," according to a police complaint filed against her.[150] Building upon the debunked fears circulating that "jihadis"[151] had tortured the young man found in the pond, Karandlaje tweeted again

-analysis-100-bjp-leaders-active-social-media/.

142   Deepshikha Ghosh, "BJP Leader Arrested For Spreading Fake News, Says Bengal Police," NDTV.com, July 12, 2017, www.ndtv.com/india-news/bjp-leader-arrested-for-spreading-fake-news-says-bengal-police-1723673.

143   Ibid.

144   Ibid.

145   PTI, "Delhi BJP Leader Shared Gujarat Riots Photo As From Bengal," NDTV.com, July 10, 2017, www.ndtv.com/delhi-news/delhi-bjp-leader-denounced-on-twitter-for-sharing-gujarat-riots-photo-as-bengals-1722698.

146   Ibid.

147   Meghnad Bose, "Beware: Fake News Fever in Karnataka as Assembly Polls Approach." The Quint, May 8, 2018, www.thequint.com/news/webqoof/fake-news-karnataka-assembly-election-2018-jihadi-murder

148   Ibid and TA Ameerudheen, "BJP Continues to Fan Communal Tensions in Coastal Karnataka over a Young Man's Mysterious Death," Scroll.in, December 18, 2017, scroll.in/article/861774/bjp-continues-to-fan-communal-tensions-in-coastal-karnataka-over-a-young-mans-mysterious-death.

149   Ibid.

150   Express News Service, "Karnataka BJP MP Booked on Charges of Promoting Communal Enmity," The Indian Express, December 22, 2017, indianexpress.com/article/india/karnataka-bjp-mp-shobha-karandlaje-booked-on-charges-of-promoting-communal-enmity/.

151   "Jihadi" as a derogatory trope in reference to Muslims serves to perpetuate the Hindutva myth that Muslims are outsiders and conquerors who have invaded India and subdued or are enemies at war with Hindus, as well as War on Terror implications.

alleging that:

"Jihadis tried to rape and murder a girl studying in 9th std near Honnavar. Why is the govt silent about this incident? Arrest those who molested and injured this girl. Where are you CM @siddaramaiah?"[152]

Rising Nationalism Adds to India's Fake News Problem

Fake News Messages Shared on Whatsapp in India in 2018, by Topic

36.5%
Scares and Scams

29.9%
Nationalism

22.4%
Current Affairs

11.2%
Others

Source BBC

"

Online Islamophobia is likely to incite religious hatred and xenophobia leading to real world crimes.

152   Ibid.

Karandlaje was consequently charged under 153, 153A and section 505 (2) for her December 14, 2017 tweet, and although it was found that the girl in question had self inflicted the wound, the circulated social media reports of the alleged attack upon the girl by "jihadis" manifested in attacks upon Muslim owned businesses and establishments in the area.[153]

Discourse analysis undertaken by Anton and Petter Törnberg regarding Islamophobic representations of Muslims and Islam found that segments of the internet actually serve as 'online amplifiers' that both reflect and reinforce "existing discourses in traditional media, which is likely to result in even stronger polarizing effects on public discourses."[154] Thus, when people in positions of power such as BJP officials share fake news and images that propagate the pro-BJP line, they stoke Islamophobia at the expense of the Muslim minority in India. Islamophobia infused with conspiracy theories goes viral and "ricochet[s] through echo chambers on Facebook, Twitter and the WhatsApp mobile messaging platform, find[ing] a receptive audience on mainstream news channels that increasingly back the government."[155] Adding to that, empirical research undertaken by Andre Oboler reveals that online Islamophobia "is likely to incite religious hatred and xenophobia leading to real world crimes."[156]

A 2018 study released by The Observer Research Foundation (ORF) revealed that Facebook users in India number more than 240 million "making India the largest audience for the social platform."[157] This means that presently India constitutes 10 percent of all Facebook's users.[158] With support from Facebook, ORF analyzed both posts and comments from mainstream news organizations, community groups, religious organizations, and prominent public personalities. The study mapped both hate speech and counter-speech on active social media accounts in India.[159]

Findings revealed that "religion and 'religio-cultural' practices related to food and dress, were the most explicit basis for hate as expressed in Indian social media: they accounted for a rise from 19 to 30 percent of the incidents over the one-year timeframe of the study."[160]

The topics stoking Islamophobia were similar to those expressed elsewhere in this report, such as interfaith marriages between Hindus and Muslims often labeled as "love jihad," beef eating and cow protection which targets Muslim religious and dietary practices, as well as general positions on universal human rights, such as Kashmir and Rohingya refugees in India.[161] Most of the hate according to the study, actually "incited bodily harm or violence against people belonging to India's Muslim community."[162]

WhatsApp owned by Facebook, has also been implicated in the dissemination of misinformation and false news. Hate speech, false news, and rumors on this platform have led to the spread of Islamophobia and violence against individuals and minority communities in India much like they have in neighboring Myanmar, where social media is attributed to the escalation of extreme violence against the Muslim Rohingya minority.[163] Just in the month of June 2018 alone, *Engadget*

153   Ibid. and The Representation of the People Act, 1951 has several applicable codes for electoral offenses by elected officials and those running for office, who create or promote enmity and hatred based on a large number of categories including religion including imprisonment, fines and disqualification. http://www.legislative.gov.in/sites/default/files/04_representation%20of%20the%20people%20act%2C%201951.pdf

154   Anton Törnberg and Petter Törnberg, "Muslims in Social Media Discourse: Combining Topic Modeling and Critical Discourse Analysis," Discourse, Context and Media, vol 13, 2016: 134.

155   Shashank Bengali, "Fake News Fuels Nationalism and Islamophobia - Sound Familiar? In This Case, It's in India." Los Angeles Times, July 11, 2017, www.latimes.com/world/asia/la-fg-india-fake-news-20170711-story.html

156   Andre Oboler, Islamophobia in Cyberspace: Hate Crimes Go Viral, by Imran Awan (Farnham, Surrey, UK: Ashgate, 2016), 41.

157   Maya Mirchandani, Ojasvi Goel, and Dhananjay Sahai, "Encouraging Counter-Speech by Mapping the Contours of Hate Speech on Social Media in India," Observer Research Foundation, August 29, 2018, https://www.orfonline.org/wp-content/uploads/2018/03/ORF_Report_Counter_Speech.pdf, 1.

158   Ibid.

159   Ibid.

160   Ibid.

161   Ibid.

162   Ibid.

163   David Lumb, "Fake News on WhatsApp Is Inciting Lynchings in India," Engadget, July 03, 2018, https://www.engadget.com/2018/07/02/india-fake-news-whatsapp-groups/.

reported that fake messages in India have spread through WhatsApp leading to the death of twelve people.[164]

Editor Shahid Siddiqui explained that fake or distorted footage have been utilized to propagate, for example, that "Muslims are murderers or rapists of Hindu women" and then those messages "are forwarded through social media" reaching "villagers and poor people with no access to any other information and they start believing that Muslims are monsters."[165] This is reflected in the 2018 case involving Muslim Google employee Mohammad Azam and his companions, who were passing through an area in on the way home. They were reportedly attacked by a large mob in southern Karnataka state's Bidar district because of WhatsApp rumors circulating on the platform about kidnappers in the area.[166] In this case, the hospitality of Azam's companion from Qatar, who offered chocolates he had brought with him to a child in the village, was criminalized and these Muslim 'others' were labeled as kidnappers. Although they escaped from the original area, they were stopped by a another larger mob as they fled.[167] As a result, Azam was murdered.

164   Ibid.
165   Vir Sanghvi,"Who Is Using WhatsApp as a Murder Weapon?" South China Morning Post, July 09, 2018, https://www.scmp.com/week-asia/society/article/2154436/indias-lynching-app-who-using-whatsapp-murder-weapon.
166   Jalees Andrabi, "32 Arrested for Lynching of Muslim Man Based on WhatsApp Child Kidnap Rumor," IndiaAbroad.com, July 15, 2018, https://www.indiaabroad.com/india/arrested-for-lynching-of-muslim-man-based-on-whatsapp-child/article_aa9e9d46-8860-11e8-bf4e-67ff98f581a6.html.
167   Sanghvi, "Who Is Using WhatsApp as a Murder Weapon?," 2018.

Populism and Media Control

Modi's War Rooms

Election war rooms are being utilized by the BJP and other parties to run election campaigns staffed primarily with people under the age of 30 from across India who are familiar with local issues. The idea is allegedly to reach out in mass to voters utilizing social media platforms such as Facebook, Twitter and WhatsApp utilizing "social media engineering" to woo votes.[168] However, an article by *The Wire* revealed that war rooms "targeting more than 300 million voters" in the run-up to the 2019 general elections are also targeting reporters and news that could defame the BJP party, including reports on lynchings.[169] As latter sections of our report demonstrate, Muslims are documented as the largest population in India that are killed in lynchings, many of which are cow or beef related.

Groups consisting of pro-BJP journalists, lawyers and graduates scour news in the war rooms for pieces that are both pro and anti-BJP and closely track the social media handles of journalists. Journalists who are too critical of the BJP and Modi are placed on a prime list and

168   Indulekha Aravind, "Social Media Engineering: How Congress & BJP's War Room Are Trying to Woo Voters in Karnataka," The Economic Times, March 25, 2018, https://economictimes.indiatimes.com/news/politics-and-nation/social-media-engineering-how-congress-bjps-war-room-are-trying-to-woo-voters-in-karnataka/articleshow/63445558.cms.

169   Ishita Mishra, "Pro-BJP or Anti-BJP: Inside the Modi-Shah Media Tracking 'War Rooms'," The Wire, August 11, 2018, https://thewire.in/politics/narendra-modi-amit-shah-bjp-india-media.

tracked further for pro or anti-BJP sentiment. Television is also tracked and listed in a similar manner and summaries on the program content are categorized, collected and scored. An article by *The Wire* includes images of the detailed information sought and the rating scale utilized. Adding to the suspicion, the project is surrounded by a sense of secrecy. For example, employees stated that they were unaware of the address of their work location until their first day, and they also do not work from the BJP headquarters inaugurated in 2018, but another location.[170]

Spokesmen from the Samajwadi Party and Congress voiced concern at the extensive media monitoring and detailed tracking of specific journalists and their social media, especially given the attacks on reporters. Congress MLA Randeep Singh Surjewala believes that such actions are beyond the norm and reflect the BJP's desire to create a surveillance state.[171] He clarified the difference between raising awareness of "issues affecting the people" and "tracking those who write against the PM or the ruling BJP in any manner."[172]

Islamophobia Monetized at the Ballot Box

In India's 2014 election, the BJP and the Sangh Parivar (the Hindu nationalist body) mobilized along communal lines. Their win is attributed in part to Hindu-Muslim polarization which was "an important aspect of the BJP's election campaign."[173] For example in Uttar Pradesh as

the election neared, the BJP and RSS "created an impression that Muslims in western Uttar Pradesh were the cause of the high crime rate, and that crimes increased after the Muzaffarnagar riots of 2013 as the number of Muslims rose in towns and villages."[174] This stereotyping of the Muslims collectively as criminals rather than victims of the attack, was mobilized to make it appear that in order to protect Uttar Pradesh and India at large from Muslim criminals, the only correct choice at the ballot box would be to elect Yogi Adityanath who would be hard on crime and Muslims.

Regarding "Hindu–Muslim strife," Zaheer Baber argues that "certain specific patterns can be identified that are strikingly similar to racial conflicts in other social contexts where religion has not been an issue."[175] Further clarifying the relationship between communalism and racialization, Sumit Sarkar a historian of modern India wrote, "communalism veers close to everyday racism, with the Muslim – like the black or colored immigrant – felt to be a biological danger" and a threat through their very existence.[176] Similar campaigns strategies and attack politics have been utilized to polarize society for electoral gains in elections beyond India. For instance in the U.S, Republicans strategically mobilized racial anxieties by constructing Willie Horton as a bogey and rhetorical weapon in the 1988 general election in an effort to brand Democrats as soft on crime. Horton was an African-American convicted of the rape and murder of a white woman while he was out of prison on a furlough program supported by Governor Michael Dukakis who was also running for U.S President on the Democratic ticket.[177] Hate and polarizing politics pay at the ballot box according to a recent Hindustan Times article

170   Ibid.
171   Ibid.
172   Ibid.
173   Milan Vaishnav, "Understanding the Indian Voter," Carnegie Endowment for International Peace, June 23, 2015, carnegieendowment.org/2015/06/23/understanding-indian-voter-pub-60416.
174   Harsh Mander, "Karwan-e-Mohabbat: Uttar Pradesh Has Found a New Excuse to Kill Muslim Men." DailyO - Opinion News & Analysis on Latest Breaking News India, Living Media India Limited, September 14, 2017, www.dailyo.in/voices/muslim-men-lynching-encounters/story/1/19496.html.
175   Zaheer Baber,"'Race', Religion and Riots: The 'Racialization' of Communal Identity and Conflict in India," Sociology, vol 38, no. 4 (2004): 703. https://libproxy.berkeley.edu/login?qurl=http%3a%2f%2fsearch.ebscohost.com%2flogin.aspx%3fdirect%3dtrue%26db%3dedsjsr%26AN%3dedsjsr.42858189%26site%3deds-live.
176   Sumit Sarkar, "Indian Nationalism and the Politics of Hindutva," In Contesting the Nation: Religion, Community and the Politics of Democracy in India, edited by Steve E. Ludden, Pennsylvania: University of Pennsylvania Press,1996, 290.
177   Richard L. Berke, "The 1992 Campaign: Political Week; In 1992, Willie Horton Is Democrats' Weapon." The New York Times, August 25, 1992, www.nytimes.com/1992/08/25/us/the-1992-campaign-political-week-in-1992-willie-horton-is-democrats-weapon.html.

that claims "candidates accused of communal crimes win their elections at a rate more than four times greater than those who have not been accused of any crimes."[178] Milan Vaishnav, a senior fellow at the Carnegie Endowment of International Peace argues that criminality is mobilized by candidates to help establish "credibility to protect their own community."[179] For example, in 2017 BJP MLA T. Raja Singh was booked under section 295A of the Indian Penal Code (deliberate and malicious acts intended to outrage religious feelings of any class by insulting its religion or religious beliefs) by police for an Islamophobic speech that he made where he "threatened to "behead" the "traitors" opposed to the construction of a Ram temple in Ayodhya."[180] This was directed toward Muslims in India who are often called "traitors," "anti-nationalists," and those who would be strongly opposed to the construction of Ram temple in Ayodhya given the contention around it. Yet although Singh had eight other prior communal crimes charges against him, he won the 2014 election by "twice as many votes" than the runner up.[181] Singh's mobilization of Islamophobia as an election platform actually enhanced his appeal. One supporter said "Raja Singh stands for Hindutva, so we vote for him."[182]

Utilizing self-sworn affidavits of hopeful political candidates, the Association of Democratic Reforms (ADR) and National Election Watch (NEW) revealed that several of India's elected officials and lawmakers have self-reported their own roles in hate. The report claimed that the "BJP has the largest number of lawmakers in the country with declared cases of hate speech against them."[183] In 2018, it was reported that of the "58 current MPs and MLAs with declared

cases of hate speech against themselves, 27 are from the BJP."[184] The report also found that by "giving tickets to candidates who are charged with cases related to hate speech, political parties have been in a way abetting circumstances that lead to events such as communal riots and violence between different groups of people."[185]

In the lead up to the upcoming 2019 elections in India, three men accused of lynching Muslims in separate high profile cases are being backed by wealthy businessman Amit Jani and Navnirman Sena, a Hindutva outfit based in Meerut to contest Lok Sabha elections.[186] The three include: Shambu Lal Raigar who videotaped himself hacking a Muslim man to death while claiming vengeance for "love jihad" in 2017, and Naresh Kumar Sehrawat, the prime accused in the brutal mob lynching of 16-year-old Junaid Khan. They are poised to run along with Hariom Sisodia who allegedly took part in the 2015 lynching of Mohammad Akhlaq. In response, the head of the Uttar Pradesh Navnirman Sena claimed that he is nurturing "a new generation of 'Hindutva warriors' to fight Islam."[187] Criminal Justice scholar Arvind Verma claims that "Indian law prohibits a person from contesting election if he or she has been convicted of any criminal charges."[188] However, he explained that the provision is often circumvented allowing a "large number" of people to contest and even win elections with serious crimes such as "murder" on their records. He refers to this "criminalization of politics" as "a peculiar phenomenon of Indian politics."[189]

178   Harry Stevens,"Let's Talk about Hate: In Indian Politics, Candidates Who Stoke Communal Hatred Thrive," Hindustan Times, July 27, 2017, https://www.hindustantimes.com/india-news/let-s-talk-about-hate-does-stoking-communal-hatred-guarantee-electoral-victory-for-politicians-yes-says-data/story-VVmK9r6hG2xeoWQxlySUbP.html.
179   Ibid.
180   Ibid. and Rao Apparasu,"BJP's Raja Singh Booked for His Threat to Behead Those Opposing Ram Temple," Hindustan Times, April 10, 2017, https://www.hindustantimes.com/india-news/bjp-s-raja-Singh-booked-for-threatening-to-behead-traitors-who-oppose-ram-temple/story-y7zwpStDdHyFL00NFNKL8I.html.
181   Stevens, "Let's Talk about Hate," 2017.
182   Ibid.
183   'BJP MPs, MLAs Top List of Hate Speech Makers,' Association for Democratic Reforms, April 25, 2018, adrindia.org/content/bjp-mps-mlas-top-list-hate-speech-makers.
184   Ibid.
185   Ibid.
186   Sharma Betwa, "Meet The UP Businessman Giving Lok Sabha Tickets To Hindus Who Have Lynched Muslims." HuffPost India, October 02, 2018, www.huffingtonpost.in/2018/09/30/meet-the-up-businessman-giving-lok-sabha-tickets-to-hindus-who-have-lynched-muslims_a_23546403/.
187   Ibid.
188   Arvind Verma,"Policing Elections in India," 2005, India Review, 4 (3/4): 361. doi:10.1080/14736480500302217
189   Ibid, 362.

Statistics

Sitting MP/MLAs with declared cases of hate speech.

Uttar Pradesh	15
Telangana	13
Karnataka	5
Maharashra	5
Bihar	4

10 of 15

Sitting Lok Sabha MPS that have declared cases related to hate speech against themselves are from the BJP.

17 of 43

Sitting MLAs with declared cases of hate speech are from the BJP.

Islamophobic Statements

BY LEADING OFFICIALS, LEGISLATORS AND POLITICIANS IN INDIA

These statements by officials demonstrate in part, systematic otherization and Islamophobia. The statments clear the way for discriminatory legislation, policies and actions toward this vulnerable population. As a result, people may face discrimination, harassment, acts of physical violence, criminalization, imprisonment, deportation, and death.

Narendra Modi
PRIME MINISTER

"Congress leaders are speaking in a language that is not acceptable in a democracy...This is insulting. This is nothing but a mindset of the Mughals."

Surendra Singh
BJP BAIIRIA MLA

"There are a very few Muslims who are patriotic. Once India becomes a Hindu rashtra, Muslims who assimilate into our culture will stay in India. Those who will not are free to take asylum in any other country."

Banwari Lal Singhal
BJP LEGISLATOR

"Muslims are worried (sic) about how to take over the nation by increasing their population; education and development have no significance to them. It's my personal opinion."

Ajay Sharma
BJP GHAZIABAD

Descended upon a wedding reception between families of a Hindu woman and Muslim man, along with members of Bajrang Dal, Hindu Raksha Dal and Dharam Jagran Manch citing "love jihad," making threats and causing a ruckus.

Subramanian Swamy
BJP LEGISLATOR

"Muslims should take an oath declaring that their ancestors were Hindu if they want to prove their citizenship."

Sakshi Maharaj
BJP MP

"Those with four wives and 40 children are responsible for the rapid population growth in the country."

Suchait Singh
RSS PRANT SANGHCHALK

"Why shoud we tolerate them (Rohingya refugees) when they pose a security threat to the nation as well as the state."

Gopal Parmar
BJP MLA

"There are some goonda (hired thug) elements in Muslim community whoo adopt Hindu names to exploaut girls in the name of 'love jihad'."

Vinay Katiyar
BJP MP

"The incident of mob lynching in Alwar is highly condemnable but people from the Muslim community should abstain from touching cows and provoke aggressive Hindus. There are a lot of Muslims who are sheltering cows but are also killing them. Cow meat is also being consumed by them."

Yogi Adityanath
BJP

Praised U.S. President Donald Trump's 'Muslim Ban' and stated that "similar action is needed to contain terror activities in this country (India)."

Sanjay Patil
BJP Lawmaker

"This election is not about roads, water or other issues. This election is about Hindus vs. Muslims, Ram Mandir vs. Babri Masjid."

Giriraj Singh
BJP Union Minister

"The growing population of the country, especially Muslims, is a threat to the social fabric, social harmony, and development of the country."

Electioneering in India consists of "running negative campaigns to denounce the opposition" and the targeting of "banners, billboards, and vehicles of their opponents, tearing them down or destroying them."[190] It also incorporates "catchy slogans, songs, skits and banners" as well as organized processions, rallies and mass meetings throughout the country.[191] In 2017, electioneering also included the screening of an Islamophobic video. Legislator Sangeet Som of the BJP, who is well known for giving inflammatory speeches including referencing the Taj Mahal as a "blot on history,"[192] was charged with "instigating communal hatred in his constituency in Uttar Pradesh."[193] In the lead up to elections he was reported for screening a highly polarizing, anti-Muslim documentary. Police seized a pen drive containing the documentary and Som was charged under Section 188 of the Indian Penal Code and booked under the People's Representation Act, according to reports.[194] Prior to that, Som was also booked in 2013 for his role in inciting emotions in the lead up to the Muzaffarnagar Riot that killed 107 people, the majority of which were Muslims.[195]

Islamophobic documentaries have also been strategically mobilized in elections in the U.S and Europe. In 2008 U.S presidential election, 28 million Islamophobic DVDs were "distributed as advertising inserts in 70 newspapers, primarily in critical swing states such as Colorado, Florida and Ohio."[196] In the 2016 election, Facebook and Google targeted voters in American swing states with Islamophobic video political advertisements.[197] One video in particular entitled, "The Islamic States of America," propagated the Islamophobic imaginary of a Muslim takeover of America reflected in the replacement of the iconographic Hollywood Hills sign with a new one that read "Allahu Akbar," an Arabic term used to express the greatness of God that has been rebranded by politicians, media pundits and Islamophobes who have linked it to terrorism.[198] The video also included the repetition of commonly mobilized stereotypes such a the 'jihadi,' 'refugees,' 'creeping sharia,'and 'hijab,' especially around election cycles.[199]

In 2018, the European Parliament was called upon to stop Islamophobic election ads in their new £29m thistimeimvoting.eu campaign. One specific point of contention was a giant banner posted in Brussels depicting Muslims and a woman in hijab (head scarf) next to the words "Because we need to work together to manage migration."[200] The campaign has been accused of pushing far right tactics and "encouraging people to vote for political groups and politicians that rely on Islamophobia and anti-migrant rhetoric."[201]

In the lead up to European elections in May 2019, Steve Bannon a known Islamophobe, propagator of the alt-right and the former chief strategist to U.S President Donald Trump, has committed to the creation of a political project entitled "The Movement" in Brussels. He will coordinate and "direct "war rooms" across Europe to ensure that anti-EU and anti-immigrant parties would succeed in gaining up to a third of the total seats in the 27-nation member bloc's parliamentary elections," which has been referred to as "a

190   Ibid, 364.
191   Ibid, 365.
192   The Quint, "BJP MLA Sangeet Som Calls Taj Mahal 'a Blot on History,' YouTube, October 16, 2017, www.youtube.com/watch?v=NHOJ-MPP5Jo.
193   "U.P: BJP MLA Sangeet Som Booked For Showing Anti-Muslim Documentary," Telugu Global, www.bing.com/cr?IG=C80218B76E474AD7BD3B851CA1508AB6&CID=2E15FC221372649
4383FF022128F65BD&rd=1&h=PqvGLt8h1iDPewqloTUH1yfEhURDODnK2Dq8_5XCI-E&v=1&r=https%3a%2f%2fwww.teluguglobal.in%2fu-p-bjp-mla-sangeet-som-booked-for-showing-anti-muslim-doc-
umentary%2f&p=DevEx.LB.1,5311.1
194   Ibid.
195   "BJP MLA Sangeet Som Calls Taj Mahal 'a Blot on History," 2017 and "107 Killed in Riots This Year; 66 Muslims, 41 Hindus," Hindustan Times, https://www.hindustantimes.com, September 24, 2013, www.hindustantimes.com/delhi-news/107-killed-in-riots-this-year-66-muslims-41-hindus/story-uqHMNT093ZqMa0WAsWdIpJ.html
196   Deborah Feyerick and Sheila Steffen, "Muslim DVD Rattles Voters in Key Battleground States," CNN, October 15, 2008, http://www.cnn.com/2008/US/10/14/muslim.dvd/index.html.
197   Max De Haldevang, "Trump's Billionaire Backers Funded These Islamophobic Facebook Ads," Quartz, April 05, 2018, https://qz.com/1245777/trump-funder-robert-mercer-also-paid-for-
islamophobic-facebook-and-google-ads/.
198   Ibid.
199   Ibid.
200   Luke James,"Exclusive: EU Told to Scrap 'Islamophobic' Election Advert by British MEP," Yahoo! Finance, September 28, 2018, https://finance.yahoo.com/news/exclusive-eu-told-drop-is-
lamophobic-election-advert-british-mep-113911379.html?_fsig=jMHhroSnCtExIt6Wfp0YIQ--.
201   Ibid.

declaration of political warfare."[202] Muslims will continue to be targeted and Islamophobia will be mobilized as part of the political warfare to come in the lead up to European elections and elsewhere.

Handbill with three men accused of lynching Muslims in high profile cases to run in 2019 election.

202   Finian Cunningham,"Steve Bannon Declares 'War Rooms' to Win European Elections – and That's Not Meddling?" MintPress News, September 25, 2018. https://www.mintpressnews.com/steve-bannon-declares-war-rooms-win-european-elections-thats-not-meddling/249823/.

The Public Lynching of Media in India

India's constitution guarantees freedom of speech, but it continues to be threatened by the Modi Administration and BJP. The Reporters Without Borders World Press Freedom Index produces an annual report on its findings annually regarding the "level of freedom available to the media in 180 countries."[203] Seven indicators used to score countries are "pluralism, media independence, abuses, environment and self-censorship, legislative framework, transparency, and the quality of the infrastructure that supports the production of news and information."[204] Once data is collected, nations are ranked and scored ranging on a scale from the freest to least free. The higher the ranking number, the less media freedom there is. In 2018, India ranked 138 out of 180 in the latest annual report. In 2017 India's score was 136.[205] This number indicates that there is less media freedom this year compared to the year prior.

The Reporters Without Borders World Press Freedom Index has revealed that mainstream media and journalists are "increasingly the targets of online smear campaigns by the most radical nationalists, who vilify them and even threaten physical reprisals."[206] The co-founder of India's first private news channel NDTV Prannoy Roy claimed that "India is going through an aggressive variant of McCarthyism against the media."[207] The company is presently under investigation by the federal police for fraud, which the company considers "a witch-hunt."[208] *The Wire's* Siddharth Varadarajan said that government ministers created the word "presstitute" in order to "describe journalists who are unfriendly to them or who don't do their bidding."[209]

Some journalists have claimed that they face intimidation if they are critical of Modi or his administration.[210] It was reported that "three senior editors have left their jobs at various influential media outlets in the past six months after publishing reports that angered the government or supporters of Modi's Hindu nationalist Bharatiya Janata Party (BJP)."[211] Reporters and others also face the threat of prosecution for 'sedition' which is punishable by life imprisonment if they are "overly critical."[212] Television anchors "have been threatened with physical harm, abused on social media and ostracized by Modi's administration."[213]

Female journalists report being threatened with gangrape against themselves and family members.[214] Recently, the United Nations intervened and called upon the government of India to protect Muslim journalist Rana Ayyub, whose life they deemed "is at serious risk."[215] In 2016, Ayyub published a book entitled the 'Gujarat Files: Anatomy of a Cover-Up' which uncovers "government complicity in anti-Muslim violence during the 2002 riots when Modi was chief minister of Gujarat."[216] Since then, she has faced harassment and threats both online and offline by Hindu nationalists.[217] In an Al Jazeera

203   "Our Activities | Reporters without Borders," RSF, April 05, 2018, accessed September 13, 2018, https://rsf.org/en/our-activities.
204   "RSF Issues Warning to India in First World Press Freedom Index Incident Report." Reporters Without Borders For Freedom of Information, July 4, 2018, https://rsf.org/en/news/rsf-is-sues-warning-india-first-world-press-freedom-index-incident-report.
205   "RSF Index 2018: Hatred of Journalism Threatens Democracies," RSF, April 26, 2018, rsf.org/en/rsf-index-2018-hatred-journalism-threatens-democracies.
206   "RSF Index," 2018, https://rsf.org/en/india.
207   Reuters,"Aggressive Variant Of McCarthyism vs Media, Says Prannoy Roy," NDTV.com, April 26, 2018, https://www.ndtv.com/india-news/india-falls-in-world-press-freedom-index-pran-noy-roy-says-aggressive-variant-of-mccarthyism-vs-media-1843406.
208   Raju Gopalakrishnan,"Indian Journalists Face Consequences If Critical of Modi's Administration," The Christian Science Monitor, April 26, 2018, www.csmonitor.com/World/Asia-South-Central/2018/0426/Indian-journalists-face-consequences-if-critical-of-Modi-s-administration.
209   Ibid.
210   Gopalakrishnan,"Indian Journalists Face Consequences," 2018.
211   Ibid.
212   Ibid.
213   Ibid.
214   Zeenat Saberin, "The Perils of Being a Journalist in Modi's India," Al Jazeera, June 14, 2018, https://www.aljazeera.com/indepth/features/perils-journalist-modis-in-dia-180614103115577.html.
215   Ibid.
216   Ibid.
217   Ibid.

article entitled "The Perils of Being a Journalist in Modi's India," Ayyub claimed that because she is a Muslim reporting on the Hindu nationalist government, this has brought on abuse related to her Muslim identity.[218] Islamophobic verbal attacks include calling her "Islamist," "Jihadi Jane" and "ISIS sex slave."[219]

Further, four reporters were murdered in 2017.[220] A recent *India Today* article stated that the 2017 murder of female reporter Gauri Lankesh was planned a year in advance.[221] Her murderer Parashuram Waghmare was affiliated with members of a "nameless underground organization that has members from Sanathan Sanstha, Hindu Janjagruthi Samithi, and many other right-wing organisations, according to the Special Investigation Team (SIT)."[222] The article also reports that Waghmore was ordered to execute her "for the sake of saving Hindu dharam."[223] Additionally, the Committee to Protect Journalists (CPJ), report that three journalists were murdered in India in 2017 and four in 2018.[224] Since 2014, when Modi took office 12 reporters have been killed.[225]

The Hate Tracker and #LetsTalkAboutHate

In 2015 under the direction of former editor of Hindustan Times (one of the exposed media houses by Operation 136) Bobby Ghosh, "Hate Tracker" a crowd-sourced database of hate crimes was begun by the media house.[226] Prior to its creation, there was "no national database of hate crimes," which made it difficult to gauge Islamophobia and also the depth of the problem

overall, necessary to enact laws to protect all affected members of civil society.[227] The short-lived website tracked "acts of violence, threats of violence, and incitements to violence based on religion, caste, race, ethnicity, region of origin, gender identity and sexual orientation" since September 2015.[228] However, the site was removed in October 2017 after Modi reportedly met with the owners.[229]

In July of 2017, *Hindustan Times* promoted animated video shorts in English. One is entitled, "Does Inciting Communal Hatred Pay In Politics?" with a tagline that reads "does spewing venom or inciting communal hatred pay in politics? Many politicians have launched their careers from the pulpit of hate."[230] Another relevant video was entitled "Kashmiri Students Face Verbal And Physical Abuse"[231] and "The brutal lynching of Mohammad Ikhlaq" with the tagline "The brutal lynching of Mohammad Ikhlaq ripped apart Dadri, where communities had lived in harmony earlier. Let's fight the divisive forces before hate sets in like the rot."[232] Using the hashtag #LetsTalkAboutHate *Hindustan Times* linked to worldwide discussions on the topic of hate.

The Institutionalization of Paid Media

In an effort to promote a Hindutva agenda and "polarize voters in the run-up to the 2019 election," a recent media exposé entitled Operation 136 (named after the ranking India received from the World Press Freedom Index of 2017) was

218   Ibid.
219   Ibid.
220   Gopalakrishnan,"Indian Journalists Face Consequences," 2018.
221   Nagarjun Dwarakanath,"Gauri Lankesh's Murder Was Planned a Year Before: Exclusive Details," India Today, August 29, 2018,https://www.indiatoday.in/india/story/gauri-lankesh-s-murder-was-planned-a-year-before-exclusive-details-of-the-killing-1326868-2018-08-29.
222   Ibid.
223   Ibid.
224   Committee to Protect Journalists, https://cpj.org/asia/india.
225   Ibid.
226   Hindustan Times, "Hate Tracker: "India's First National Database to Track Hate Crimes," YouTube, July 27, 2017, www.youtube.com/watch?time_continue=45&v=go0d8hmN-Qow.

227   Niha Masih, "HT Hate Tracker: A National Database on Crimes in the Name of Religion, Caste, Race." Hindustan Times, https://www.hindustantimes.com/, July 28, 2017, www.hindustantimes.com/india-news/ht-hate-tracker-a-national-database-on-crimes-in-the-name-of-religion-caste-race/story-xj2o03dKF9PsW4IYIEvdgI.html.
228   Ibid.
229   Staff, "After Editor's Exit, Hindustan Times Pulls Down Controversial 'Hate Tracker'," The Wire, October 25, 2017, thewire.in/media/hindustan-times-hate-tracker.
230   Hindustan Times, "#LetsTalkAboutHate: Does Inciting Communal Hatred Pay in Politics?" YouTube, July 27, 2017, www.youtube.com/watch?v=J2I3bpoQMlM.
231   Hindustan Times, "Let's Talk About Hate: Kashmiri Students Face Verbal and Physical Abuse," YouTube, July 26, 2017, www.hindustantimes.com/videos/india-news/let-s-talk-about-hate-kashmiri-students-face-verbal-and-physical-abuse/video-NbRBhGvSfmPgZQg9vxLrmL.html.
232   Hindustan Times," #LetsTalkAboutHate: The Brutal Lynching of Mohammad Ikhlaq," YouTube, July 23, 2017, www.youtube.com/watch?v=0xQpRjTFVgk.

undertaken by *Cobrapost.*"[233] The exposé revealed that payments were offered to over two dozen various media companies to promote a Hindutva agenda in order to "polarize voters in the run-up to the 2019 election."[234] All but two media outlets reportedly accepted, including major media houses. A series of undercover exposes revealed that "news organizations were willing to not only cause communal disharmony among the citizens but also tilt the electoral outcome in favour of a particular party."[235] This included "newspapers, radio stations, TV channels and websites" as well as "advertorials and events."[236]

India's powerful corporate media houses were set to "mobilise the electorate on communal lines" by promoting the hate speech of Hindu extremists such as "Vinay Katiyar, Uma Bharti and Mohan Bhagwat," while targeting certain opposition leaders. The exposé also revealed that "the arrangement included running the campaign on all platforms – print, electronic, radio or digital including, e-news portals, websites and social media such as Facebook and Twitter."[237] Operation 136 uncovered that several media houses are actually owned or patronized by politicians, especially regional media, and that "it was natural for them to become their master's voice."[238] RSS and Hindutva ideology have become embedded within the "newsrooms and boardrooms of Indian media houses."[239]

Manufacturing the Muslim Menace: Rohingya Refugees

Refugees are an important group to consider when discussing Islamophobia across many parts of the world today. Often Muslims are collectively stereotyped and criminalized as outsiders coming to disrupt society, take jobs from citizens and enact violence against society either as 'illegals,' 'criminals,' 'security,''demographic threats,' 'terrorists' or 'rapists' and 'anti-nationals.' This has also been the case across North America, and Europe. For instance, the U.S has banned Muslim refugees from seven Muslim predominant countries, while Europe has restricted their influx and movement. With regards to India, Rohingya refugees who have fled Islamophobia and genocide in Myanmar, face Islamophobia in India where many have sought refuge. Similar to some refugees in European nations, the Rohingya refugees in India reside on the periphery of society, primarily in "refugee camps or makeshift homes with poor access to basic necessities" that are under "constant surveillance...by Indian intelligence agencies."[240] Further complicating issues is the fact that India is not a signatory of the UN Refugee Convention. A 2017 *Outlook India* article revealed that "the government and a section of media are trying to project that the increasing number of Rohingya refugees in the country will encourage Islamic fundamentalism" and that they are attempting to brand "all Rohingyas as terrorists."[241] They have also been accused of having ties "to terrorist groups based in Pakistan as well as the Islamic

233   Staff, "Cobrapost Sting: Big Media Houses Say Yes to Hindutva, Black Money, Paid News." The Wire, May 26, 2018, thewire.in/media/cobrapost-sting-big-media-houses-say-yes-To-hindutva-black-money-paid-news.
234   Staff, "Cobrapost Sting: Big Media Houses Say Yes to Hindutva, Black Money, Paid News." The Wire, May 26, 2018, thewire.in/media/cobrapost-sting-big-media-houses-say-yes-To-hindutva-black-money-paid-news.
235   Ibid.
236   Ibid.
237   Ibid.
238   Ibid.
239   Ibid.
240   Ibid.
241   Ashok Swain, "Rohingya Refugees: India Should Not Pass The Buck To Muslim World By Adopting A False And Blinkered Narrative," https://www.outlookindia.com/, OutlookIndia.com, September 9, 2017, www.outlookindia.com/website/story/rohingya-refugees-india-should-not-pass-the-Buck-to-muslim-world-by-adopting-a-f/301498.

State (IS)."[242]

Utilizing common Islamophobic framing of Muslims and refugees as 'foreigners,' 'illegal' and 'security threats,' Suchait Singh of the RSS Prant Sanghchalk expounded that "we do not consider them (Rohingyas and Bangladeshis) as refugees as they are foreigners and have entered in our country illegally."[243] He continued, "why should we tolerate them when they pose a security threat to the nation as well as the state."[244] The sensationalism around the Rohingya as a security threat in this manner can be seen as one way Hindu nationalists "appease its hardline supporters."[245] In fact, the claim of the Rohingya as security threats is a blatant misrepresentation of the facts and is not uncommon among Hindu nationalist circles. As of 2017, it was estimated by the UN Refugee Agency that 20,000 Rohingya refugees that fled ethnic cleansing in Myanmar, now live in India.[246] However, the Indian government estimates this figure to be at 40,000, twice the amount.[247]

In a multi-city investigation undertaken by *NDTV*, reporters went to four areas with a high concentration of Rohingya: Jammu, Delhi, Jaipur, and Haryana. They interviewed refugees in the camps that verified that they have been repeatedly vetted by police. The reporters viewed documents, collected details on FIR's filed against Rohingyas and interviewed police and officials about the actual threat. In Jammu, out of a roughly 6000 people Rohingya population, 14 FIRS were filed.

---

242   Mohammed Sinan Siyedh, "India's Rohingya Terror Problem: Real or Imagined?" South Asian Voices, 9 Feb. 2018, southasianvoices.org/indias-rohingya-terror-problem-real-imagined/.
243   PTI,"Rohingyas a Security Threat, Deport Them: RSS," The Indian Express, May 03, 2018, indianexpress.com/article/india/rohingyas-a-security-threat-deport-them-rss-5101212/.
244   Ibid.
245   Ibid.
246   Swain,"Rohingya Refugees," 2017.
247   Sreenivasan Jain, et al. "Rohingyas A Terror Threat? NDTV Finds Little Evidence Of Government Claim." NDTV.com, September 16, 2017, www.ndtv.com/india-news/rohingyas-a-terror-threat-ndtv-finds-little-evidence-of-government-claim-1751114.

"The criminal process itself is the punishment."

Nitya Ramakrishnan - Lawyer

"I drew a series of cartoons and uploaded in on a website called Cartoons Against Curruption, some of them were critical of the Parliament, politicians, the system and the bureaucracy so they slammed me with sedition charges, they said because my cartoons insulted the parliament, it amounted to sedition. I was locked up for two days....the kind of problems people face, their voice of dissent is crushed, their work is disturbed, all you energy goes into fighting that case and it is not only about the time you spend in jail, or financial losss or professional loss. Socially people see you as 'anti-national.'"

Aseem Trivedi, Cartoonist

"I was editor of the Hindu for about two years and during those two years, I collected three or four criminal defamation suits, so you can imagine that and the editor or reporter operating in the kind of environment would think 100 times before they write certain things if you worried that the government will file a criminal defamation case or even worse that the law of sedition may be invoked. This has an affect... they have created an atmosphere that is not conducive to vigirius debate, independent journalism, and kind of no holds barred public space that any democracy particularly one like Inida needs and deserves."

Siddharth Varadarajan, Editor The Wire

Source:
India: Government Critics Jailed and Harassed, 2016

"

In India, 'local and national governments are using overbroad and vague laws such as criminal defamation, sedition, hate speech or those dealing with national security issues for political ends stifling free speech.'

HUMAN RIGHTS WATCH

5,743
JAMMU

14 FIRs Total: Eight cases for lack of visa, two cases of rape, one case of cow slaughter, one case for causing injury, one case for selling goods in the black market and one for stealing railway property.

1,000
DELHI

Police officials reported that they had no data on FIRs registered against Rohingyas in the city, or any evidence of radicalization. Given the condition of the Rohingyas, they added, it seems highly unlikeley that they will be drawn to extremism.

350
JAIPUR

One FIR was filled of a rape charge by a Rohingya woman against a Rohingya man.

N/A
HARYANA

Police in Faridabad told NDTV that no cases are registered against Rohingyas. Officials in Chandigarh said they have no state-wide data on crimes by Rohingyas.

NDTV claimed that the cases consisted of:

> 8 of the cases for lack of visa, 2 cases of rape, 1 case of cow slaughter, 1 case for causing injury, 1 case for selling goods in the black market and 1 for stealing railway property. In Delhi, the population was 1,000, no data on cases against them. Out of Jaipur's 350 Rohingya, only 1 FIR was filed by another Rohingya alleging rape. Haryana had no FIRs. Police interviews also confirm that the Rohingya were "peaceful" and concerned with working and surviving. The clarified that any crimes that have been committed have constituted petty crime. Further, there was no evidence of extremism.[248]

In December 2017 the Minister of Home Office was presented with a request for a response on the Rohingya. Among the requests was to state:

1. whether it is a fact that nearly 40000 Rohingyas are staying in India and;
2. the basis on which Government is saying that those who are seeking refuge are all insurgents or illegal migrants

The response of the Home Office regarding the number of Rohingya in India revealed that there was not "accurate data" and that the number of 40,000 was merely an "estimate." The Home Office did not present any basis for the statement that "those who are seeking refuge are all insurgents."[249]

In reality, facts demonstrate that the Rohingya pose an extremely low level of threat, if any, to India and sensationalism and fear mongering serves particular political agendas. However, the threat against the Rohingya in India is underreported. For example, there have been attempts to push for their deportation, including those who are registered with the United Nations High Commissioner for Refugees (UNCHR) as refugees, anti-Rohingya Muslim protests by ultra-nationalist groups, and acts of violence such as the razing of a Rohingya refugee camp by BJP youth wing leader Manish Chandela and associates, who proudly boasted of the attack on social media in April of 2018.[250]

The fictional security threat narrative is essential to consider because discourse makes realities knowable. This sort of discourse attempts to solidify the link between Rohingya refugees and criminality, militancy and terrorism, potentially removing certain guaranteed protections, clearing the way for discriminatory legislation, policies, and actions toward this vulnerable population. It also conveys the possibility that through discourse and policy, 40,000 plus people may be criminalized, imprisoned, deported and possibly ethnically cleansed.

Propaganda by Hindu nationalists is strategic. Singh's labeling of the Rohingya as "foreigners" who enter the country 'illegally" rather than as "refugees" and BJP leader Yogi Adityanath's calls for "similar action" regarding the banning of Muslims from seven nations under the Trump Administration during an election rally "to contain terror activities in [India]," does more than just appeal to segments of the Hindu majority at election time.[251] It perpetuates the nationalist narrative of Muslims as invaders of India and a threat to Hindu culture, as well as the nation.
It has also been reported that BJP rule in India has created its own political refugees who have fled persecution from Modi's government. Findings by the Asian Human Rights Commission, suggest that out of 550 cases of reported custodial torture in India occurring over a ten year period between 2005-2015 that:[252]

248   Ibid.
249   Unstarred Question 534,"Stand of Government on Rohingyas,"Government of India Ministry of Home Affairs, December 20, 2017.
250   Outlook Magazine,"Hindu Sena Protests against Rohingya Muslims at Jantar Mantar," YouTube, September 11, 2017, https://www.youtube.com/watch?v=J3A7bqAr0Io and "All Rohingya Muslim Refugees Are Illegal Immigrants, Will Be Deported despite UN Status, Says Centre." Scroll.in, August 14, 2017, scroll.in/latest/847215/all-rohingya-muslim-refugees-are-illegal-immigrants-will-be-deported-despite-un-status-says-centre.
251   NDTV, "BJP's Yogi Adityanath Praises Trump Ban, Compares Western UP To Kashmir," YouTube, January 31, 2017, www.youtube.com/watch?v=UPZ4QIX0Yb0.
252   Narendra Modi officially took power in 2014 as Prime Minister, and custodial torture has continued under his leadership creating political refugees.

State agents in India resort to torture to force persons in custody to confess to crimes, to extract bribes and to intimidate and silence them so they do not speak out against state agencies, powerful politicians, or financially or politically influential persons. It does not provide any figures for 2017.[253]

In 2017 it was reported that 7,400 Indians have sought asylum in the United States.[254] That same year it was reported that "2,227 Indians were apprehended specifically trying to cross the U.S-Mexico border."[255] That number was surpassed by April 2018 as more than 3,750 Indian nationals had been arrested by US Border Patrol.[256] The number of Indian asylum seekers crossing the US-Mexico border are increasing, and they now account for the "fifth-largest group after immigrants from Mexico, Honduras, Guatemala and El Salvador."[257] However, very few of the requests by Indian nationals for asylum are granted.[258]

Among the asylees from India are Sikhs, Christians, Hindus claiming to have faced persecution by the governing BJP party, as well as "Muslims claiming persecution by Hindus in the aftermath of Hindu-Muslim sectarian violence in parts of Gujarat in 2002."[259] Human Rights Watch has issued a warning against "'vigilante violence" aimed at critics of the ruling BJP, and "extremist Hindu groups" that are BJP aligned committing "numerous assaults against Muslims and other minority communities, especially as a response to rumors over the selling, purchase or consumption of cows or beef."[260] HRW held the government of India responsible for both their failure to stop and investigare "vigilante attacks against minority religious communities" and the role of BJP leaders in promoting "Hindu supremacy and ultra-nationalism, which in turns exacerbates more violence.[261]

253   Suman Guha Mozumder, "Asylum America: Why More Indians Are Seeking Refuge," IndiaAbroad.com, July 01, 2018, https://www.indiaabroad.com/indian-americans/asylum-america-why-more-indians-are-seeking-refuge/article_e77cee36-7c65-11e8-9a24-c7bdc2307751.html.

254   PTI, "Over 7,000 Indians Sought US Asylum in 2017: Report - Times of India," The Times of India, June 20, 2018, https://timesofindia.indiatimes.com/india/over-7000-indians-sought-us-asylum-in-2017-report/articleshow/64672874.cms.
255   Hitender Rao, "Immigrants from India Increasing at US-Mexico Border," VOA, August 20, 2018, https://www.voanews.com/a/immigrants-india-us-mexico-border/4533007.html.
256   Chantal Da Silva, "Nearly Half of All Immigrants Detained in Federal Prison Are Indian Asylum Seekers," Newsweek, August 14, 2018, https://www.newsweek.com/growing-number-asylum-seekers-india-showing-us-mexico-border-1072329.
257   Rao, "Immigrants from India, 2018.
258   Da Silva, "Nearly Half of All Immigrants Detained," 2018.
259   Mozumder, "Asylum America," 2018.
260   Da Silva, "Nearly Half of All Immigrants Detained," 2018.
261   Ibid.

Attacks Against Bodies: Beef Attacks, Lynching, and Cow Vigilantism

India's 'Anti-Sharia' Legislation[262]

Prime Minister Narendra Modi's ascension to power has had significant consequences upon the physical welfare and religious freedom of India's Muslim minority. In particular, there has been an increase in Islamophobia and violence against Muslims in the name of 'cow protection' and concerns regarding Hindu sensitivities, which runs counter to the claims of a secular government. In reality, a Brahmanical form of Hinduism ie 'Hindutva' is being propagated across India today by ultra-nationalist parties such as the BJP and their affiliates, posing a threat to both Muslims and democracy. In an effort to 'purify' the body politic, Muslims have been excluded from civil society and the targeting, harassment, surveillance, arrest, abuse and murder of them has been sanctioned.[263] As

a result, Muslims have reported living in fear.[264]

Though cow protection and regulations have a long history in India, it has been mobilized as an election platform utilized by the BJP in the lead up to elections.[265] In particular, Modi campaigned on a "pink revolution" platform in 2014 in opposition to the profitable and robust beef industry in India that thrived under the Congress party.[266] However, in the years since Modi was elected to office, beef sales in India have doubled and presently India is leading the global beef industry.[267] India also has a highly profitable billion dollar leather industry that employs millions of people.[268] In addition, BJP official Sangeet Som, the Islamophobe "charged with making inflammatory speeches ahead of the 2013 riots in UP's Muzaffarnagar," that killed 66 Muslims, injured 703 and displaced many more, was a partner in two halal meat company/processing plants in India.[269]

---

262   Anti-Sharia legislation is used here to denote similarities with bills introduced in several U.S state legislatures, stoking Islamophobia by conjuring fear of Muslims and Islam, including an imagined infiltration of not only U.S courts, but society at large. The U.S, Canada and Europe also have legislation, bans and restrictions on minarets, halal meat, calls to prayer, street praying, mosque building, wearing of hijab, circumcision etc, that distinctly target Islam and Muslims, as well as, some other faith traditions.

263   Amar Diwakar, "How "Cow Vigilantes" Launched India's Lynching Epidemic," The New Republic, July 26, 2017, https://newrepublic.com/article/144043/cow-vigilantes-launched-indias-lynching-epidemic.

264   Samar Halarnkar, "'Maybe It Is Time to Change My Son's Name': The New Reality of Being Muslim in India," Scroll.in, July 08, 2017, https://scroll.in/article/843074/maybe-it-is-time-to-change-my-sons-name-the-new-reality-of-being-muslim-in-india and Murali Krishnan, "Undeclared War: India's Muslims 'in Constant Fear' as Vigilante Murders Increase," ABC News, July 29, 2017, http://www.abc.net.au/news/2017-07-30/fear-growing-among-muslims-in-india/8751380.

265   Michael Safi, "Cow Slaughter to Be Punishable by Life Sentence in Gujarat," The Guardian,14 Mar. 2017, www.theguardian.com/world/2017/mar/14/indian-state-government-life-sentence-cow-slaughter.

266   NDTV, "Government's 'Pink Revolution' Destroying Cattle, Says Narendra Modi," YouTube, April 02, 2014, https://www.youtube.com/watch?v=1ElnjqtBbuc.

267   Rahul Kumar, "Beef Exports From India Doubled Under Modi Government," Asian Independent, July 27, 2018, https://www.theasianindependent.co.uk/beef-exports-from-india-doubled-under-modi-government/.

268   "Brand India," IBEF:India Brand Equity Foundation. July 2018, https://www.ibef.org/exports/leathe-industry-india.aspx.

269   Tanima Biswas, "BJP Leader Sangeet Som's Links With Meat Export Firms Exposed by Documents," NDTV.com, October 10, 2015, https://www.ndtv.com/india-news/documents-expose-bjp-Leader-Sangeet-soms-link-with-meat-export-firms-1230567 and Bharti Jain, "Government Releases Data of Riot Victims Identifying Religion, Times of India, September 24, 2013, https://timesofindia.indiatimes.com/india/Government-releases-data-of-riot-victims-identifying-religion/articleshow/22998550.cms.

Beef bans and cow legislation divide segments of society based on religious difference and are mobilized to divide India's Muslims and Hindus in the name of 'protecting' Mother Cow. They are exclusionary and unjustly target Muslims and Dalits who tend to consume beef as a religiously lawful meat and an inexpensive form of protein. Both groups also tend to work in the beef and dairy trade. Further, these discriminatory laws often drive the lethal vigilantism that has caused the violent lynchings of several Muslims over the years since Modi has been in office.

Aakar Patel the Executive Director of Amnesty International India has drawn a link between increasing cow legislation that predominantly targets Muslims and the "growing trend of Islamophobia that needs to be stopped in its tracks."[270] Patel also pointed to the BJP's campaign for cow protection and what he called "emboldened vigilante groups, who seem to be operating in some cases with the tacit approval of state authorities."[271] He has called upon Indian Prime Minister, senior BJP leaders, and Chief Ministers to condemn the attacks and bring the perpetrators to justice.[272]

Article 48 in the Constitution of India delineates that states shall take steps to prohibit the "slaughter of cows and calves and other milch and draught cattle."[273] This constitutional provision has provided what has been referred to by advocates as "a cloak of legitimacy to violence and discrimination against religious minorities."[274] For example, the provision has provided the legal grounds for several of the bills

and legislation leading to beef bans currently making their way across India.[275] Laws vary by state and most states currently have some form of cow legislation. For example, in Uttar Pradesh eating beef is prohibited and in Chandigarh consumption of beef, buffalo, bullock and ox is also banned.[276]

The Guardian claims that "a number of BJP-led states have extended bans or tightened punishments against cow slaughter since Modi became prime minister in 2014."[277] According to *India Spend,* as of 2017 the slaughter of cows was "prohibited in 84 percent of India's states and union territories (UTs), which account for 99.38 percent of the country's population."[278]

Cow legislation, ranging from slaughter to possession and transport of beef, criminalize and otherize Muslims and it has led to violence against them. The laws have been championed by "Hindu nationalists, including the BJP and its affiliates such as the RSS."[279] In Gujarat, Bharatiya Janata Party (BJP) member Vijay Rupani announced that a bill was introduced in his state to make the slaughter of cows and the transport of beef punishable by a life sentence.[280] Subramanian Swamy of the BJP introduced a bill making the death penalty a possibility in cases over cow slaughter that was recently withdrawn.[281] Swamy has also made Islamophobic statements in the past such as calling upon Muslims in India to "take an oath declaring that their ancestors were Hindu if they want to prove their citizenship."[282] There is no doubt that the BJP has "direct bearing on decision making at present and thus policy

270   "India: Hate Crimes against Muslims and Rising Islamophobia Must Be Condemned, "Amnesty International, June 28, 2017, www.amnesty.org/en/latest/news/2017/06/india-hate-crimes-against-muslims-and-rising-islamophobia-must-be-condemned/.
271   Ibid.
272   Ibid
273   "The Constitution Of India 1949,"Article 15(4) in The Constitution Of India 1949, indiankanoon.org/doc/237570/.
274   CSSS, "A Narrowing Space," 12.
275   Ibid.
276   "States Where Cow Slaughter Is Banned So Far, and States Where It Isn't." News18, May 26, 2017, www.news18.com/news/india/states-where-cow-slaughter-is-banned-so-far-And-states-where-it-isnt-1413425.html.
277   Safi, "Cow Slaughter," 2017.
278   Alison Saldanha, "99.38% Indians Now Live In Areas Under Cow-Protection Laws," IndiaSpend, April 15, 2017, http://www.indiaspend.com/cover-story/99-38-indians-now-live-in-areas-under-cow-protection-laws-42787
279   CSSS, "A Narrowing Space," 12.
280   Safi, "Cow Slaughter," 2017.
281   Anahita Khanna,"Bill Seeking Death Penalty For Cow Slaughter Introduced in RS By Subramanian Swamy." HuffPost India, March 25, 2017, www.huffingtonpost.in/2017/03/25/bill-seek-ing-death-penalty-for-cow-slaughter-introduced-in-rs-by_a_22011334/.
282   ' Muslims Should Not Live in This Country,' Says BJP MP Vinay Katiyar,"Scroll.in, February 7, 2018, scroll.in/latest/867827/muslims-should-not-live-in-this-country-says-bjp-mp-vinay-kati-yar.

formation impacting the lives of the citizenry."[283] Smitha Rao wrote in "Saffronisation of the Holy Cow: Unearthing Silent Communalism" that bills of this kind are "symptomatic of the silent communalisation of the Indian state at the hands of the Hindu right and is not motivated by compassion towards animals."[284]

Islamophobia not only exists within the very creation of the bills and laws themselves but the discriminatory legislation signal a "greater entrenchment and institutionalization of Hindu nationalism and anti-minority sentiment."[285] Cow legislation has also "created an increased state surveillance and punishment" and "suspicions that Muslims are engaging in anti-Hindu, criminal activities."[286] But there is also majoritarian surveillance where Hindu neighbors watch Muslims and even stop and question them regarding activities, especially those that relate to beef. Human Rights Watch (HRW) has claimed that the government in Haryana reportedly set up a version of America's *See Something, Say Something,* where citizens can report cow related suspicions to an appointed police task force via a 24-hour helpline.[287]

The legislation, in part, also has emboldened right-wing nationalist groups such as the RSS, VHP and Bajrang Dal to "engage in violence against Muslims whom they suspect of slaughtering cows."[288] Anti-cow legislation has also played an increasing role in the incitement of 'witch-hunts' and vigilante violence in India.[289]

Cow Related Violence

Cow related violence at the hands of vigilantes (*gau rakshaks*) who take the law into their own hands in the name of 'cow protection' is among the leading recorded source of violence against Muslims in India. It has increased annually since Prime Minister Modi took office in 2014 and 2017 was its highest number of recorded incidents yet. IndiaSpend revealed that according to their data recorded up until June 25, 2017:

As many of 97 percent of these attacks were reported after Prime Minister Narendra Modi's government came to power in May 2014, and half the cow-related violence—30 of 60 cases—were from states governed by the Bharatiya Janata Party (BJP) when the attacks were reported.[290]

In 2018, IndiaSpend recorded 31 incidents of cow-related violence involving 57 victims, of which 29 were identified as Muslim.[291] The data further reveals that "Muslims were the target of 52 percent of violence centered on bovine issues over nearly eight years (2010 to 2017) and comprised 84 percent of 25 Indians killed in 60 incidents."[292] Reportedly the majority of the attacks (52 percent) "were based on rumours."[293]

The lynchings of two unrelated Muslims, Pehlu Khan, and Junaid Khan are important cases that garnered global attention in 2017 and propelled conversations, advocacy and legislation forward around lynching and cow vigilantism.

283   Smitha Rao,"Saffronisation of the Holy Cow: Unearthing Silent Communalism," Economic and Political Weekly, vol. 46, no. 15, 2011, pp. 80–87. JSTOR, www.jstor.org/stable/41152321, 81.
284   Ibid, 80.
285   CSSS, "A Narrowing Space," 8.
286   Amrita Basu, Violent Conjunctures in Democratic India, (Cambridge: Cambridge University Press, 2015), 45.
287   "India: 'Cow Protection' Spurs Vigilante Violence." Human Rights Watch, 12 May 2017, www.hrw.org/news/2017/04/27/india-cow-protection-spurs-vigilante-violence.
288   Basu, "Violent Conjunctures in Democratic India," 45.
289   CSSS, "A Narrowing Space," 8.
290   Delna Abraham and Ojaswi Rao,"84% Dead In Cow-Related Violence Since 2010 Are Muslim; 97% Attacks After 2014," IndiaSpend, December 8, 2017, www.indiaspend.com/cover-story/86-dead-in-cow-related-violence-since-2010-are-muslim-97-attacks-after-2014-2014.
291   Abraham and Rao,"84% Dead In Cow-Related Violence, 2017.
292   Ibid.
293   Ibid

Cow Related Violence by the Numbers

2018

73%
of the 57 victims in cow related violence were Muslim. 3% are unknown.

13
deaths recorded

31
incidents of cow related violence

2017
43 Incidents

108 Victims | 60% Muslim | Deaths: 13

In 70% of the incidents, BJP was the state party in power.

2016
30 Incidents

67 Victims | 42% Muslim | Deaths: 9

In 53.5% of the incidents, BJP was the state party in power.

2015
13 Incidents

49 Victims | 50% Muslim | Deaths: 11

In 31% of the incidents, BJP was the state party in power.

2014
3 Incidents

11 Victims | 73% Muslim | Deaths: 0

In 33.3% of the incidents, BJP was the state party in power.

CASE STUDY
JUNAID KHAN

Muslim teen lynched by mob in Ramadan 2017 on train ride home.

One significant case in 2017 was that of sixteen-year-old Junaid Khan. Khan was a young student home from school for the Muslim religious holiday Eid. On June 23, Khan and his brother left their Khandawali village, district of Palwal, Haryana headed for Delhi by train to shop for the Eid holiday. As he was returning home with his brother and two friends, he was lynched to death by a mob of young men on a public train.

They flung our skull caps, pulled my brother's beard, slapped us, and taunted us about eating cow meat. Beef is not even cooked in our village. Once we reached Ballabhgarh, they took out knives. They were older than us — probably in their 30s — so we couldn't do anything," Shaqir Khan[294]

294   Juggernaut Books Blog, "#NotinOurName: Why You Should Support the #NotinMyName Protests," The Lowdown, June 28, 2017, http://blog.juggernaut.in/not-in-my-name/.

Junaid's other brother Hashim who was also attacked recounted that the initial attack began with about 20-25 men but that many jumped in thereafter shouting "you are Muslims, you are anti-nationals."[295] No one intervened to stop the violence.

In a video by *The Quint*, Khan's family and friends shared their memories of Khan as a young man who always had a smile on his face, memorized the entire Quran and led his community in prayer and who dreamed of becoming an imam at the masjid one day.[296] But confusion and fear were also expressed among the community as were concerns that his murder has brought to reality.

Junaid's grieving mother Saira asked, "how can any random stranger do such a thing?" Mohd Azah a neighbor stated that "people are scared here..they are worried that something like this might happen to them...or our children who study in the city...are also scared to go to college" and Khan's uncle Abdul Sayyid said "we've never seen such hatred in India before ...they call us 'Pakistani' that's wrong...we are also Indians[...] this discrimination began after the BJP came to power."[297] He also explained how the murder has divided this community from their Hindu neighbors with whom they used to visit and celebrate. He recalled how they did not come to the Eid following Junaid's death.[298]

Locally, the lynching of young Junaid led to public mourning by his predominantly Muslim community. They did not celebrate the Islamic holiday of Eid, the celebration marking the end of the Ramadan fast that year. Additionally,

the villagers and Muslims in neighboring areas wore black bands around their arms on Eid in solidarity and a hashtag #blackeid was used to bring attention to the increasing mob violence targeting minority groups in India.[299] One organizer stated that "silence is tantamount to complicity, especially at a time where the events are happening with increasing frequency."[300]

Khan's murder and the photo of his lifeless body on a train platform also caused public outrage in India and gained worldwide attention. His lynching has also forced larger conversations around what has been called India's shift toward 'mobocracy.'[301] A Facebook post by filmmaker Saba Dewan regarding the lynching of young Junaid is cited as a source in the mobilization of an online campaign #notinmyname, as well as physical protest marches across India on June 28, 2017. The event page on Facebook describes Not in My Name as "a citizens protest against the recent spate of targeted lynchings of Muslims in India" and refers to the recent stabbing of Junaid Khan.[302] The event page refers to the attacks on Muslims as "part of a pattern of systemic violence against Dalits, Adivasis, and other disadvantaged and minority groups across the country" and refers to the "brazen silence" that the government has exhibited around "heinous crimes."[303] Via the Facebook event, a call is made for the "citizens of India reclaim and protect our Constitution."[304] Similar protests were also reportedly held in London, Boston, and Toronto on June 29, 2017.[305] While Modi has remained silent on the lynchings of Muslims, and members of the BJP selectively pay lip service on occasion, protestors have reportedly sent apologies to Junaid's father via statements such as "we are

295   The Quint, ""We Are Scared & Angry": Khandawli Villagers After Junaid's Death," YouTube, June 28, 2017, https://www.youtube.com/watch?v=PnqLLEvRAKM
296   Ibid.
297   Ibid.
298   Ibid.
299   Huizhong Wu,"Indian Muslims Are Hashtagging This Holiday #BlackEid," CNN, June 28, 2017, https://www.cnn.com/2017/06/26/asia/black-eid-india-muslim/index.html and Yusra Husain, "Men in Lucknow at #Eid Namaz in Solidarity with Those Lynched #StopKillingMuslims #EidWithBlackBand, @TOIIndiaNews pic.twitter.com/DbSlZvoVUF." Twitter, 26 June 2017, twitter.com/yusrahusainTOI/status/879182128726126593.
300   Wu, "Indian Muslims Are Hashtagging This Holiday #BlackEid," 2017. https://www.cnn.com/2017/06/26/asia/black-eid-india-muslim/index.html.
301   NDTV, "'Black Eid' In Junaid's Village: India Shifting To 'Mobocracy?" YouTube, June 26, 2017, https://www.youtube.com/watch?v=W7mxH2vwBo4.
302   Saba Dewan, Sanjay Kak, and Rahul Roy, "Facebook," Not In My Name, June 28, 2017, https://www.facebook.com/events/832175993606631.
303   Ibid.
304   Ibid.
305   Juggernaut, "#NotinOurName," 2017.

together in your grief" and "we are sorry we could not keep your son safe."[306] Twitter users took to the social media platform to show support tagging their tweets with the #notinmyname hashtag.

However, the #notinmyname hashtag has drawn criticism from some in India as a distraction from the structural injustice and toxic Brahmanism at the center of the issue. In a recent opinion piece Rajesh Rajamani penned for *The News Minute,* he claimed that elite, liberals have utilized the #notinmyname hashtag to compartmentalize their own privilege, allowing them to benefit from their caste position while condemning the lynching of Muslims, rather than address the need to dismantle the problematic Brahmanical Hindu structure that both allows such violence and from which they benefit.[307]

Official narrative claims that the attack that led to Junaid's murder occurred due to an argument over a seat on the train, though the FIR acknowledges that the attack "took on a violent and communal hue."[308] However, the accounts of witnesses including Khan's own brother who was severely beaten and injured in the same attack, clearly demonstrate that they were attacked because they were Muslim. Markers of identity such as skull caps, beards and accusations of beef consumption were factors in the attack, and the reason why no one intervened to stop the attack or protect the youth. A few months later on a train in the Palwal

district, in the state of Haryana, an area close to Junaid's, three Muslim clerics were beaten under similar circumstances by a group of men. Similar to young Junaid, they too were not allowed by the men to deboard at their stop similar to Junaid's case and the police have stated that this incident too could also be a 'dispute over

seats' on the train, rather than targeted acts of Islamophobia.[309]

Yet Khan's murder does not appear in cow related violence data collected by seminal sources on the topic such as *IndiaSpend,* although several articles on Junaid's lynching do refer to beef eating accusations made by the attackers, similar to those launched against those lynched in cow related mob violence. Again and again, young Junaid's name constantly appears among and alongside that of Muslim victims of cow lynchings, debates on the topic of cow violence and in protests.

The police arrested six men shortly after the lynching who admitted to participating in the beating, but not the stabbing of Junaid. Yet the end of March 2018, less than a year after Junaid's murder all of the accused have been released from prison except for the main person Naresh Kumar. The *Indian Express* reports that Junaid's father has claimed that Haryana police helped Rameshwar Dass one of the two key perpetrators accused in the murder of Junaid, obtain bail by subverting the investigation.[310]

Junaid's murder resonated beyond spectacular or isolated incidents, it solidified a sense of ongoing vulnerability for Muslims engaging in everyday activities. *The Quint* collected tweets by young Muslims in India that reflect the fears and anxieties that they experience in the increasing climate of Islamophobia, and the tweets were read off one by one in a video. The fears expressed by young Muslims included:

carrying meat or eating any kind of meat in lunch boxes when traveling by train to visit family or returning to campus lest it be confused for beef and threaten their loves, giving Islamic salutations on the phone or keeping a beard or wearing

306   "Silence on Mob Lynchings Broken at #NotInMyName Protest," The Quint, YouTube, June 28, 2017, https://www.youtube.com/watch?v=ywQBloQAxWQ
307   Rajesh Rajamani, "The Savarna Redemption: Why 'Not In My Name' Campaign Is a Part of the Problem," The News Minute, June 28, 2017, https://www.thenewsminute.com/article/savarna-redemption-why-not-my-name-campaign-part-problem-64288
308   "Junaid's Last Moments - The Train Journey That Killed Him," The Quint, YouTube, July 13, 2017, https://www.youtube.com/watch?v=g3zC4kZ614U.
309   The Quint, "Three Muslim Clerics Allegedly Attacked on a Moving Train in U.P.," YouTube, November 24, 2017, https://www.youtube.com/watch?v=VBLME8z1N6U and The Quint, "Junaid's Last Moments," 2017.
310   Express News Service,"Junaid Khan Lynching: 53-year-old Key Accused Granted Bail," The Indian Express, March 28, 2018, https://indianexpress.com/article/india/junaid-khan-lynching-53-year-old-key-accused-granted-bail-5115187/.

certain clothing affiliated with Muslims.[311]

The Tweets below were taken from the same thread used by *The Quint* around @AngellicAribam's post on Twitter July 23, 2018. The tweets reflect a sense of being under siege as well as the need to self-discipline regarding their words and actions, such as public displays of Muslimness for themselves and family members. Some tweets specifically mention Junaid and also train travel while Muslim. Places of public transport such as the train in Junaid's case and the highway in Pehlu Khan's case indicate serious mobility issues for Muslims as they attempt to move from one space to another and engage in everyday activities such as school and work.

311   Arpan Rai, "No Namaz, No Salaam: Muslims in Modern India Forced to Self-Censor," The Quint, July 27, 2018. https://www.thequint.com/videos/indian-muslims-twitter-on-lynchings-bigotry-and-hate.

Angellica Aribam ✔
@AngellicAribam

In today's India, while such fear would never enter the consciousness of the majority Hindus, it has become an everyday reality for the Muslims as they're "demonised".

3:51 AM - 23 Jul 2018

Mir Adnan
@mirradnan17 · Jul 23

Since 2015 I don't carry any mutton even in Delhi :-(

> **Angellica Aribam** ✔
> @AngellicAribam
>
> A dear friend said, "I've stopped carrying mutton in my lunchbox nowadays. You never know someone might say I am carrying beef and I might get lynched". A fear that is justified in today's times especially

ursila ali
@UrsilaAli

Demonised/othered/marginalized. From politics of food, space, language to identity! A question I have heard way too much--so do you idenitfy as a Muslim or an Indian? As if the two are mutually exclusive!

3:14 AM - 25 Jul 2018

Riin (ʘ‿ʘ)*:.. ..:* @hiei900 · Jul 23

Even if we don't eat anything, sanghis will still attack us as soon as they know our identity. That is the scary reality ☹ Remember that Delhi 15 yrs old kid travelling on train b4 Eid... justice was never served to his family

⟳ Angelica Aribam Retweeted

Shamshir @shamshir_gaya · Jul 23
Replying to @aageSeLeftLelo @AngellicAribam
Muslims have left the demand for equality, now they are fighting for survival. Persecution & nothing else.

⟳ Angelica Aribam Retweeted

Shamshir @shamshir_gaya · Jul 23

I have travelled a lot through train in recent time & have promised myself that I will not argue with anyone over anything. My idetity as a Muslim is the biggest worry for me & my family.

mehz khan @mehzkhan · Jul 25
Replying to @AngellicAribam
And also add from my Real Life Experiences, I have friends from Top Univeristies working at MNC's who fear buying a house in Majority Domniant Areas with the Fear if Organised Riots just like Gujarat.

mehz khan @mehz khan · Jul 25
Replying to @AngellicAribam
With fear of being left unemployed, thousands of Muslim workers migrating to cities from Low Income Group, often Hide their Religious Identity or Adopt a Neutral Name in orderto fit in, Well this never the case with Majority!

312

312   Angelica Aribam, Twitter Post. July 23 16, 2018, https://twitter.com/AngellicAribam/status/1021347130135506944, Mir Adnan, Twitter Post, July 23, 2018, https://twitter.com/mirradnan17/status/1021337951794368512, Riin, Twitter Post, July 23, 2018, https://twitter.com/hiei900/status/1021434569726148608, Mehz, Khan,Twitter Post, July 17, 2018, https://twitter.com/

CASE STUDY
PEHLU KHAN

The attack and murder of Pehlu Khan, a dairy farmer from Nuh district of Haryana, by a group of 200 cow vigilantes affiliated with right-wing Hindutva groups in Alwar, Rajasthan, India.

In April 2017 Pehlu Khan, a 55-year-old, impoverished, Muslim dairy farmer who cared for his blind mother, wife and sons, was lynched in Alwar by a group of *gau rakshaks* (ultra-nationalist cow protectors) as he transported some cattle in the back of his truck.[313] Alwar is located in the state of Rajasthan and has a predominantly Hindu population at 82.72 percent and is 14.90 percent Muslim, according to India's 2011 census data.[314] The attack was

mehzkhan/status/1022067694953267202, Pepper Smoker, Twitter Post, July 23, 2018, https://twitter.com/pepper_smoker/status/1021336758468964352, Shamshir_Gaya, Twitter Post, July 23, 2018, https://twitter.com/shamshir_gaya/status/1021339625779023872, https://twitter.com/shamshir_gaya

313   Abhishek Angad, "Alwar Attack: Gau Rakshaks Killed a Dairy Farmer, Not Cattle Smuggler," The Indian Express, April 07, 2017, https://indianexpress.com/article/india/alwar-Gau-rakshaks-killed-a-dairy-farmer-not-cattle-smuggler-4601434/.

314   "Alwar District: Census 2011 Data," Jaisalmer District Population Census 2011, Rajasthan Literacy Sex Ratio and Density, http://www.census2011.co.in/census/district/429-alwar.html.

recorded via cell phone video and it captured the confiscation of his cows. They were seized and taken to a Hindu run *gaushala* (cow shelter).[315] While in the hospital Khan was able to name his attackers in an FIR before succumbing to his injuries two days later.[316]

Officials have claimed that Khan, his sons and companions had engaged in "cow smuggling" after police said that they were unable to produce a proper receipt for the animals they were transporting.[317] Khan's son Irshad has offered a receipt for the cows with a stamp of the Jaipur Municipal Corporation and the proper date to officials and media.[318] It has also been reported by the *Indian Express* that Khan was indeed one of ten dairy farmers in his village that provided milk and longtime customers have confirmed that.[319] Khan's companions, including his sons, were charged with Section 5 of the 1995 Rajasthan Bovine Animal (Prohibition of Slaughter and Regulation of Temporary Migration or Export Act). The act prohibits the transport of cows for slaughter, but the cows in question were "expensive milch cattle with calves," and not cows for slaughter.[320]

The video footage of Khan's attack went viral and it was covered in the news across the globe, but that did not stop a few officials in Parliament from denying that the attack took place at all. Deputy Chairman PJ Kurien stated that they could not rely on media reports and called for an official report to be presented to the House regarding the attack by gau rakshaks.[321] Cow related violence is often met with "inaction on the part of state officials"

or as in Khan's case, cross-case charges being filed against victims of such crimes.[322] There have also been reports of "victim and witness intimidation" and "excessively slow investigation and judicial processes."[323] Shedding light on police corruption when it comes to Muslims and Dalits, the Deputy Superintendent of Police was recorded in a viral video in 2018 explaining how she actually has filed "false cases against Dalits and Muslims" who have tried to file cases at her station under Scheduled Castes and Scheduled Tribes (Prevention of Atrocities) Act.[324] She also claims to have withheld arrest of the accused in those cases, advised the accused how to file counter-cases against Dalits, and has filed cases under Section 307 of the Indian Penal Code, attempt to murder, against Muslims, so that they do not get bail easily.[325]

In other cases police have been accused of standing nearby or are participants in the attacks. Regarding a recent lynching in 2018, BJP Union Minister Jayant Sinha went as far as honoring eight men convicted in the cow related lynching of a Muslim man named Alimuddin Ansari in Jharkhand, by placing flower garlands around their necks and hugging them during a ceremony after they were released on bail.[326]

Criminalization of the victims of cow vigilantism through labels such as 'beef eaters' and 'cow smugglers' is common in the otherization utilized by police, officials and vigilantes in such cases. Criminal charges are often filed against victims of lynchings either exclusively or in tandem with their attackers. Cow legislation that targets Muslims

315   CSSS, "A Narrowing Space," 8.

316   See article for actual FIR naming individuals and also the stamped receipt) Aarefa Johari, "Why Has the Rajasthan Police Filed an FIR Against the Victims of the Alwar Lynching?" Scroll. n, April 07, 2017, , https://scroll.in/article/833929/why-has-the-rajasthan-police-filed-an-fir-against-the-victims-of-the-alwar-lynching.

317   Angad, "Alwar Attack: Gau Rakshaks Killed a Dairy Farmer," 2017.

318   Aarefa Johari, "Why Has the Rajasthan Police Filed an FIR Against the Victims of the Alwar Lynching?" Scroll.in, April 07, 2017, https://scroll.in/article/833929/why-has-the-rajasthan-police-filed-an-fir-against-the-victims-of-the-alwar-lynching

319   Angad, "Alwar Attack: Gau Rakshaks Killed a Dairy Farmer," 2017.

320   Harsh Mander, "Pehlu Khan, One Year Later," The Indian Express, April 21, 2018, , https://indianexpress.com/article/opinion/columns/pehlu-khan-rajasthan-cow-lynching-5145631/.

321   "Alwar Gau Rakshak Attack Did Not Happen: Minister Mukhtar Abbas Naqvi." The Indian Express. April 07, 2017. https://indianexpress.com/article/india/alwar-gau-rakshak-attack-did-not-happen-minister-mukhtar-abbas-naqvi-4601726/.

322   Ibid.

323   Oral Statement Minority Rights Group Human Rights Council, 36th session. "MRG, Citizens Against Hate and People's Watch Reacts to the UPR of India." Minority Rights Group, September 21, 2017, minorityrights.org/advocacy-statements/mrg-citizens-hate-peoples-watch-reacts-upr-india/.

324   Scroll Staff, "Beed: Storm over Video Purporting to Show Police Officer Saying She Files False Cases against Dalits," Scroll.in, December 2, 2018, scroll.in/latest/904259/beed-video-of-police-officer-saying-she-targets-dalits-muslims-with-false-cases-goes-viral.

325   Ibid.

326   "Union Minister Jayant Sinha Garlands 8 Convicted for Ramgarh Mob Lynching," India Today, https://www.indiatoday.in/india/story/union-minister-jayant-sinha-garlands-8-convicted-or-ramgarh-mob-lynching-1279601-2018-07-06.

facilitates this injustice. The *Indian Express* reported in a recent article that criminalization of the victims of cow lynching occurred in states across the country.[327] Commenting on the Alwar lynching, BJP leader and Islamophobe Vinay Katiyar seemed to criminalize Muslims in general and placed responsibility for lynching at their feet when he said, "The incident of mob lynching in Alwar is highly condemnable but people from the Muslim community should abstain from touching cows and provoke aggressive Hindus. There are lot of Muslims who are sheltering cows but are also killing them. Cow meat is also being consumed by them."[328] This statement encourages perpetrators and can be understood as government support for lynching.[329]

The strategy of criminalizing the victims causes confusion around incidents of lynchings, which should be clear cut cases of criminal violence. Additionally, in some cases more effort is put into the forensic testing of the meat in question rather than in conducting the necessary and thorough investigations to find, arrest and properly charge the perpetrators of such violence. Meat becomes the center of such cases rather than human life, or in most cases
of cow lynching, Muslim life. In fact, a revealing *Hindustan Times* article reported that police officers found that in most cases the meat in question was not beef.[330]

The media, key players in the dissemination of Islamophobia to the masses, also utilize these dangerous tropes in reporting. These stereotypes are generally deployed to create the violent Muslim menace although beef consumption and slaughter is permissible in Islam, as is owning butcher shops and running halal meat companies and processing plants within India's lucrative beef industry. The Islamophobic tropes contribute to the concept of the 'Muslim problem,' as they facilitate the construction of the Muslim minority as culturally opposite to the Hindu majority and therefore they are then cast as a threat to not only 'mother cow' in need of protection, but also to an ultra-nationalist conception of a Hindu nation. But who is protecting the Muslims in India?

In Pehlu Khan's case it has been reported that villagers believe that his testimony was disregarded in order to protect "influential protect cow vigilantes affiliated to Sangh organisations."[331] An independent investigative team endorsed by the Alliance for Justice and Accountability, Human Rights Law Network, and South Asia Solidarity Group have identified all of the accused in Khan's death as local Hindutva activists and have called for the arrest of all six men named by Khan before he died, as well as the filing of a new FIR and an investigation into the involvement of the two named cow vigilante groups: Vishwa Hindu Parishad and Bajrang Dal for their involvement.[332]

A year after Pehlu Khan's violent lynching by Hindutva vigilantes, the community reportedly remains under siege and justice has not been served. The six men identified by Khan before he succumbed to his injuries "all been absolved by the police of any guilt."[333] In fact their names have reportedly been removed from the case entirely.[334] Khan's case is a textbook example of the culture of impunity that exists regarding lynchings under the guise of cow protection.

327   Ibid.
328   Nelanshu Shukla, "Muslim Community Should Abstain from Touching Cows, Provoking Hindus: BJP Leader on Alwar Lynching," India Today, July 23, 2018, https://www.indiatoday.in/india/story/muslim-community-should-abstain-from-touching-cows-provoking-hindus-bjp-leader-on-alwar-lynching-1294041-2018-07-23.
329   Ibid.
330   Ritesh Mishra, "40,000 cows saved since 2009 in Madhya Pradesh, claims VHP," Hindustan Times, July 28, 2016, Newspaper Source, EBSCOhost (accessed March 30, 2018).
331   Mander, "Pehlu Khan, One Year Later," 2018.
332   "Rajasthan Police Deliberately Weakened Pehlu Khan Lynching Case, Says Independent Fact-finding Team," Scroll.in, October 27, 2017, https://scroll.in/latest/855578/rajasthan-po-lice-deliberately-weakened-pehlu-khan-lynching-case-says-independent-fact-finding-team.
333   Mander, "Pehlu Khan, One Year Later," 2018.
334   Ibid.

"

In most cases that we investigated, we found the police either stalled investigations, or in some cases were even complicit in the cover-up of murder. In quite a few instances police filed cases under cow protection laws against the victims or their families and associates.

Jayshree Bajoria
Research Consultant, Human Rights Watch

Modi's Cash Cows

A 2017 investigative report by Reuters uncovered how 'Cow protection' turned out to be lucrative for the BJP party. The report offered the "first in-depth look at how the actions of cow vigilantes are also leading to further economic marginalization of the country's Muslim minority."[335] It uncovered that Hindu nationalist gau rakshaks seize cows after they stop and beat farmers that transport them, as in Pehlu Khan's case. The gau rakshaks steal the cows from the farmers, who are generally Muslim or Dalit, and then redistribute their wealth in the form of a cow, through BJP led gaushalas (cow shelters) where "the stolen cows are being given to Hindu farmers."[336]

The investigative report further revealed that "states governed by Modi's party have seen a marked increase in cow theft from Muslims as well as funding for cow shelters that in many cases take in the stolen cattle."[337] The report estimates that in northern India 190,000 cows have been seized since the election of Prime Minister Modi to office in 2014. Some of the property seizures reportedly occurred in the presence of police and "almost every single one of them from Muslims."[338] A Reuters investigative report entitled "In Modi's India, Cow Vigilantes Deny Muslim Farmers Their Livelihood" surveyed 110 cow shelters led by BJP chief ministers throughout six states prior to or just after the election in 2014.[339] The report claimed that there was an increase in cattle holdings from 84,000 (2014) to 126,000 (2017) although these number only represent a small amount of shelters in the country.[340] According to the report, "of the 110 cattle facilities surveyed, all but 14 said they receive cows from the Hindu vigilante groups.

About a third said they sell or give cows away, nearly all to Hindu farmers and households."[341] In comparison, the report uncovered that only three of 24 non-BJP ruled facilities stated that "they sold or gave away cattle - mainly to Hindus - after receiving them."[342]

Although the report clarifies that it is difficult to evaluate, it estimates that of 190,000 cows taken by BJP groups in northern India ranging in value between 0 to 25,000 rupees ($385) depending on the cow, the amount of loss equates to more than $36 million.[343] Add to that the fact that some families also make a living by selling the milk that the animals provide, such as lynching victim Pehlu Khan and his family. Thirty-six million dollars is a significant amount of monetary loss in a nation with extreme poverty and where Muslims are among those with the lowest income statistically.

Additionally in March 2017, three Muslim owned butcher shops were razed in Uttar Pradesh, a predominantly Hindu state led by Hindutva extremist Yogi Adityanath. Adityanath is "known for his polarizing and inflammatory speeches against Muslims, and has railed for harsher penalties for the slaughter of cows."[344] Since his election reportedly "dozens of butcher shops deemed illegal by the government have been sealed off across the state."[345] Uttar Pradesh has topped the charts for communal violence three years in a row. In 2018 it witnessed 195 cases of communal violence. With ten reported incidents of cow related violence from 2010-2017 according to IndiaSpend data, Uttar Pradesh shared the lead position for cow vigilantism with Haryana.

335   Special Report, "In Modi's India, Cow Vigilantes Deny Muslim Farmers Their Livelihood,"Reuters, Thomson Reuters, November 6, 2017, www.reuters.com/investigates/special-report/india-Politics-Religion-cows/.
336   Ibid.
337   Ibid.
338   Ibid.
339   Ibid.
340   Ibid.
341   Ibid.
342   Ibid
343   Ibid.
344   AFP, "Butcher Shops Razed amid Crackdown on Beef in India," Arab News, March 22, 2017, www.arabnews.com/node/1072471/world.
345   Ibid.

'Love Jihad' and Conversion Laws

Defining *'love jihad'*

The 'love jihad' conspiracy argues that Muslim men are waging Jihad in India by luring Hindu women into marriages through trickery, in order to convert them to Islam.[346] Proponents of 'love jihad' claim that these young men are waging war the capture of innocent Hindu women's hearts, referred to as 'Love Romeos'. Right-wing nationalists in particular, construct 'love jihad' as a strategy employed by Muslim fundamentalists to boost population numbers in a supposed ongoing demographic war to outnumber Hindus in India.[347] Hindutva groups and forces have consistently expressed a "fear" that Hindu women are being converted to Islam in the name of "false love".[348] Associate Professor of History, Charu Gupta from Delhi University brings attention to the way in which these anxieties around the conversion of Hindu women can be traced to the 1920's.[349] However in the more recent wake of terrorist threats and Muslim fundamentalism, increasing images of a violent and virulent Muslim have intensified anxieties of a more 'global' Islamist conspiracy. In particular, it has been professed that there is a foreign influence on these 'false love conversions', and that "Muslim youth are receiving funds from abroad to lure Hindu women in these marriages of trickery and false love".[350] Proponents even profess that "Muslim youth are receiving funds from abroad for purchasing designer clothes, vehicles, mobile phones and expensive gifts to woo Hindu women and lure them away".[351] It was further "alleged that beautiful, well-dressed young Muslim men were posing as Hindus... with red pūjā (worship) threads on their wrists and with ambiguous nicknames, it was claimed they were hanging around girls' schools and colleges".[352] The 2010 Foreign (Contribution) Regulation Act thus attempts to regulate the inflow use of such alleged funding received from foreign individuals, associations, and companies that may be "detrimental to the national interest".[353]

The first public appearance of the term 'love jihad' can be traced to around 2009, mainly in the southern states of Kerala and Karnataka. It's formulation, while originating in the early twentieth century, combines contemporary anxieties around loss of identity and conversion with stereotypes linking Muslims with terrorism and extremism.[354] Gupta summarizes that "'love jihad', which is actually a jihad against love, is a 'delicious' political fantasy, a lethal mobilisation strategy, a vicious crusade, and an emotive mythical campaign. It is an attempt by Hindutva

346   Gupta, Allegories of love Jihad; Khalid, "The Hadiya Case".
347   Mohan, "Love Jihad and demographic fears."
348   Gupta "Allegories of love Jihad".
349   Ibid; Charu Gupta, "Hindu women, Muslim men: Love Jihad and conversions", Economic and Political Weekly (2009): 13-15. https://www.jstor.org/stable/25663907
350   Gupta, "Hindu women, Muslim men", 13.
351   Gupta, Allegories of love Jihad, 295.
352   Ibid, 295.
353   USCIRF. "2017 Annual Report".
354   CSSS, "A Narrowing Space".

forces for political and communal mobilisation in the name of women."[355]

Historical Context

Fears around the supposed religious warfare of 'love jihad' have circulated in various forms of propaganda and anxieties across India for over a century. According to Associate Professor Charu Gupta who has published widely about Hindu-Muslim marriages in India, Muslim rulers have been historically portrayed as decadent manipulators in the popular literature of the late nineteenth century.[356] This longstanding history of anxieties about Muslim numbers out-growing the Hindu population, can be traced back to as early as 1909 when N. Mukherji wrote the book 'Hindus: A Dying Race'. This book proceeded to influence many tracts and publications by the Hindu Maha Sabha, the parent organization of the RSS.[357] However, the earliest connection to 'love jihad' can be traced to similar abduction and conversion campaigns launched by Arya Samaj and other Hindu revivalist bodies in the 1920s in north India, that drew sharper lines between Hindus and Muslims. As Gupta highlights:[358]

...in certain ways 'love jihad', and the various issues it touched on, had an uncanny resemblance to the "abduction" and conversion campaigns launched by the Arya Samaj and other Hindu revivalist bodies in the 1920s in UP, at a time when there was a spate of Hindu-Muslim riots in the region. Similar idioms have been repeatedly conjured up in a variety of ways, for example in 2009, thus revealing the wider continuity of such fabricated metaphors.

355   Charu Gupta, "When Society Is Threatened by Love", The Tribune, 2014, 9, http://www.academia.edu/10306613/When_Society_is_threatened_by_love.
356   Ishita Bhatia, "Right-Wing Men Assault Youth, Brothers in Court For 'Love Jihad'. The Times of India, January 15, 2018. https://timesofindia.indiatimes.com/city/meerut/right-wing-men-assault-youth-brothers-in-court-for-love-jihad/articleshow/62498624.cms; Gupta "Allegories of love Jihad".
357   Mohan, "Love Jihad and demographic fears."
358   Gupta "Allegories of love Jihad", 293.

It was such abductions that provided 'one of the glues for Hindu unity' in a country divided by caste. Such fears around 'love jihad' particularly increased following the 1947 Partition of India, whereby women on both sides of the conflict were impacted and 'recovered' from opposing religious groups.[359] This tension and cultural pressure against interfaith marriage on either side has cultivated an social environment of hostility and fear that amplifies the recent efforts against 'love jihad'. With the emergence of Hindu nationalists as a dominant political force in India[360], these allegations of 'love jihad' rose to national awareness in September 2009, initially alleged to have been conducted in Kerala and Mangalore in the coastal Karnataka region. Gupta highlights that:

> ...the ogre of 'love jihad' became a public citation of Hindu communalists in BJP ruled Karnataka in August 2009 when the 18 year old Silija Raj ran away with the 24 year old Asgar Nazar from Chamarajnagar, a small Karnataka town around 180 km from Bangalore. In 2009, a division bench of the court ordered a CID investigation into the cases of 21,890 girls who went "missing" between 2005 and 2009. It was discovered that 229 girls had married men of other faiths, but that conversion had occurred only in 63 cases.[361]

Following this initial flare-up in 2009, concerns with 'love jihad' emerged again in 2010, 2011 and 2014, however most of these claims were deemed baseless with no evidence to support them. The unprecedented victory of the BJP in 2014, however, intensified Hindutva socio-religious cries against 'love jihad', and for *ghar vāpasī* (return to home).[362] For example, "Rashtriya Swayam Sevak Sangh's sarkaryawah Suresh Bhayyaji Joshi stated in a press conference as late as October 20, 2014, that the 'Hindu samaj (society) has been facing the 'shame' of 'love jihad' since long, and the Uttar Pradesh government should take a 'serious view' of it, as it 'hurts the dignity of women'".[363] Further, "The September 7, 2014, issues of RSS's mouthpieces, Panchjanya and Organiser, had their cover stories on 'love jihad'. They urged people to raise the slogan 'love ever, 'love jihad' never!' We have witnessed an aggressive campaign around 'love jihad' in various villages, mofussils and towns of western UP in the months of August and September, particularly prior to the recent elections, by Hindutva organisations like the Dharma Jagran Manch, the Vishwa Hindu Parishad and the Bajrang Dal".[364]

The current socio-political context is thus shaped by this history of fear around 'love jihad', creating a hostile and divisive environment. This environment has encouraged political and communal mobilization in the name of Hindu women via increasingly aggressive metaphors against interfaith marriage.[365]

359 Ibid.
360 Bhatia, "Right-Wing Men Assault Youth".
361 Gupta, "Allegories of love Jihad", 390.
362 Ibid.
363 Gupta, "When Society Is Threatened by Love", 9.
364 Ibid, 9.
365 Gupta, "Allegories of love Jihad".

'Love Jihad' and the Politics of Gender in India

The political landscaping of communalism has historically, and continues to draw on the figure of vulnerable Hindu women to carry on orchestrated campaigns against 'love jihad'.[366] Indeed, through campaigns against alleged 'love jihad', "Hindu men have been asked to assert their prowess, protect their women and avenge such wrongs...[and]...move the centre of sexual violence from men in general and Hindu men in particular, towards the Muslim male".[367] This section therefore provides an overview of how 'love jihad' is both shaped by, and continues to shape the Hindutva politics of gender in India.

First, the 'love jihad' myth exacerbates fears of 'breeding Muslims' overtaking Hindu population in India[368] through what has been labelled as a 'population Jihad'.[369] According to proponents of 'love jihad', these forced conversions of Hindu women in the name of love are part of an international conspiracy to increase Muslim population at the cost of a supposed decline in Hindu numbers through the potential loss of child-bearing Hindu wombs.[370] For example, in 2016, high-ranking BJP parliamentarians, such as Yogi Adityanath and Sakshi Maharaj, reportedly called for laws to control the Muslim population.[371]

In addition, Hindu patriarchal notions appear deeply entrenched in discourse campaigns against 'love jihad', which reinforce images of passive victimized Hindu women at the hands of inscrutable Muslims abound.[372] This is accompanied by stereotypes of the hyper-sexuallzed, evil, licentious, and sexually violent Muslim male that must be punished by the hyper-masculine Hindu male:

> The 'love jihad' campaign, while focusing its anger on Muslims, received its emotional bonding from the "victimized" Hindu woman. The Hindu woman has often been regarded as an exclusive preserve of the Hindu man, and safeguarding her virtue is identified as his exclusive prerogative. In the name of protecting "our" women, which the women themselves have never asked for, they justify all forms of violence.[373]

Such allegations of Muslim youth trapping Hindu women 'through love' to convert to Islam has been a potent propaganda tool by right-wing Hindu nationalists, to exacerbate anti-Muslim sentiment. Indeed, "as part of the motif of 'love jihad', Hindus were constantly asked to be brave, to avenge past wrongs, and to be the warriors of a strong Hindu race".[374]

Hindu nationalists have actively responded to the perceived problem of Hindu women marrying outside their community with a campaign of *bahu lao, beti bachao* ('bring in the daughter-in-law, save the daughter') – an initiative to 'protect' Hindu men married to Muslims or Christians and to encourage women from those communities to marry into Hinduism.[375] Launched in 2015 in Uttar Pradesh by Bajrang Dal (a wing of the VHP and part of the broader Sangh Parivar), this campaign effectively emulates the alleged 'love

---

366   Gupta, "When Society Is Threatened by Love.
367   Ibid, 9.
368   Gupta, "Allegories of love Jihad".
369   Muhammed Mashkoor, "The Number Question: Muslim Demography and Islamophobia in India", Islam And Muslim Societies: A Social Science Journal 11, 11 (2018) 32-39.
370   Gupta, "Hindu women, Muslim men".
371   USCIRF. "2017 Annual Report".
372   Gupta, "When Society Is Threatened by Love".
373   Gupta, "Allegories of love Jihad", 298.
374   Ibid, 294.
375   Gourav Mishra, "Love Jihad Incidents In 2017 Which Went Beyond Religion to Alleged Terrorist Links", International Business Times India Edition, December 30, 2017, https://www.ibtimes.co.in/love-jihad-incidents-2017-which-went-beyond-religion-alleged-terrorist-links-754996

jihad' and has also reached other states such as West Bengal, where in recent years the BJP has increased their influence. In July 2015, an RSS activist reportedly distributed pamphlets at schools warning pupils that Hindu women had to be protected from Muslim men who were tricking them into marriage and then selling them at Arab markets.[376]

The body of the Hindu woman in such campaigns and warnings, become a site for both claims to community homogeneity and honor, as well as for cracks within its articulation[377], whereby "tales of abducted and converted Hindu women were metamorphosed into a symbol of both sacredness and humiliation. Simultaneously, images of passive victimized Hindu women, duped at the hand of inscrutable Muslims were used in an attempt to silence and erase female subjectivity and desire".[378] Indeed, the converted Hindu woman is a potential site of outrage of family order and religious sentiment, strengthening the drive for Hindu nationalist mobilization. Allegations of abductions have caused a number of localized affrays, and even occasional riots, tracing back to Kanpur in June 1924 and in Mathura in March 1928, where it was reported that a Muslim man had eloped with a Hindu woman.[379] This communalized, gendered anxiety around the 'abduction' of Hindu women was also evident in epidemics of rumors before the Gujarat carnage in 2002.[380] Whether in 1920, or 2018, any possibility of women exercising their legitimate right to love and their right to personal choice is ignored within these campaigns that demonize inter-religious love and intimacies and undermine female free choice.[381] Fitting neatly into this gendered anxiety was the communalization of the issue of the 'abduction' of Hindu women, particularly based on the premise that female conversion is subject to family and communal approval, without individual autonomy. This ultimately "undermines the status of women in India with the old patriarchal notion that women are not self-sufficient to make their own decisions".[382] Thus, the embedding of patriarchy, 'nationhood' and violence against women in discourses on population numbers has continued to make reproductive women's bodies a site of communal anxiety about the future of Muslim versus Hindu population numbers[383], manifesting in fears around 'love jihad' and the way in which it regulates and controls the everyday lives of Hindu women. [384]

Anti-Conversion Laws and Ghar Vāpasī

Alongside 'love jihad', the other issue that gained momentum at the end of 2014 was that of *ghar vāpasī*. "*Ghar vāpasī* signaled a synchronized vocabulary of anti-conversion by the BJP and of reconversion by the VHP and Dharm Jagran Samiti, an affiliate of the Rashtriya Swayamsevak Sangh" (Gupta, 2018, p. 291).

376   Ibid.
377   Gupta, "When Society Is Threatened by Love".
378   Gupta, "Allegories of love Jihad", 297.
379   Gupta, "When Society Is Threatened by Love".
380   Mohan, "Love Jihad and demographic fears."
381   Ibid.
382   Sahel Md Delabul Hossain, Seema Kumari Ladsaria, Rajni Singh, "'Love-Jihad'; Protection of Religious Proximity an Indian Situation", International Journal of Humanities and Cultural Studies 2, 4 (2016), 672 https://www.ijhcs.com/index.php/ijhcs/article/view/211
383   Mohan, "Love Jihad and demographic fears."
384   Gupta, "Allegories of love Jihad".

"

"Ghar vāpasī has been touted as the return to authentic origins, the starting point, the abode of birth. It produces and enforces notions of a primordial religious identity, whereby all and everyone are declared Hindus. Thus states Praveen Togadia of the VHP: "At one point of time, the entire world was Hindu. There were seven billion Hindus, and now there are just one billion." The shift from the whole world to the Hindu nation is swift, as ghar vāpasī denationalizes Islam and Christianity, facilitating their "othering".[385]

Further, a "common thread that links both 'love jihad' and ghar vāpasī is the obsession with the numerical strength of Hindus. The numbers game, and constructed fears around it, has been central to the modern politics of Hindutva... religious conversions have been regarded as not only challenging an established community's assent to religious doctrines and practices, but also altering demographic equations and producing numerical imbalances".[386] Religious conversions and re-conversions, two sides of the same coin, have thus acquired political prominence in more contentious ways at the end of 2014.[387] This can be connected directly to discourses around 'love jihad', whereby Hindu nationalists have responded to the perceived problem of Hindu women marrying outside their community by introducing, and in some states, implementing anti-conversion Laws, named "Freedom of Religion" Acts. The Hindu Right have introduced anti-conversion laws in an attempt to control 'forced conversions', and claim to have no objection to 'voluntary' conversions. Despite this claim that the laws only target 'forced conversions', an increased number of Indian states have written laws that make it virtually impossible for Hindus to convert to other religions, particularly Abrahamic faiths.

These laws have been passed by six legislatures in Chhattisgarh, Himachal Pradesh, Gujarat, Rajasthan, Madhya Pradesh, Arunachal Pradesh and Odisha. These laws generally require government officials to assess the legality of conversions and disbar conversions by use of "force," which is defined as a show of force or threat of injury or threat of divine displeasure or social ex-communication. Infringement of these laws results in fines and imprisonment for anyone who uses force, fraud, or "inducement" to convert another.[388] Alternatively, inter-religious couples who wish to marry without conversion, must apply one-month in advance under the 'Special Marriage Act' where the legality of their

385   Ibid, 302.

386   Ibid, 302.
387   Ibid.
388   USCIRF, "2017 Annual Report".

marriage is assessed, and often dismissed. Many eloping couples are afraid to apply for legal marriage under this act, and thus take conversion as the way out of utilizing this legislation.[389]

Anti-conversion laws thus disproportionately target Abrahamic faiths, as conversion to any religion that has the concept of hell or heaven is implicitly assumed to be a forcible conversion.[390] Further, "inducement" or "allurement" that disqualify conversions are defined to include "the offer of any gift or gratification, either in cash or in kind and shall also include the grant of any benefit, either pecuniary or otherwise." These specifically target Christian missionaries whose schools, hospitals and other charitable works provide free services to all, including non-Christians.[391] Although the anti-conversion laws do not explicitly ban conversions, in practice these laws both by their design and implementation, infringe upon the individual's right to convert, favor Hinduism over minority religions, and represent a significant challenge to Indian secularism.[392]

Most laws require that government be notified of the conversions 30 days in advance. If the government official determines that the conversion was forced then the guilt is liable to a punishment of up to three years' imprisonment, which is seven years in the case of tribals. Despite thousands of Christians and Muslims being converted to Hinduism, not one case of forced conversion is known to have been applied to conversions into Hinduism.[393] As Gupta highlights: "when a Hindu man marries a Muslim woman, it is always portrayed as "romance" and "love" by Hindu organizations, while when the reverse happens it is depicted as "coercion".[394] An explicit example of this double-standard is reflected in the 2008 ethnic cleansing of a Christian population from Kandhamal in Odisha in 2008 by Hindu ultra-nationalist militias, who were only allowed to return on the condition that they renounce Christianity.[395] Despite this example, there remain no cases of forced conversion applied on the Hindu groups or individuals. These laws are therefore critiqued as being one-sided, only concerned with conversions away from Hinduism but not toward Hinduism.[396] Sample cases relating to conversion are provided in the table below, including preventing conversion to Islam, threats against other religious groups, such as Christians to convert to Hinduism, and attacks against a Church on the basis of alleged forced conversions to Christianity.

389   Gupta, "Allegories of love Jihad".
390   Alliance for Justice & Accountability, "Minority Rights Violations in India".
391   Ibid.
392   Gupta, "Allegories of love Jihad".
393   Gulam Jeelani, "From Love Jihad, Conversion To SRK: 10 Controversial Comments by UP'S New CM Yogi Adityanath", Hindustan Times, April 6, 2017. https://www.hindustantimes.com/assembly-elections/from-love-jihad-conversion-to-srk-10-controversial-comments-by-up-s-new-cm-yogi-adityanath/story-5JW2ZFGZzAdIZeIcjcZCNM.html.
394   Gupta, "Allegories of love Jihad", 289.
395   Menon, "'Security', Home, And Belonging in Contemporary India".
396   Gupta, "Allegories of love Jihad"; CSSS, "A Narrowing Space".

Table No. 1: Sample Cases relating to Conversion in India

#	Date	Place	Event
1	September 2014	Shivpuri, Madhya Pradesh	Members of the Bajrang Dal and VHP put pressure on district officials to reject nine Hindu Dalits' petitions to convert to Islam.[397]
2	December 2014	Madhunagar, Uttar Pradesh	RSS-related groups, the Dharma Jagran Samanvay Vibhag and Bajrang Dal, converted 200 Muslim persons to Hinduism. The new converts later stated they had been misled, told that they were receiving help to get ID cards.[398]
3	February 2016	Across India	The RSS allegedly put up threatening signs across India in train stations stating Christians need to convert to Hinduism or leave the country by 2021, or risk death.[399]
4	April 2017	Maharajganj, Uttar Pradesh	Members of the group Hindu Yuva Vahini called police to a Christian church by alleging forced conversions, causing disruption to a prayer service involving Ukrainian and U.S tourists. While Hindu Yuva Vahini members surrounded the church during the disruption, the police visit found no evidence of forced conversions.[400]

Table Source: Dr. Angana P. Chatterji and cited material

397   United States Department of State, "International Religious Freedom Report for 2014 – India", Bureau of Democracy, Human Rights and Labor, 2014, http://www.state.gov/j/drl/rls/irf/religiousfreedom/index.htm?year=2014&dlid=238494.

398   United States Commission on International Religious Freedom, "2015 Annual Report", Washington DC: United States Commission on International Religious Freedom, 2015, 151 http://www.uscirf.gov/sites/default/files/India%202015.pdf.

399   USCIRF. "2017 Annual Report", 152.

400   Suhasini Raj, and Nida Najar, "Hindu Group Claims Christians Tried Forced Conversions in India", New York Times, April 8, 2017, https://www.nytimes.com/2017/04/08/world/asia/india-uttar-pradesh-hindu-christian-church-conversions.html.

Hindu nationalist groups have been able to operate such assertive *Ghar Vāpasī* campaigns targeting minorities for conversion with apparent impunity. These so-called 'homecomings' are justified by the RSS as 'reconversions' on the basis that their predecessors were themselves supposedly converted from Hinduism through proselytization or force by other 'foreign' religions, including Islam.[401] Observers note that these laws create a hostile and, on occasion, violent environments for religious minority communities because they do not require any evidence to support accusations of wrongdoing.[402] Despite the shortcomings of these laws, BJP President Amit Shah has advocated for a nationwide anti-conversion law.[403] In spite of the absence of credible data to support laws restricting religious conversions in India, there are voices within the government which have called for a national anti-conversion law.[404] In April 2015, for example, Union Home Minister Rajnath Singh of the BJP called for a national level anti-conversion law, ostensibly to protect communal harmony, though critics have pointed out that this would violate basic religious freedoms.[405]

On the flipside, *Ghar Vāpasī* or Conversion to Hinduism ceremonies are initiated on the view that all individuals born in India are Hindus by default, even if their communities have practiced other faiths for several generations.

"Ghar vāpasī has been touted as the return to authentic origins, the starting point, the abode of birth. It produces and enforces notions of a primordial religious identity, whereby all and everyone are declared Hindus. Thus states Praveen Togadia of the VHP: "At one point of time, the entire world was Hindu. There were seven billion Hindus, and now there are just one billion." The shift from the whole world to the Hindu nation is swift, as ghar vāpasī denationalizes Islam and Christianity, facilitating their "othering."[406]

401   CSSS, "A Narrowing Space".
402   USCIRF. "2018 Annual Report".
403   USCIRF. "2017 Annual Report".
404   CSSS, "A Narrowing Space".
405   Ibid.
406   Gupta, "Allegories of love Jihad", 302.

There have been ongoing reports of *Ghar Vāpasī* ceremonies in 2017, although their number and nature were impossible to confirm.[407] In 2014, following the BJP national victory, the RSS announced plans to "reconvert" thousands of Christian and Muslims families to Hinduism as part of a so-called *Ghar Vāpasī* (returning home) program, and began raising money to do so. The Dharm Jagran Samiti (Religious Awakening Council) is an RSS-VHP affiliate dedicated to converting Muslims and Christians to Hinduism. According to a report by *India Today*, this organization said it would expedite its *Ghar Vāpasī* campaign: "Muslims and Christians don't have any right to stay here [in India]," one of its leaders said in December 2014. "Our target is to make India a Hindu nation by 2021... Muslims and Christians must convert to Hinduism "if they want to stay in this country".[408]

This statement is connected to the organizations' claims that they converted 57 Muslim families to Hinduism in Uttar Pradesh. Such conversion ceremonies have led to panic among Muslims and the displacement of Muslim communities from their homes. However, after domestic and international outcry, the RSS postponed its plans. Nevertheless, in its annual report presented of 2015, the VHP claimed to have converted nearly 34,000 people to Hinduism over a year and "prevented" nearly 49,000 Hindus from converting to other religions. These conversions and "preventions" were carried out in the states of Odisha, Gujarat, Chhattisgarh, Jharkhand and Assam. The Dharm Jagran Samiti also distributed pamphlets for its fundraising drive where the cost of converting a Muslim was fixed at Rs. 500,000 ($7,500) and of converting a Christian at Rs. 200,000 ($3,000). BJP MP Satish Gautam welcomed the announcement.[409] Smaller-scale forced conversions of religious minorities were also reported in 2016. In addition, in February 2016 the RSS reportedly placed signs in train stations throughout India that said Christians had to leave India or convert to Hinduism or they will be killed by 2021.[410]

As Gupta highlights, the language of Ghar Vāpasī is not motivated by a desire to promote spirituality and religious values but is imbued with a strong anti-Christian and anti-Muslim conviction and passion, adopting language that frames all other religions as anti-national, and in a domain of exile. Further, it adopts a language that views all non-Hindu religions as anti-national, and thus exacerbates the othering of non-Hindu religious groups, such as Muslim in India. Simultaneously, anti-conversion and reconversion campaigns, along with 'love jihad', fortify Hindutva politics around religious identities and boundaries, and impose a creed of Hindu masculinity and violence, particularly against women.[411]

'Love Jihad' propaganda and Implications

This propaganda and fear around 'love jihad', has been falsified in multiple contexts and periods over the last decade, as mere conspiracy and myth. Indeed, as Gupta also brings to our attention: "in actual practice, 'love jihad' was an emotive mythical campaign, a "delicious" political fantasy, a lethal mobilization strategy and a vicious crusade – a jihad against love – for political gains in elections".[412] This myth has been propagated through pamphlets, meetings, debates, rumors and everyday conversations, sustaining 'love jihad' as an active cultural, and ultimately political issue that monopolized the everyday representation of inter-religious marriages. Such propaganda around 'love jihad' were falsified through numerous investigations, including in 2009 and 2012.

407   USCIRF. "2018 Annual Report".
408   Piyush Srivastava, "Dharm Jagran Samiti Leader Vows to Create Hindu Rashtra by 2021", India Today, December 19, 2014. https://www.indiatoday.in/india/story/dharm-jagran-samiti-leader-vows-to-create-hindu-rashtra-by-2021-231854-2014-12-19.
409   Alliance for Justice & Accountability, "Minority Rights Violations in India".
410   USCIRF. "2017 Annual Report".
411   Gupta, "Allegories of love Jihad".
412   Gupta, "Allegories of love Jihad", 292.

> **In 2009 "...the then CID DGP, D. V. Guruprasad, told the High Court: "There is no organised attempt by any group of individuals to entice girls/women belonging to Hindu or Christian religions to marry Muslim boys with the aim of converting them to Islam." Not only did the Karnataka High Court finally close the investigations into 'love jihad' in November 2013, finding no evidence of any such conspiracy, but it ruled that Silija Raj was free to go anywhere she wished. She chose to go with her husband. In 2012, the Kerala police categorically declared that 'love jihad' was a "campaign with no substance," and instead brought legal proceedings against the website hindujagruti.org for spreading religious hatred and false propaganda"[413]**

Most recently, the NDTV investigative report on 'love jihad' found that police investigations failed to find evidence of an organized 'love jihad' campaign. The Police report stated that sporadic cases of trickery by unscrupulous men were not evidence of a broader conspiracy. In Uttar Pradesh, police also found no evidence of attempted or forced conversion in five of six reported 'love jihad' cases. "In most cases we found that a Hindu girl and Muslim boy were in love and had married against their parents' will," said state police Chief A.L. Banerjee. "These are cases of love marriages and not 'love jihad'.[414] The Alliance for Justice & Accountability draws on the expose by Cobrapost and Gulail (both investigative portals) to verify that the 'love jihad' campaign is a fabrication used by Hindutva leaders to create false propaganda that girls are in danger and need to be rescued from Muslim boys.[415] Most recently, the 'Kerala Love-Jihad' investigation ordered by the Supreme Court and undertaken by the National Investigation Agency (NIA) in 2017 found that of the eighty-nine speculated cases, only eleven cases of 'love jihad' were confirmed by Kerala Police Chief Loknath Behera. Further, four of these eleven cases of 'love jihad', involved Hindu men converting to Islam to marry Muslim Women, which was objected by the couple's families.[416] Further, the NIA informed the Supreme Court that "none of the man and women it examined in cases that emerged while investigating the Kerala 'love jihad' case were enticed by monetary benefits to convert to Islam".[417]

Despite proof of the 'love jihad' myth, Hindu nationalist groups, in particular the RSS and Vishwa Hindu Parishad (VHP), have launched counter-campaigns and initiatives that spread fear and hostility around inter-religious marriages. Gupta draws particular attention to the spike in anti-'love jihad' propaganda by Hindu publicists

414   Alliance for Justice & Accountability, "Minority Rights Violations in India".
415   Ibid.
416   Younus, "Kerala: NIA finds only 11 out of 89 'love-jihad' cases to be true", The Siasat Daily, 9 March, 2018, https://www.siasat.com/news/kerala-nia-finds-only-11-out-89-love-jihad-cases-be-true-1327711/.
417   Vijaita Singh, "No conversion money seen in 'love jihad' cases: NIA". The Hindu. November 2, 2017, https://www.thehindu.com/news/national/no-conversion-for-money-seen-in-love-jihad-cases-nia/article19966254.ece

in the 2014 national elections:

"

"the year 2014 thus saw orchestrated propaganda campaigns and popular inflammatory and demagogic appeals led by a section of Hindu publicists against 'love jihad' against the supposed 'abductions' and conversions of Hindu women by Muslim men, ranging from allegations of rape and forced marriages, to elopement, love, luring and conversion...drawing on diverse sources such as small meetings, handbills, posters, myths, rumors and gossip, the campaign against the mythical 'love jihad' operated in a public-political domain and attempted to monopolize the field of everyday representation."[418]

Such propaganda has sparked Hindu vigilantes to not only police community members and relationships but are also demand legislation to restrict inter-religious marriages all together. The Bajrang Dal, for example, intend on prohibiting any Hindu woman who marries a Muslim man, from converting to Islam, despite running their own campaigns that encourage Hindu men to marry Muslim women. The Hindu Yuva Vahini have also allegedly carried out a "reverse 'love jihad'" in an Uttar Pradesh region, with the Uttar Pradesh Chief Minister Yogi Adityanath warning that if "one Hindu girl is converted [to Islam] we will convert 100 Muslim girls [to Hinduism]".[419]

Tracing back to 2009 when the concept of 'love jihad' gained momentum, organizations like the Rashtriya Swayamsevak Sangh, Vishwa Hindu Parishad, Sri Ram Sene, Akhil Bharatiya Vidyarthi Parishad and Hindu Janjagruthi Samiti began to hold meetings, distribute pamphlets and even file court cases in Kerala, Karnataka and Delhi, declaring that the organisation, as part of an Islamist conspiracy, had devised plans for compulsive and deceitful religious conversions by winning over young women.[420] In the years to follow, media and various sections of the Hindu fundamentalist groups such as the Bajrang Dal, the Vishwa Hindu Parishad, the Rashtriya Swayamsevak Sangh (RSS) and the Akhil Bharati Vidyarthi Parishad mounted a sustained campaign, including the student wing of the Bharatiya Janata Party (BJP) in New Delhi's Jawaharlal Nehru University which distributed pamphlets, against this grand conspiracy.[421]

The year of 2014 however saw orchestrated propaganda campaigns and popular inflammatory and demagogic appeals led by a section of Hindu publicists against 'love jihad' against the supposed 'abductions' and conversions of Hindu women by Muslim men, ranging from allegations of rape and forced marriages, to elopement, love, luring and conversion.[422] Such attempts were particularly evident in Uttar Pradesh and to an extent in Bihar as well as other regions, where

418   Gupta, "Allegories of love Jihad", 294.

419   Alliance for Justice & Accountability, "Minority Rights Violations in India".
420   Gupta, "Hindu women, Muslim men".
421   Mohan, "Love Jihad and demographic fears."
422   Gupta, "Allegories of love Jihad".

'love jihad' was framed as important determinant of Hindu identity and consciousness in 2014, providing Hindu publicistis with a common reference point. An example of this publicity is highlighted below:

> "The 7 September 2014 issues of RSS's mouthpieces, Pāñcajanya and Organiser, had 'love jihad' as their cover stories. They urged people to raise the slogan "love for ever, 'love jihad' never!" Pāñcajanya's cover had an illustration of a man wearing a kaffiyeh or traditional Arab headdress, a beard in the shape of a heart, and sinister sunglasses in which red hearts were reflected. The magazine asked on the cover, "pyār andhā yā dhandhā" (love blind or trade)."[423]

Indeed, "the idioms, language and symbols invoked during the 'love jihad' campaign were not only meant to draw sharper lines between Hindus and Muslims, but were also thought to be useful in reaping a rich political harvest in the election landscape of 2014".[424] These campaigns have intensified in more recent years, whereby Hindu nationalist groups have conducted 'rescue operations' to counter 'love jihad', and reportedly deployed right-wing lawyers to identify and disclose registered cases of inter-religious marriage between Muslim men and Hindu women.[425] Such groups have also acknowledged levelling false accusations of rape and kidnapping against Muslim men, and have benefitted from legal and political patronage, with strong links to the police and certain political actors.[426]

A year-long investigation called *Operation Juliet* by Cobrapost and Gulail, published a report on the mythical nature of 'love jihad', and exposes the more extreme expressions of violence and control used by Hindutva groups in their bid to stop inter-religious marriage between Muslim men and Hindu women.[427] According to the report, Hindutva outfits (Sangh Parivar) and its splinter groups use violence, intimidation, emotional blackmail, duplicity and drugs to split the married couples. The report reveals the systematic effort across pan-India to spread propaganda and campaigns that further cause a rift between two religious communities with the objective of feeding the national and identity anxieties to win elections.[428] A primary example of this is reflected in the formation of 'anti-Romeo squads' by the police in Uttar Pradesh after winning the 2017 state elections in which the BJP campaign had consistently drawn on references to 'love jihad'.[429] In July, even after Prime Minister Narendra Modi finally condemned violent mob attacks, an affiliate organization of the BJP, the Rashtriya Swayamsevak Sangh (RSS), announced plans to recruit 5,000 "religious soldiers" to "control cow smuggling and 'love jihad'".[430] Further, in early 2018, the *Times of India* reported that Hindu nationalist groups utilize people to spy on interfaith couples in order to target the couples with 'love jihad' tactics of assault, threats, and possible arrests.

The ramifications of such campaigns and initiatives are wide-reaching, in not only fostering hate, further suppressing women to control

423   Gupta, "Allegories of love Jihad, 293.
424   Ibid, 293.
425   CSSS, "A Narrowing Space", 21.
426   Guarav V. Bhatnagar, "BJP, RSS Leaders Caught Using 'Love Jihad' Bogey to Fuel Communal Polarisation", The Wire, October 5, 2015. https://thewire.in/communalism/bjp-rss-leaders-caught-using-love-jihad-bogey-to-fuel-communal-polarisation
427   Cobrapost, "Operation Juliet: Busting the Bogey of "Love Jihad"", Cobrapost. 4 October, 2015, https://www.cobrapost.com/blog/operation-juliet-busting-the-bogey-of-love-jihad-2/900
428   Ibid.
429   CSSS, "A Narrowing Space", 8.
430   Human Rights Watch, "World Report 2018".

and limiting their agency,[431] but more seriously contributing to riots such as the 2013 riots in Muzaffarnagar, as well as provoking smaller-scale communal tensions and violence in India, such as extremists blocking an interfaith marriage between a Muslim man and a Hindu woman who had converted to Islam.[432] The in-depth piece on love-Jihad and communal riots in Uttar Pradesh by the Hindustan Times highlights that "Inter-religious couples, however, say they are being hunted. Of the more than 12,000 low-key communal incidents recorded in UP since 2010, nearly 15 percent are spurred by cases involving women: from alleged sexual violence to elopement".[433] Indeed the negative impacts of propaganda against 'love jihad' on the current socio-political environment in India highlights the way in which "representation, performance, and events fed into each other, providing one of the primary sources of communal power"[434] to Hindutva forces and communities across the nation.

'Love Jihad' in 2017

Cases and issues relating to 'love jihad' in the year of 2017 represented a peak in political discourse, propaganda and campaigns. As a means of further fuelling public anxieties around 'love jihad', the BJP formed 'anti-Romeo squads' in Uttar Pradesh after winning the 2017 state elections. Symbolic of a new level of securitization of this issue, these squads signified the formalization of initiatives and campaigns against the alleged activity of 'love jihad'. This was accompanied by an affiliate organization of the BJP, the Rashtriya Swayamsevak Sangh (RSS), announcing plans to recruit 5,000 "religious soldiers" to "control cow smuggling and 'love jihad'".[435] In the same year, the Times of India reported that Hindu nationalist

groups utilize people who spy on interfaith couples in order to target the couples with 'love jihad' tactics of assault, threats, and possible arrests. As reflected in Table 2, 'love jihad' in 2017 was emboldened by this formalization of counter-initiatives and campaigns, implemented through vigilante attacks against interfaith marriages or neighborhoods suspected of being home to such couples, and the death of an elderly man who was accused of facilitating 'love jihad'. In addition, there was an increased distribution of official propaganda against 'love jihad'. For example educational pamphlets, directed towards warning young Hindus against 'love jihad' were distributed at a spiritual fair in the state capital of Jaipur. Similarly, in early 2018, Bajrang Dal and Durga Vahini, the women's wing of the VHP, organized an awareness program for parents of young women across many regions of coastal Karnataka on 'love jihad'. This included visiting households, schools, colleges and distributing handbills across Mangaluru city and other parts of Dakshina Kannada, Udupi and Kasargod. In addition to propaganda and education against 'love jihad', 2017 to early 2018 was occupied by intensified public discourse and discussions on various mediums. Namely, In January, a Facebook posting 'exposed' a list of 100 interfaith couples where readers were encouraged to take violent action against them in accusation that the couples were formed as a result of "'love jihad".[436] This posting which included profiles and personal contact information, made couples and family members vulnerable to social pressure, and in some cases, receiving death threats.[437]

431   Gupta, "Hindu women, Muslim men".
432   CSSS, "A Narrowing Space", 21.
433   Appu E. Suresh. "Love Jihad: UP's forbidden couples", Hindustan Times. October 19 2016, https://www.hindustantimes.com/static/uttar-pradesh-communal-riot/love-jihad-uttar-pradesh/
434   Gupta, "Allegories of love Jihad", 295.
435   Human Rights Watch, "World Report 2018".
436   Kim Arora, "Facebook post lists interfaith couples, calls for attacks", The Times of India, February 6, 2018, https://timesofindia.indiatimes.com/india/facebook-post-lists-inter-faith-couples-calls-for-attacks/articleshow/62796340.cms.
437   Ibid.

Table 2: Cases and Events relating to 'love jihad' in 2017

#	Date	Place	Event
1	March 2017	Rajasthan	RSS-VHP-Bajrang Dal leaders called a massive gathering of Hindus from several villages in Rajasthan which decided to boycott Muslims in the villages because a Hindu woman had eloped with a Muslim man a night before she was to be married off to a Hindu. The police traced the runaway couple in New Delhi and then took the man in custody.[438]
2	March 2017	Uttar Pradesh	The BJP campaign drew on references to 'love jihad' during the 2017 state elections in Uttar Pradesh and, in March 2017, following their electoral success, so-called 'anti-Romeo squads' were formed by the police.[439]
3	April 2017	Meerut, Uttar Pradesh	Members of the Hindu Yuva Vahini forcibly entered a house in Meerut to accost a Muslim man and a Hindu woman belonging to another faith. The couple were forcibly taken to a police station, where the man was booked on charges of obscenity. The vigilantes were not reprimanded by the government.[440]
4	May 2017	Nandrauli, Uttar Pradesh	Following news that a married Hindu woman and Muslim man had eloped, there were attacks on the homes of Muslims living in Nandrauli, an area in Sambhal District of Uttar Pradesh. This led to an exodus of the majority of Muslims from the village to nearby area.[441]
5	May 2017	Bulandshahr, Uttar Pradesh	Members of the VHP-affiliated Hindu Yuva Vahini beat to death Gulam Ahmad (60 years old) in an Orchard in village Sohi, accusing him of aiding another Muslim man to elope with a Hindu woman on May 2. The killers also harassed, molested, and threatened Ahmad's family members, leading to their exodus from the village. The local community was unsympathetic and subjected the family to a social boycott, which displaced them to Aligarh.[442]
6	May 2017	Kerala	The Kerala High Court annulled the marriage of Hadiya, a 24-year-old woman who had converted to Islam from Hinduism, with Shafin Jahan, labelling her "weak and vulnerable... capable of being exploited".[443] Meanwhile, India's National Investigation Agency alleged the relationship to be a 'love jihad' and Jahan to have terrorist connections.[444] The NIA's accusations have not been substantiated and the Supreme Court overturned the annulment in 2018, allowing the couple to be together.[445]
7	Nov 2017	Jaipur	The Rajasthan government has asked schools in the state capital Jaipur to take students and teachers to a spiritual fair, where they can learn about 'love jihad'. This five-day fair intended for the social transformation of students' patriotism distributed pamphlets on 'love jihad'. The pamphlet talks about how prominent actors like Saif Ali Khan and Aamir Khan have been ensnaring Hindu women. It states that it's better to die in one's own religion than converting. Finally, it listed the places where 'love jihad' happens, including beauty parlors, mobile recharge shops, ladies' tailors, Muslim hawkers, and few others.[446]

438   Salik Ahmad, "Love Jihad: Muslims of Rajasthan Village Boycotted after Man Elopes with Hindu Woman", Hindustan Times, March 22, 2017, https://www.hindustantimes.com/jaipur/love-jihad-muslims-of-rajasthan-village-boycotted-after-man-elopes-with-hindu-woman/story-MOsm6qcSc692GXfiZPBbpI.html

439   Sidharth Pandey, "UP Elections 2017: BJP Promised Anti-Romeo Squads to Stop Love Jihad, says its Meerut Leader", NDTV, February 05, 2017, https://www.ndtv.com/india-news/up-elections-2017-bjp-promised-anti-romeo-squads-to-stop-love-jihad-says-its-meerut-leader-1656250

440   Indian Express, "Hindu Yuva Vahini Harasses Interfaith Couple in Meerut." Indian Express, April 12, 2017, https://indianexpress.com/article/india/hindu-yuva-vahini-harassed-a-interfaith-couple-in-meerut-4610464/

441   Mohamad Ali, "Exodus of Nandrauli's Muslims Continues", The Hindu, May 20, 2017 http://www.thehindu.com/news/national/exodus-of-nandraulis-mulims-continues/article18516533.ece.

442   Saurabh Sharma, "A Year After Lynching of Man in Bulandshahr over 'Love Jihad' Issue, Victim's Family Members Live Like Refugees", Firstpost, June 7, 2018, https://www.firstpost.com/india/a-year-after-lynching-of-man-in-bulandshahr-over-love-jihad-issue-victims-family-members-live-like-refugees-4501227.html; The Wire Staff, "Hindutva's 'Love Jihad' Obsession Leads to Murder of Muslim Man in UP", The Wire, May 3, 2017,https://thewire.in/politics/hindutvas-love-jihad-obsession-leads-to-murder-of-muslim-man-in-up

443   Indian Express, "For the Record: 'It Is Absolutely Unsafe to Let (24-Year-Old) Be Free To Do As She Likes,'" Indian Express, May 31, 2017. http://indianexpress.com/article/india/for-the-record-it-is-absolutely-unsafe-to-let-24-year-old-be-free-to-do-as-she-likes-4681708/.

444   Kavita Krishnan, "SC Should Defend Women's Privacy, Autonomy, Not Perpetuate 'Love Jihad' Myth," The Wire, August 20, 2017. https://thewire.in/communalism/love-jihad-nia-probe-kerala-court.

445   BBC, "India Supreme Court restores 'love jihad' marriage", BBC, March 08, 2018,https://www.bbc.com/news/world-asia-india-43327380

446   Financial Express Online, "Rajasthan Government Wants Students, Teachers to Learn about Love Jihad; Here Is How", The Financial Express. November 19, 2017, https://www.financial-express.com/india-news/rajasthan-government-wants-students-teachers-to-learn-about-love-jihad-here-is-how/939167/

8	Nov 2017	Mumbai	Bandra police registered a First Information Report (FIR) against the husband of former model Rashmi Shahbazker after she filed a complaint that he had been forcing her to convert to Islam for the past 12 years. The police indicated that Ms. Shahbazker claimed her husband Asif Shahbazker was on a 'love jihad' mission.[447]
9	Nov 2017	Kerala	A petition was filed in the Kerala High Court (HC), by 25-year-old Akshara Bose, alleging that she was subjected to forced conversion, sexual exploitation and fraudulent marriage. She also claimed that the woman's husband tried to sell her to Islamic State (ISIS).[448]
10	Dec 2017	Online / Rajasthan	A Hindu named Shambhulal Regar used 'love jihad' as an obfuscating cover for his murder of a Muslim for his own personal reasons. Regar killed the Muslim Mohammad Afrazul with an axe and torched the body, then posted the torching and his justification online.[449] However, the Rajasthan police charge sheet states that Regar had had an illicit relation with a woman, whom he referred to as his "Hindu sister" in the video of him murdering Mohammed Afrazul, but she had a liking for a Bengali Muslim man, the chargesheet states. Regar was upset and angry about it and thus went on a murderous rampage. Regar had earlier revealed to the police that Afrazul was not his target, but that he wanted to kill another man named Ajju Sheikh, who allegedly was in touch with this woman who police believe, Regar had illicit relations with.[450]
11	Jan 2018	Online / India	In January, a Facebook posting of a list of 100 interfaith couples surfaced where readers were encouraged to take violent action, claiming that the couples were results of 'love jihad'. The posting included profiles and personal contact information, subjecting couples and family members to social pressure and undermining their safety, including one couple who reported receiving death threats.[451]
12	Jan 2018	Karnataka	Right-wing organizations, including Vishwa Hindu Parishad (VHP), Bajrang Dal and Durga Vahini, the women's wing of the VHP, organized an awareness program for parents of young women across many regions of coastal Karnataka on 'love jihad'. This included visiting households, schools, colleges and distributing handbills across Mangaluru city and other parts of Dakshina Kannada, Udupi and Kasargod.[452]
13	Jan 2018	Baghpat	A Muslim youth and his two brothers were beaten up by members of Hindu Yuva Vahini and Vishwa Hindu Parishad on at a Baghpat court for carrying out 'love jihad', as the youth was set to marry a Hindu woman from Punjab there.[453]

Source: Miscellaneous sites/reports as cited, and Dr. Angana P. Chatterji.

447   Rachna Dhanrajani, "Former Model Accuses Husband Of 'Love Jihad'", The Hindu. November 18, 2017, http://www.thehindu.com/news/cities/mumbai/former-model-accuses-husband-of-love-jihad/article20553502.ece
448   Mishra, "Love Jihad Incidents in 2017".
449   Shruti Menon, "Behind Rajasthan Killing, Mistaken Identity, 'Love Jihad' Lie, Hate Clips." NDTV, December 26, 2017, https://www.ndtv.com/india-news/behind-rajasthan-killing-mistaken-identity-love-jihad-lie-hate-videos-1792369.
450   Times Now Digital, "Rajasthan Hacking: Accused Made 'Love Jihad' Claim to Cover His Affair With 'Hindu Sister', Say Police", Jan 15, 2018, Times Now News, http://www.timesnownews.com/india/article/rajsamand-hate-crime-accused-shambhu-lal-regar-killed-afrazul-khan-love-jihad-claims-to-hide-illicit-relationship-rajasthan/189165.
451   Gowen, "India's Hindu right intensifies".
452   Sharan Poovana. "Right-Wing Outfits Campaign in Karnataka Against 'Love Jihad'". Livemint. January 04, 2018. https://www.livemint.com/Politics/T4DS9yZjZVOIDSH4xHTc1M/Right-wing-outfits-campaign-in-Karnataka-against-love-jihad.html.
453   Ishita Bhatia, "Lawyers, Drivers, Students, Waiters, Kiosks in 'Love-jihad' Spy Network", Times of India, January 16, 2018, https://timesofindia.indiatimes.com/city/meerut/lawyers-drivers-students-waiters-kiosks-in-love-jihad-spy-network/articleshow/62514200.cms.

The case of Hadiya-Akhila (2017)

The key case of 'love jihad' in 2017 was the Case of Hadiya-Akhila which occupied news headlines and public debate in India during the months of her court proceedings. This controversial case, which falsified claims of 'love jihad', became India's top story where "everyone wanted to save a woman who showed no signs of wanting to be saved".[454] Hadiya, a young Hindu woman who claimed to have converted to Islam in 2012 under her own free will, faced legal proceedings after her father in January 2016 filed a habeas corpus petition after she disappeared from the campus where she studied. He claimed that his daughter was forcefully converted to Islam and that she had expressed being held against her will by two of her Muslim classmates. However, after she was found, Hadiya claimed that she was following Islam since 2012 and left her home out of her own will. The court later dismissed Ashokan's petition in June 2016 after she produced records of her admission to Satyasarani hostel in Manjeri. By December 2016 after marrying a Muslim man, her father filed another petition and alleged that she had converted to Islam through 'love jihad' and feared that she would be taken to join ISIS in Afghanistan, citing two cases of Kerala women joining the group after conversion and marriage to Muslim men. Despite Hadiya presenting her marriage certificate and marriage registration certificate, the judgment from the Kerala High Court, in the last week of May 2017, sided with her father Ashokan. The judges were unimpressed by Hadiya, a "gullible" and "ordinary girl of moderate intellectual capacity," who had "apparently memorized" Arabic verses. Hadiya's five-month marriage to Jahan was annulled; Hadiya was put in the care of her parents.[455] In August, the National Investigation Agency, the Indian government's top antiterrorism organization, began investigating Hadiya's conversion and marriage. One news channel, *Republic*, states that more than twenty-five thousand tweets had shared a link to an investigation it had conducted into 'love jihad'. After the judgment, Hadiya became a celebrity, with media's hunger being fueled by the difficulty of catching a glimpse of her. Her appearances on television were furtive and fleeting: unauthorized recordings, glimpses through a phalanx of policemen hurrying her along.[456] While being held by her father, Hadiya expressed her desire to return to her husband stating: "I need the freedom to meet the person I love…I am asking for fundamental rights".[457] She also spoke about how her parents had tried to convert her back to Hinduism. She wanted to complete her education and continue on with her life.[458] After over a year of court proceedings, the Supreme Court on 8 March 2018 overturned the annulment of Hadiya's marriage by the Kerala High Court on the basis that the she had married out of her own free will, not as a result of 'love jihad'.[459] It did, however allow the NIA to continue investigation into the allegations of a terror angle.[460] The case of Hadiya reflects the ways in which generalizations have been made about 'love jihad' without concrete proof about the actual abduction and conversion of Hindu women and the way in which stories and examples of 'love jihad' have repeatedly been falsified.[461]

454   Bhatia, "Right-Wing Men Assault Youth".
455   Ibid.
456   Ibid.
457   Ibid.
458   Ibid.
459   BBC, "India Supreme Court restores 'love jihad' marriage".
460   India Today, "Hadiya's Marriage Restored, Supreme Court Says No Love Jihad", India Today, March 8, 2018, https://www.indiatoday.in/india/story/hadiya-s-marriage-to-shefin-stays-supreme-court-overturns-kerala-high-court-order-1184561-2018-03-08.
461   Gupta, "Allegories of love Jihad".

'Love jihad' and Islamophobia

'Love jihad' utilizes exclusionary principles for political and communal mobilization through the creation of a common "enemy other" in the name of 'protecting' Hindu women. Far-right Hindu nationalists have constructed 'love jihad' as an organized conspiracy, whereby Muslim men are aggressively converting vulnerable Hindu women to Islam through trickery and marriage. In actual practice, however, there is a lack of evidence supporting the legitimacy of 'love jihad'. Propaganda against 'love jihad' has thus been a mere lethal mobilization strategy against love, for political gains in elections.[462] This vicious crusade against interfaith marriage, and demonization of Muslim men has further intensified the marginalization of Muslims in India and exacerbated a hostile, anti-Muslim political and social climate.

As reflected in the preceding sections of this report, the increased mobilization and political focus on 'love jihad' in the last decade must be understood within the longstanding and fruitful history of anxieties about Muslims out-growing Hindu populations, which can be traced to as early as 1909 when N. Mukherji wrote the book 'Hindus: A Dying Race', and more pronounced connection to 'love jihad' can be traced to similar "abduction" and conversion campaigns launched by Arya Samaj and other Hindu revivalist bodies in the 1920s, as well as tensions around the recovery of Muslim and Hindu women from opposing parties in the 1947 partition of India and Pakistan.[463] First appearing in 2009 in political and public discourse, the term 'love jihad' has gained more momentum since 2014, to the advantage of far right-wing nationalists. As exemplified in the previous paragraphs of this section, 'love jihad' has built traction by exacerbating the ongoing fears of 'breeding Muslims' set to overtake

462   Ibid.
463   Gupta, "Hindu women, Muslim men".

Hindu population in India. This is complimented by a highly patriarchal nationhood of violence against women, that simultaneously constructs reproductive women's bodies a site of communal anxiety about the future of the Hindu race, in a demographic war against other minorities.[464] This ultra-Hindu nationalism and emphasis on the dominance of a Hindu population is also inseparable to anti-conversion laws and the *ghar vāpasī* (returning home) program which restricts the ability for Hindus to convert to other religions, while simultaneously advancing and encouraging the conversion, often forced conversions of other religious groups, to Hinduism. As emphasized by Gupta, a "...common thread that links both 'love jihad' and *ghar vāpasī* is the obsession with the numerical strength of Hindus. The numbers game, and constructed fears around it, has been central to the modern politics of Hindutva".[465]

More deeply, Gupta brings attention to the inextricable link between 'love jihad', *ghar vāpasī* and rising Hindu Nationalism in India, ultimately reflecting the national "shift in electoral politics to the right".[466] The hostile anxieties and opposition to Hindu conversion to Islam, particularly from women who are responsible for the reproduction of Hindu children, thus manifests via the 'love jihad' propaganda and initiatives detailed in this report. As Gupta highlights: "the twin strategies of anti-conversion/reconversion can also be seen as an attempt to harden religious identities and boundaries, while undermining syncretic cultural practices and religious pluralities in our everyday life. The anxieties of the Hindu Right and a section of Hindu men have coalesced around threatened religious collectivities as well as intimate matters of family and the individual".[467] Most importantly, "campaigns such as 'love jihad' and ghar vāpasī signify a shift in electoral politics to the right, and the marginalization of non-communal forces, whereby discourses of religious "othering" and hatred have persisted and gained a new lease

of life".[468] Cases and events around 'love jihad' in 2017 in particular, reflect the impact of this electoral politics, evident in the fortification of propaganda and public fears around the issues. Such rhetoric is materialized in educational awareness campaigns warning students against 'love jihad', political commitment to forming 'Romeo Squads' that fight against 'love jihad', and various attacks against interfaith couples and any individuals suspect of facilitating such unions. In particular, the controversial and widely broadcasted case of Hadiya, which captured nationwide interest, reinforces the false and mythical nature of the 'love jihad' campaign, and that the concerning degree to which Hindu women are stripped of their agency or free-will to choose who to love, and what religion to follow in their daily life.

Notably, the impact of 'love jihad' campaigns and initiatives is most significant in heightening Islamophobia and intensifying anti-Muslim sentiment across the nation. Indeed, 'love jihad' is predicated on exclusionary principles, and reproduces historical references to the aggressive and libidinal energies of the Muslim male, thus creating a common "enemy other." 'Love jihad' has not only resulted in hostile communal tensions but also results in experiences of structural, as well as everyday discrimination among Muslims in their neighborhoods and daily life. The ultra-nationalist right-wing Hindutva war against supposed 'love jihad' has led to the displacement of some Muslim communities, built fear and insecurity and led to the intensified and increased securitization, policing and community vigilantism against Muslims in India.

---

464   Mohan, "Love Jihad and demographic fears."
465   Gupta, "Allegories of love Jihad", 306.
466   Ibid, 310.
467   Ibid, 307.
468   Ibid, 310.

Politically-Stoked Violence and The Geography Of Islamophobia In India

Politically-Stoked Violence

Commonly referred to as 'communal violence', this section of the report provides a critical overview of 'politically-stoked violence' against Muslim spaces, neighbourhoods and communities across India. We adopt the terminology of 'politically-stoked violence', to more explicitly identify the role of political actors and forces in both instigating, and exacerbating communal tensions that result in mass-violence against Muslim communities across the nation. Framing an event as mere 'communal violence' fails to account for the power dynamics inherent in the plotting of group violence, often pursued for political purposes. This broad term normalizes such violence as mere natural communal tensions that appear to result from historical grievances, or disagreements that occur at the societal level without the influence of external factors. Such framing problematically silences the role of broader structural, political and institutional actors, such as the State and government officials in instigating communal tensions that lead to violence against minority communities in India.

The *Minority Rights Violations in India* report by the Alliance for Justice and Accountability clarifies that "violence has traditionally visited India's religious minorities in the form of "communal riots," a euphemism employed to describe targeted and organized violence against there minorities."[469] Further, the report indicates that such violence against Muslim communities, is "often instrumentalized for political gains" and it also "disproportionately affects India's religious minorities – in particular Muslims."[470] Such connections have been drawn by Union Minister of State for Home Affairs Hansraj Gangaram Ahir who attributed "religious factors," among others as one of the perpetuating issues of 'communal violence'.[471] Therefore we adopt the term 'politically- stoked violence' to explain this phenomenon.

This section contextualizes and documents politically-stoked violence against Muslim communities in India. In doing so, the report exposes the negative impact of such attacks on the general security of Muslims in their everyday existence, as well as within Muslim spaces. Islamophobia in India not only affects individuals, but operates broadly to discriminate Muslim communities and the spaces that they navigate, leading to a general insecurity of Muslims within various private and public spheres. Documenting various cases of spatialized Islamophobia in

2017 onwards exposes the impacts of politically stoked violence on Muslim residential patterns, internal displacement, and subsequent patterns of ghettoization and segregation. Such negative spatial outcomes are situated as a byproduct of experiences of Islamophobia, which are sustained through discriminatory behaviors, policies and legislation that further restrict the social and spatial mobility of Muslims in India.

Background

Historically, India has suffered various outbreaks of large-scale politically-stoked violence against religious minorities, particularly against Muslim communities and their spaces which remain unresolved years later.[472] The major periodic outbreaks include Uttar Pradesh in 2013, Odisha in 2007–2008, Gujarat in 2002, and Delhi in 1984. Among the most serious attacks against a Muslim space took place in 1992, when Hindutva activists destroyed the Babri Masjid in Uttar Pradesh, nearly 2,000 people lost during months of rioting.[473] A decade later in 2002, three days of violence in Gujarat left 790 Muslims and 254 Hindus dead according to government reports, while other organizations and scholars have reported that nearly 2,000 people lost their lives. In 2007 in Odisha, Christians suffered several months of unrest that killed 100 people and destroyed 300 churches and 6,000 homes. In 2013, the Muzaffarnagar district of Uttar Pradesh saw communal clashes that killed 42 Muslims and 20 Hindus, along with the displacement of 50,000 people.[474]

These persistent instances of politically-stoked violence against religious minorities have often been incited by politicians or religious leaders, advocating a nationalistic and exclusionary

469   Alliance for Justice & Accountability,"Minority Rights Violation in India," 29.
470   Ibid.
471   PTI, "Uttar Pradesh Tops the List of Communal Violence Hit States in 2017, Says Government." The Indian Express, Thursday, May 03, 2018, indianexpress.com/article/india/uttar-pradesh-tops-the-list-of-communal-violence-hit-states-in-2017-says-government-5097651/.; Also see: United States Commission on International Religious Freedom. 2017. "2017 Annual Report". Washington DC: United States Commission on International Religious Freedom. http://www.uscirf.gov/sites/default/files/2017.USCIRFAnnualReport.pdf
472   USCIRF. "2018 Annual Report", 163.
473   Ibid.
474   Ibid.

message against non-Hindu minorities.[475] Not only have politicians propagated such violence but have failed to serve justice for the attacks against Muslim bodies and spaces over the last few decades.

A significant case of communal violence which affected Muslims in India took place in 2013 in Kawal, a village on the outskirts of the town of Muzaffarnagar in the state of Uttar Pradesh. In August 2013, three young men – one Muslim and two Hindus – were killed in the course of an altercation in Kawal, a village on the outskirts of the town of Muzaffarnagar.[476] Some claimed the Hinduboys killed the Muslim in an argument that began as a traffic accident, and others say the argument was ignited by the harassment of a Hindu girl.[477] In the weeks of community tension that followed, both the BJP and the Samajwadi party, then Uttar Pradesh's ruling party, provoked and exacerbated such tensions by sending their representatives to deliver inflammatory speeches before angry crowds.[478]

In the subsequent course of the riots that swept the western Uttar Pradesh countryside through the end of September, at least 62 people had died, majority of whom were Muslim, several women were raped and over 50,000 mostly Muslim villagers were displaced from their homes. A year on from the attacks, Sethi reported that riot relief camps of displaced Muslims remained dispersed in small villages around Muzaffarnagar that Muslims were too afraid to return to.[479]

A more recent incident of right wing violence against minorities in India took place in seven districts of Bihar state who witnessed communal violence during the Hindu religious festival of Ram Navami.[480] Tension triggered violence during the festive procession in Bhagalpur on March 17 which has now engulfed seven districts of the state, resulting in hundreds of shops owned by a particular community being turned to ashes and over 100 people – including policemen – suffering injuries over 10 days in March 2018.[481] Such massive violent incidents are thus more likely to occur in existing geographies of violence, and potentially spread to other regions if the Modi Administration and state governments continue to fail to punish individuals who engage in violence and incitement to violence against religious minorities.

Although the government of India has attempted to establish special structures to investigate and adjudicate crimes stemming from these incidents of mass violence, the effectiveness of these investigations has been undermined in the ability to serve justice. This is attributed to a number of factors including limited capacity, an antiquated judiciary system, inconsistent use, political corruption, and religious bias - particularly at the state and local levels.[482]

A 'lackadaisical attitude' of the government towards these riots has led to , the police, along with the media, overplaying the involvement of Muslims in violent activities whilst underplaying the involvement of other right-wing Hindu groups or organizations in these incidents.[483] A lack of legal accountability, for these killings has intensified climate of aggression and provided perpetrators with permission to further incite violence against religious minorities in India.[484] Dr. Angana P. Chatterji, a researcher from the UC Berkeley 'Political Conflict, Gender and Peoples Rights Project' contextualizes how "conflicted democracies frequently and sufficiently serve segments of the population yet are unable to

475   USCIRF. "2017 Annual Report", 149.
476   Sethi, "Love Jihad in India".
477   Ibid.
478   Ibid.
479   Ibid.
480   Tarique Anwar, "Hindu Extremists Attack Mosque, Communal Clashes In 7 Districts In India's Bihar", The Dawn News, March 29, 2018, http://www.thedawn-news.org/2018/03/30/hindu-extremists-attack-mosque-communal-clashes-in-7-districts-in-indias-bihar/.
481   Ibid.
482   USCIRF, "2017 Annual Report".
483   Human Rights Watch, "World Report 2018".
484   USCIRF, "2018 Annual Report".

effectively provide justice and accountability to subordinated groups, especially those entangled in, and impacted by, conflict and upheaval" the negative impact.[485] It is within this environment of conflict, that government on national, state and local levels have failed to provide justice for Muslim communities in India under attack, with the adequate assistance required for repairing the damage of the violence on neighborhoods, homes and places of worship destroyed throughout these attacks.

Geography of Politically-Stoked Violence

There is a pronounced geographic pattern of where politically-stoked violence occurs, which can be traced to ten states. The states with the highest incidents of communal violence include Uttar Pradesh, Karnataka, Maharashtra, Madhya Pradesh, Bihar, Rajasthan, West Bengal, Jharkhand, Telangana and Assam. Collectively these ten states accounted for the majority of politically-stoked violence during the period of 2015-2017.[486]

Data released in 2017 by the Ministry of Home Affairs reveals that there were 822 communal incidents in 2017, compared to 703 in 2016 and 751 in 2015.[487] These attacks occurred in regions with a largely predominant Hindu population and small Muslim population. The CSSS report entitled "A Narrowing Space: Violence and Discrimination Against India's Religious Minorities" found that "religious minorities are especially vulnerable to the threat of communal violence. Muslims, in particular, while making up less than 15 percent of the population, have typically made up the large majority of victims."[488] Similarly, data by

area reveals that most 'communal' incidents occur in areas where there is an overwhelmingly Hindu majority.[489]

According to statistics presented by *The Quint,* the largest geographical concentration of politically-stoked violence incidents took place in Uttar Pradesh during the year of 2017. It numbered 195 communal incidents resulting in the death of 44 people and injuries to 452, compared to 162 incidents in 2016 and 155 in 2015. Uttar Pradesh was followed by Karnataka experienced 100 'communal riots,' including 9 deaths and 229 injuries.[490] It is important to note that the BJP rules a significant proportion of these states, where a steady rise in politically-stoked violence has taken place. Such instances are, however, beginning to occur in other regions across India including rural areas and small towns.

> These persistent instances of politically-stoked violence against religious minorities have often been incited by politicians or religious leaders, advocating a nationalistic and exclusionary message against non-Hindu minorities.

485   Chatterji, Conflicted Democracies and Gendered Violence, 24.
486   Data for tables from Ministry of Home Affairs 2017 and Hindu and Muslim population data from Census India, 2011.
487   Data for tables from Ministry of Home Affairs, 2017.
488   Ibid, 2.
489   Ibid.
490   "Communal Violence Spikes in 2017, UP Records Most Number of Riots," The Quint, February, 7 2018, www.thequint.com/news/india/communal-violence-spikes-in-2017.

Table 3: Number of Communal Incidents and Hindu-Muslim Population Ratios for the Top Ten Areas of Communal Violence in India[491]

State	2015	2016	2017	Hindu Population	Muslim Population
Uttar Pradesh	155	162	195	79.73%	19.26%
Karnataka	105	101	100	84.00%	12.92%
Maharashtra	105	68	46	79.83%	11.54%
MP	92	57	60	90.89%	6.57%
Bihar	71	65	85	82.69%	16.87%
Rajasthan	65	63	91	88.49%	9.07%
West Bengal	27	32	58	70.54%	27.01%
Jharkhand	28	24	49	67.83%	14.53%
Telangana	11	8	19	n/a	n/a
Assam	3	12	15	61.47%	34.22%

Data gathered by *Coastal Digest* on Karnataka reveals that although Muslims form a minority of the local population, they have been arrested for 'communal violence' more than Hindus or any other religious group. However, religious minorities including Muslims are often the targets of such communal violence. A *National Herald India* article entitled "Communal Riots: Heads Muslims 'Lose', Tails They Are the 'Losers'," verified that "communal violence is a double whammy for the Muslim community as targets of violence as well as victims of the subsequent police actions."[492] The data revealed that of the 1,254 people arrested for 'communal violence' in the state from the period of 2013-2017, 670 were Muslims, compared with 578 Hindus and 6 Christians.[493] As reflected in the data presented in the table below, there is a significant disproportionate policing of Muslim communities, with India's 2011 Census counting that Karnataka's population is 84 percent Hindu versus only 12.92 percent Muslim.[494]

491   Data for tables from Ministry of Home Affairs 2017 and Hindu and Muslim population data from Census India, 2011.
492   Neha Dabhade and Suraj Nair, "Communal Riots: Heads Muslims 'Lose', Tails They Are the 'Losers'," National Herald, June 28, 2017, www.nationalheraldindia.com/minorities/csss-report-on-communal-violence-2016-muslims-found-to-be-worst-victims-of-both-rioting-and-subsequent-police-action.
493   "670 Muslims, 578 Hindus, 6 Christians Arrested for Communal Violence in 2013-17,"Coastaldigest.com, January 6, 2018, www.coastaldigest.com/news/670-muslims-578-hindus-6-christians-arrested-communal-violence-2013-1
494   India Census, 2011.

Table 4: Karnataka Hindu and Muslim Population and Arrests for Communal Violence[495]

Religion	Population (%)	Arrests
Hindu	84%	578
Muslim	12.92%	670

Although limited in its scope, disaggregated data on religion collected by the Centre for the Study of Society and Secularism (CSSS) in some of the 2016 cases is useful to gauge the proportionality and impact of politically-stoked violence upon Muslim communities.

Table 5: Hindu and Muslim Data Drawn From 62 Communal Riots of 2016[496]

Number of Riots	Type of Violence	Hindus	Muslims
12	Arrests	75	178
5	Injuries	11	46
4	Death	0	7
3	Car	0	6
3	Homes	1	67
3	Shops	3	56

The CSSS, a civil society organization in India, provided empirical evidence that Muslims suffer more from communal riots in all areas: arrests, injuries, death and damage to property.[497] Further, Muslims are more often victims of "coercive force used by the state as a riot control measure, post riot arrests, and launching of prosecutions" further diminishing the likelihood that the Muslim minority are enacting violence against Hindus.[498]

It should also be taken into account that anti-cow legislation has also played a role in the incitement of "vigilante violence along communal lines in India."[499] Of the top ten Hindu dominated areas that have experienced violence, nine of them have also enacted anti-cow legislation, including the state of Bihar which also has restrictions related to cows. Anti-cow legislation has been linked to vigilantism, politically-stoked violence and lynching against Muslims and Dalits.

---

495   "670 Muslims, 578 Hindus, 6 Christians Arrested," Coastal Digest, 2018.
496   Centre for the Study of Society and Secularism (CSSS) cited in Dabhade,"Communal Riots: Heads Muslims 'Lose', 2017.
497   Ibid.
498   Ibid.
499   Ibid.

Documenting Attacks on Muslim Neighborhoods and Spaces in 2017

Politically-stoked violence inflicted against Muslim neighborhoods and spaces have led to the general insecurity of Muslims in everyday, as well as Muslim spaces. Far right Hindu nationalists provoke and encourage attacks against Muslim spaces in order to assert Hindu dominance, and ultimately exclude Muslim bodies, symbols, places of worship from the national space. Politically-stoked violence is often directed towards Muslim communities, neighborhoods and places of worship, undermining and threatening the right for Muslim bodies, sites or neighbourhoods to exist, 'belong' or be placed in the national space.

The spatialized Islamophobia experienced by Muslim communities' ranges from attacks against mosques, violence against Muslim neighborhoods, the contestation over the 'right to land' for sites of worship, and the distribution of anti-Muslim propaganda in Muslim spaces or neighbourhoods to invoke fear and exclusion among Muslim communities. For example, part of the Madani Masjid, located in Faizabad's Mughalpura locality, was gutted in an attack against this neighborhood in August 2016. The mosque houses a *Madrasa*[500] and the local office of *Jamat-e-Ulema Hind*, a national organization of Muslim clerics.[501] Bottles full of gasoline were thrown inside the mosque which were then set on fire and a portion of the mosque that housed religious texts and books of madrasa was completely burnt down.[502] Alarmingly, Qari Badshah, the imam of the mosque, claimed that he informed the police as soon as he noticed flames, but the police took nearly two hours to reach the spot despite the police station being located only 500 meters (3 feet) away from the building under attack.[503]

Muslim religious spaces are not only attacked physically through riots and violence, but are also often monitored, infiltrated or trespassed by right-wing Hindu nationalist groups. Muslim community leaders and members reported that mosques are monitored for 'terrorism' and results in the regular detainment of young boys and men who are indiscriminately held without charges on the pretext of countering terrorism.[504] An example of such prying, and imposition of authority occurred in July 2016, when members of a right-wing Hindu group were charged with trespassing at a Karnataka school and disrupting Arabic class, based on the suspicion that the school was spreading extremism via the textbooks that the trespassers confiscated from teachers.[505] This enforcement of power and infiltration of Muslim spaces cultivates insecurity and fear in Muslim communities, making it increasingly difficult to find safety the public sphere. Muslim spaces also become places of danger in such circumstances, which are subjected to ongoing Islamophobia. Such infiltration of Muslim spaces characterizes Sayyids sixth cluster of Islamophobia, which alludes the intensified state surveillance of Muslim populations through use of secret police against Muslim populations as an Islamophobic act.

Islamophobia was spatialized from 2017 onwards in a variety of ways. These included incidents of politically-stoked violence, the vandalism of Muslim sites, disputes and contentions over land, and the symbolic infiltration of Muslim sites. Prior to 2017, the Indian government's Union Ministry of Home Affairs reported in January 2017 that in the first few months of 2016 there

---

00   Madrasa is the Arabic word for any type of educational institution, however is commonly associated with places of education for Islamic instruction.
01   Dhirendra Jha, "Attack on Mosque in India Ignites Fears of a Larger Communal Design", Dawn, August 20, 2015, https://www.dawn.com/news/1201687.
02   Ibid.
03   Ibid.
04   United States Commission on International Religious Freedom, "2016 Annual Report", Washington DC: United States Commission on International Religious Freedom, 2016, http://www.scirf.gov/reports-briefs/annual-report/2016-annual-report.
05   Alliance for Justice & Accountability, "Minority Rights Violations in India".

were 278 incidents of 'communal violence'.[506] Recent attacks from 2017 onwards were mostly directed towards Muslim communities, however the extent to which these incidents had increased is difficult to determine, as minorities have reported being afraid or believed it to be useless to report them.[507] Table 6 documents a number of attacks and incidents that have been reported from 2017, particularly in news media relating to Muslim spaces, Muslims neighborhoods and places of worship.

506   USCIRF, "2017 Annual Report".
507   Ibid.

Table 6: Incidents relating to Muslim spaces in India (January 2017- April 2018)

#	Date	Place	Event
1	March 2017	Uttar Pradesh	A group of men celebrating the victory of the BJP in a village in Uttar Pradesh attempted to plant a flag on top of a mosque in the area.[508]
2	March 2017	Mumbai	On the 2017 anniversary of the Babri Mosque demolition, Indian Muslims in demonstrate in Mumbai, demanding the reconstruction of the mosque on the disputed site where the ancient mosque was torn down by Hindu nationalists in 1992.[509]
3	March 2017	Gujarat	In March 2017, a Hindu mob attacked a Muslim neighborhood in Gujarat killing one person.[510] Over 50 Muslim families fled as their homes were armed with country-made revolvers and sharp-edged weapons, a nephew of the man killed told NDTV news station. Victims claimed the police refused to intervene to save them and families have continued to stay away from the village out of fear.[511]
4	August 2017	Gujarat	The Supreme Court of India rejected a petition for the Gujarat state government to allocate compensation funds for the repair of religious structures damaged in the 2002 anti-Muslim pogrom, which was led by Sangh Parivar members. However, the Supreme Court did accept the state government's decision to include religious structures in the victim compensation program for up to Rs. 50,000 (~$740 USD) per damaged structure.[512]
5	October 2017	Uttar Pradesh	The central government controversially removed UNESCO world heritage site - the Taj Mahal from India's tourism brochure.[513] USCIRF connects this with Hindutva-nationalist attempts to erase or downplay the influence of non-Hindus in Indian history, including the Taj Mahal which was built by a Muslim ruler in the 17th Century. A prominent BJP party member, Yogi Adityanath, reportedly said the Taj Mahal claimed that the Taj Mahal "does not reflect Indian culture".[514]

508   CSSS, "A Narrowing Space", 17.
509   Annie Gowen, "India's Hindu right intensifies a religious battle over a demolished mosque", The Washington Post, 12 March, 2018. https://www.washingtonpost.com/world/asia-pacific/indias-hindu-right-intensifies-a-religious-battle-over-a-demolished-mosque/2018/03/11/7a35de6a-170b-11e8-930c-45838ad0d77a_story.html?noredirect=on&utm_term=.6aca6c9f69fb
510   Hiral Dave, "One Killed in Gujarat Village as Students Clash Sparks Communal Riot", Hindustan Times, March 26, 2017, https://www.hindustantimes.com/india-news/one-killed-in-gujarat-village-as-students-clash-sparks-communal-riot/story-TyoyOKiMXk2YsCFnfZbN1J.html
511   Bhan, Rohit, "'5,000-Strong Crowd Came with Pistols, Weapons': A Gujarat Village, Seared", NDTV, March 28, 2017, https://www.ndtv.com/india-news/day-before-riot-gujarat-village-split-sarpanchs-term-for-muslim-hindu-1674486
512   The Telegraph, "SC Refuses Damages for Shrines", The Telegraph, August 30, 2017,   https://www.telegraphindia.com/1170830/jsp/nation/story_169903.jsp.
513   Saif Khalid, "Taj Mahal Dropped from Tourism Booklet of Uttar Pradesh", Aljazeera, October 9, 2018, https://www.aljazeera.com/news/2017/10/taj-mahal-dropped-tourism-booklet-uttar-pradesh-171008161648332.html
514   USCIRF, "2018 Annual Report".

6	**March 2018**	Aurangabad	Communal violence broke out on March 25 with rioters setting ablaze 31 shops, according to official figures, however locals claim that over 50 shops were burned down. More than 25 people were injured. The violence began after someone allegedly threw stones at a Ram Navami procession, which was being carried out by Hindu Akhadas, at Muslim-majority Qazi Muhalla in Nawadih area. Police sources claim that objectionable slogans provoked people of the locality. The clashes ensued when members of the Muslim community objected to the slogan. A mosque was destroyed, a Karbala was damaged, and havoc was raged at a graveyard by the rioters with saffron headbands who were proclaiming victory with loud chants of '*Jai Shri Ram*'.[515]
7	**March 2018**	Samastipur	Hundreds of people gathered around a mosque at local Gudri Bazar demanding instant punishment for an unknown man who had allegedly thrown a flip-flop at a procession on March 26. The mob entered the mosque and set parts of it on fire, ransacked the mosque, waved tricolor along with saffron flags at the religious place, and tied a saffron flag to one of the mosque minarets. The rioters also torched a nearby *madrasa* and destroyed the religious scriptures. After being pacified, the mob returned and looted the shops owned by Muslims before setting them on fire.[516]
8	**April 2018**	Hyderabad	A special NIA court in Hyderabad acquitted five suspects accused of the Makkah Masjid bomb blast case, after almost 11 years ago where an improvised explosive device ripped through a Friday congregation, killing 9 people and injuring 58 others. The accused acquitted by the court included Naba Kumar Sircar alias Swami Aseemanand, a former member of the RSS in Gujarat, and other members of the group.[517]

515   Anwar, "Hindu Extremists Attack Mosque".
516   Ibid.
517   Mohammad Siddique, "Five Accused in India Mosque Blast Acquitted", Gulfnews. April 16, 2018, https://gulfnews.com/news/asia/india/five-accused-in-india-mosque-blast-acquitted-1.2206499

The above incidents, events and attacks can be connected to the increasing politicization of land ownership, and the 'right to place' being exclusively constructed as one reserved to Hindu citizens. Indeed, in many cases, the presence of places of worship belonging to religious minorities has been politicized. For example, members of the Sangh Parivar in Uttar Pradesh have spread rumors that Muslims are carrying out a so-called 'land jihad', or an allegedly coordinated land-grab, by illegally setting up religious structures on public property during the night.[518] Some incidents, such as the attacks against Muslims in Samastipur can also be attributed to the increasing politicization of religious festivals such as Rama Navami with the heavy participation by saffron outfits' activists, resulting in Communal conflagration. The history and context of such contestation over space, which can be connected to the case of the Babri Masjid, that symbolizes the Hindu nationalist demand to control and occupy land to the detriment of providing land for religious minority spaces.

The Case of the Babri Masjid

The ancient Babri masjid was brought down by Hindu fanatics in 1992 claiming it had been built by razing a Hindu temple. The demolition of the mosque triggered nationwide communal riots claiming hundreds of lives in the following days of its demolition.[519] This remains a 'disputed site', whereby both Hindus and Muslims are claiming the site for their respective religious places of worship. In 2010, the high court in the state of Uttar Pradesh, where Ayodhya is located, ruled that the mosque had been built on the ruins of a Hindu temple and ordered that the site be divided into three parcels – two for Hindu groups and the third for Muslims. Hindu and Muslim litigants have since proclaimed a division is unacceptable and emphasized the way such division further cultivates an environment of polarization and communal disharmony, for what Muslims claim is for political gain.[520]

This violence, as well as rhetorical attacks on Muslim sites and the right to 'be in place' has led to greater insecurity Muslims, some of whom have recently fled areas of Uttar Pradesh on account of rising hostility.[521] Such incidents of Islamophobia also have spatial implications on where Muslims are placed or have the right to be in place in India. This has resulted in a wide range of socio-spatial issues including the ghettoization, segregation and internal displacement of Muslims struggling to find their place in an anti-Muslim socio-political environment.[522]

The Implications of Spatial Islamophobia: Ghettoization, Segregation and Displacement

Residential segregation along religious lines, particularly for Muslims in India has been an ongoing area of concern among scholars, human rights activists and community members[523], and was first brought to attention by the Sachar report that documented discrimination and socio-economic disadvantage being experienced by Muslim

518   Rohan Venkataramakrishnan, "A Brief History of Love Jihad, From Jodhaa Akbar to the Meerut Gang-Rape". Scroll.In. August 15, 2014. https://scroll.in/article/674314/a-brief-history-of-love-jihad-from-jodhaa-akbar-to-the-meerut-gang-rape
519   Gowen, "India's Hindu right intensifies".
520   Ibid.
521   CSSS, "A Narrowing Space", 13.
522   Raphael Susewind, "Muslims in Indian cities: Degrees of segregation and the elusive ghetto", Environment and Planning A 49, 6 (2017): 1286-1307, https://doi.org/10.1177/0308518X17696071; Sachar, "Report on…Status of The Muslim".
523   Susewind, "Muslims in Indian Cities", 1287.

populations.[524] Susewind draws attention to the way in which prolonged and unresolved histories of communal violence, and the states negligence towards Muslims has led to this large-scale 'ghettoization' of Muslims.[525] On the other hand, some scholars refer to the long-standing pattern of residential clustering of Muslims in enclaves and claim that these have always been voluntary. The terms ghetto' and 'enclave' are commonly used if spaces are primarily segregated along ethnic, racial, communal or caste lines.

The term 'ghettoization' is commonly is used to describe the impacts of politically-stoked riots, violence, and general attacks against minorities on their residential patterns and choices.[526] Susewind brings attention to way in which such incidents of violence against Muslims in India have resulted in the formation of Muslim 'ghettos' - 'a bounded, ethnically uniform socio-spatial formation born of the forcible relegation of a negatively typed population'.[527] India's Muslims are thus especially excluded from national growth by being forced to move into ghettos in order to seek refuge from physical violence. Unlike other forms of residential clustering, segregation of Muslims in urban India is thus increasingly perceived to be problematic, and commonly attributed to the state's negligence towards this religious minority, prolonged histories of so-called 'communal' violence between religious groups and ensuing security concerns[528] and prejudices.[529]

The impact of politically-stoked violence on Muslim residential patterns in India is reflected in the segregated and dilapidated neighbourhoods of Juhapura in Ahmedabad and Shivaji Nagar in Mumbai, where ghettoization indeed seems to increase following each new communal riot.[530] Susewind's study similarly found that the cities where the marginalization of Muslims is understood to be primarily an outcome of communal (politically-stoked) riots are among the most highly (Ahmedabad), or moderately segregated (Mumbai and Aligarh city).[531] Further, the negative implications of violence against Muslim communities on the spatial distribution of Muslim populations is reflected in the large-scale rural- to-urban migration following violence in Muzaffarnagar in 2013. This conflict led, to the largest internal displacement in India since Partition leaving a large number of Muslims in camps since 2013 who continue to face barriers with being resettled today.[532]

The "ghettoization" of poor Muslims has resulted in this group being the most excluded of India's poor from growth. This has resulted in Muslims being neglected by municipal and government authorities, failing to access water, sanitation, electricity, schools, public health facilities, banking facilities, child care centers, ration shops (subsidized public food distribution shops), roads and transport facilities within their respective residential areas.[533] The increasing ghettoization of Muslims implies a shrinking space for Muslims communities in the public sphere subsequently excluding Muslims them from India's high growth rate, whilst simultaneously isolating them from the cultural and social mainstream.[534]

This can be connected with the Sachar Report's findings on discrimination against Muslims in buying and renting accommodation in the locality of their choice that limits their spatial, and thus social mobility within and across various regions

524   Sachar, "Report on...Status of The Muslim".
525   Susewind, "Muslims in Indian cities", 1287.
526   Loïc Wacquant, Urban Outcasts: A Comparative Sociology of Advanced Marginality, Oxford: Wiley, 2008.
527   Susewind, "Muslims in Indian cities", 1289.
528   Laurent, Gayer and Christophe Jaffrelot. Muslims In Indian Cities. London: Hurst & Company, 2012.
529   Anuradha Banerjee, Firdaus Rizvi, Sukhadeo Thorat, and Vinod K Mishra, "Urban Rental Housing Market: Caste & Religion Matters in Access". Economic & Political Weekly 50, 26/27 (2015): 47-53, https://www.epw.in/journal/2015/26-27/housing-discrimination/urban-rental-housing-market.html
530   Susewind, "Muslims in Indian cities".
531   Ibid.
532   CSSS, "A Narrowing Space", 5.
533   Susewind, "Muslims in Indian cities".
534   Ibid.

in India. Housing insecurity was similarly reported in the Misra Commission report which found that 34.63 percent of the Muslims lived in 'kutcha' (temporary) houses and 41.7 percent lived in *'semipucca'* (semi-permanent) while the figures are 6.68 percent and 49.67 percent respectively, for the Sikhs.[535] Similarly, the ratio of those living in rented houses was highest among the Muslims (43.74 percent) and among minorities, only 78.78 percent of the Muslim Households had electricity as a source of lighting as compared to Parsis (99.21 percent) and Sikhs (88.81 percent).[536] The "Disturbed Areas Act" (1991), is also a law that restricts Muslims and Hindus from selling property to each other in "sensitive" areas, was intended to avert an exodus or distress sales in neighborhoods hit by inter-religious unrest. The state, headed at the time by Prime Minister Narendra Modi, amended the law in 2009 to give local officials more power in property sales. It also extended the reach of the law, saying it was doing so to protect Muslims, who make up about 10 percent of the state's 63 million people. However, critics see the act's enforcement and the addition of new districts under it as state sanctioned segregation. As a result, Muslims are confined to the filthiest corners, with no hope of upliftment. Development and progress are for everyone else in the state, but not for Muslims. The division is so marked that Juhapura, a teeming township in Ahmedabad of about 400,000 people, many who moved there after the 2002 riots, is referred to by local Hindus as "Little Pakistan". Conditions there and in other Muslim settlements in Ahmedabad, Gujarat's largest city, are similar, whereby residents lack proper roads, street lights, adequate drinking water, sewage pipes, and access to public clinics and schools.[537]

Menon draws attention to the way in which rising religious tensions and violence, increasing Islamophobia and suspicion of Muslims, and the deep entrenchment and enactment of discourses of security, have pushed Muslims to seek shelter in 'safe' neighborhoods with large Muslim populations, such as Old Delhi.[538] Muslims interviewed in Menon's study increasingly imagine Old Delhi as a refuge, and thus consciously chose to relocate to this neighbourhood, or refuse to leave this 'Muslim place'.[539] Menon warns of the dangers of such ghettoization, highlighting how in the context of an exclusionary nationalism that produces boundaries which construct Muslims as the other', Muslim containment in Old Delhi facilitates and enables easier surveillance and control by the security state.[540] While Muslims might feel safer residing in Muslim areas, Aamr Sahib notes that schools and other institutions that would usually ensure the continuing development of these communities are moving away because of their own priorities and prejudices, further marginalizing Muslims residing in these 'safe places'.[541] Most interestingly, while many Muslims complained about the poor living conditions in Old Delhi, they did not necessarily view moving out of Old Delhi as an option. Exclusionary understandings of nation and belonging have ensured that it is difficult to find housing to rent or buy outside of Old Delhi if you are Muslim, highlighting the dialectic effects of Islamophobia on the segregation of Muslim communities.[542]

The spatial impacts of Islamophobia upon Muslim sites, spaces and communities has restricted the residential options, and choices of Muslims in India. The actual and perceived threat of violence has resulted in the exclusion of Muslim communities from the national space. This has resulted in the increased ghettoization of Muslims to limited places of security and belonging that enable the survival of these communities in an increasingly hostile

535   Sachar, "Report on...Status of The Muslim".
536   Ibid.
537   Susewind, "Muslims in Indian cities".
538   Menon, "'Security', Home, And Belonging in Contemporary India".
539   Ibid.
540   Ibid.
541   Ibid.
542   Ibid.

socio-political environment of Islamophobia. As reflected in the literature discussed in this section, such violence has negative impacts on the spatial and social mobility of Muslims in India. Such reduced mobility results in limited socio-economic opportunities to participate in national economic growth, increased housing insecurity, and an intensified geographical division of Muslims from the Hindu majority in an increasingly Islamophobic national space.

Spatialized Islamophobia and the Future of Muslims in Indian Cities

As discussed in this section, Islamophobia is not only institutionalized, but also spatialized through communal violence, attacks and contestations over the right for Muslim neighborhoods and places of worship to exist in the Indian national space. Historically, India has suffered various outbreaks of large-scale politically-stoked violence against religious minorities, particularly against Muslims that remain unresolved years later. In documenting cases from 2017 onwards, it is exemplified that the BJP victory and subsequent implementation ultra-right-wing nationalist discourse and policies have intensified such attacks against Muslim sites, neighborhoods and places of worship. Most concerning, is the direct impact of such violence on patterns of segregation and the ghettoization of Muslims, further limiting their socio-economic opportunities for growth out of dire situations of poverty. This section has critically examined the impacts of communal violence on Muslim displacement, and subsequent patterns of ghettoization and segregation sustained through discriminatory policies that further restrict the social and spatial mobility of Muslims in India.

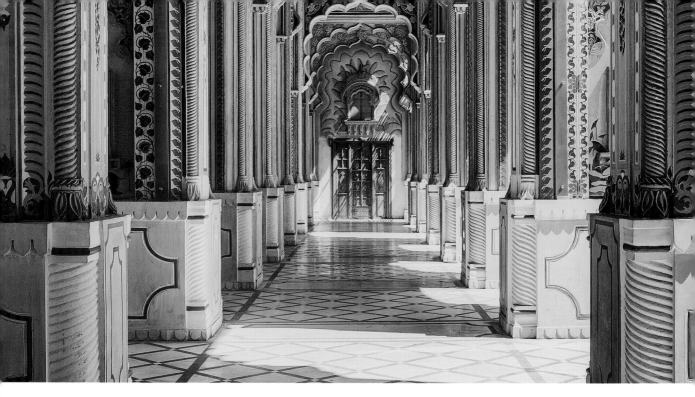

Existing Initiatives and Efforts to Challenge Islamophobia in India

Attacks Against Bodies: Beef Attacks

Scholarly Resistance

Academics such as Ram Puniyani continue to educate the public on Hindu-Muslim unity and working to dispel the myths and conspiracy theories at the heart of the Hindutva project directed at Muslims and others.[543]

Civil Society

March 2017: A national database announced its launch in March by DOTO described as a " joint civil society effort and is run by a large network of civil society organizations both at the national and at the grassroots level" covering the documentation of religious identity hate crimes post 2014.[544] Chairman of Delhi Minorities commission cited the thousands of Muslims and Dalits that suffer from "state sponsored/'saffron

---

543   Siasat Hyderabad,"Was Lord Ram Born on Babri Masjid Land? Prof Ram Puniyani Explains Conspiracy," YouTube, December 6, 2017, www.youtube.com/watch?v=kCuzRbrm_6k and Ram Puniyani, "India and Hindu Muslim Unity," TEDxTalks, YouTube, May 22, 2018, www.youtube.com/watch?v=_nj7x5N5pA8.
544   "DOTO: Database on Targeted Hate Violence in India Launched," Thepolicytimes.com, March 08, 2018, https://thepolicytimes.com/doto-database-targeted-hate-violence-in-dia-launched/.

terror" on the rise across the nation.[545]

June 2017: In response to calls for a nationwide ban on the sale and purchase of cattle from animal markets for slaughter, students at at IIT-Madras held a 'beef fest' on campus in protest as students ate and voiced dismay at the infringement on their "personal rights" and "food choice."[546] Youth Congress leaders in Kerala publicly slaughtered and cooked a cow in protest going viral on social media ending in their arrest and charges under IPC Section 428 and section (ii) of the Prevention of Cruelty to Animals Act 1960. They were also suspended by Congress.[547]

November 2017: Following mob attacks on two other Muslim victims, United Against Hate campaign held a public meeting and a press conference at Delhi Press Club to protest against communal attacks, mob lynching that receive state patronage as a united response including family members of teenager Junaid Khan.[548]

April 2018: A protest was held in New Delhi upon the one year anniversary of Pehlu Khan's lynching at the hands of Hindutva extremists entitled 'National Protest Against the Assault on Cattle Economy and Lynching of Dalits and Muslims.[549]

In August 2018 Twitterverse called out Modi for his double standard regarding cow protection when it comes to Muslims in India, yet during a visit to what Twitterverse refers to as "beef eating" Rwanda he gifted 200 cows.

People such as @memeghnad tweeted a "mass alert for gau rakshaks" (cow protectors) to hurry and go to Rwanda to protect the cows.

@MyFellowIndians posted an article about the gifting with a picture of Modi's face, reminiscent of a "Wanted" poster. Above it it said "cow smuggler spotted taking 200 cows to Rwanda."[550] @one_by_two posted "a man got lynched because he was taking a cow from one village to another...I just heard that another man is taking 200 cows from India to Rwanda. I hope nothing happens to him. I pray for him![551]

@VinayDokania tweeted: UNESCO gives "biggest cow smuggler" award to Modi for smuggling 200 cows to Rwanda! #WaModiJiWah
Dear bakhts please don't lynch our PM bcoz wo #ChowkidarNahiBhagidar..hai

Legal Resistance

Important legal events in 2017 include the resistance by states such as Kerala, West Bengal, Karnataka and Puducherry to the call for a nationwide ban on cow slaughter referring to it as "an intrusion of state rights" and "against principles of secularism and federalism" in India and upon "rights of the people."[552] Below is a brief timeline of significant occurrences:

July 2017: The draft of a new law to address mob lynching was presented to the public at the Constitution Club New Delhi. The law entitled Maanav Suraksha Kanoon (MASUKA) was proposed by the National Campaign Against Mob Lynching was founded by a group of youth "as a response to a spate of lynching incidents that have rattled the nation."[553]The draft provides a definition of "lynching" and "mob" as well as proposals regarding offenses, investigations, trials and compensation.

545   Ibid.
546   KV Lakshmana, "Students at IIT-Madras Hold Beef Festival to Protest Cattle Slaughter Ban," Hindustan Times, May 29, 2017, https://www.hindustantimes.com/india-news/students-at-iit-madras-hold-beef-festival-to-protest-cattle-slaughter-ban/story-zX0HSeCwjFEcwbk1M9uZ8I.html.
547   Ramesh Babu, "Kerala: Youth Congress Suspends Three Workers for Slaughtering Cow in Public," Hindustan Times, May 29, 2017, https://www.hindustantimes.com/india-news/congress-could-take-action-against-workers-who-slaughtered-cow-in-kerala-market/story-DkOn0Ca7Hcz5rNqtFhbtJN.html.
548   Hishma Tanseema Nazir, "Raising a Unified Voice against Hate," The Hindu, November 20, 2017, https://www.thehindu.com/todays-paper/tp-national/tp-newdelhi/raising-a-unified-voice-against-hate/article20608003.ece.
549   NewsClickin, "A Year On, Pehlu Khan's Murderers Still Not Convicted," YouTube, April 04, 2018, https://www.youtube.com/watch?time_continue=250&v=ErOz-LQEvu8.
550   "Twitter Laughs at Modi's Promise of 200 Cows to Beef-Eating Rwanda," The Quint, July 24, 2018, https://www.thequint.com/news/india/modi-gifts-200-cows-to-rwanda-twitter-reactions.
551   Ibid.
552   Shreya Kalra, "A Brief History Of India's War On Cow Slaughter And How People Have Reacted To It," Indiatimes.com, May 30, 2017, https://www.indiatimes.com/news/india/a-brief-history-of-india-s-war-on-cow-slaughter-and-how-people-have-reacted-to-it-322757.html.
553   The Quint, "MASUKA Unveiled: What Does The Anti-Lynching Bill Draft Say?" July 07, 2017, https://www.thequint.com/news/masuka-unveiled-anti-lynching.

September 2017: The Supreme Court tasked the Centre and state governments with curbing cow vigilantism.

July of 2018: Following a series of lynching attacks and efforts by advocates, the Supreme Court has recommended a law against lynching, stating that "no citizen shall be allowed to take the law into their hands."[554] The Supreme Court called for a new penal provision regarding vigilantism and lynching and cow vigilantism was at the center and the blatant "dehumanization of human beings."[555] The proposed measures includes special courts, compensation for victims and their families, and stronger disciplinary action for officers who did not follow proper conduct regarding lynching.[556] The court also called for a campaign via media to spread the word that mob violence will not be tolerated under the law and that volatile messages and those who spread them will be met with strict action. However, there are critics among varying segments of society in India who argue that mob lynching can be addressed by already existing penal codes, and that it is the lack of implementation of existing laws, as well as political forces driving the lynching that is the problem.

Journalism and Reporting

In a time of rigid curtailment of press freedoms, special acknowledgement should be given to all of those on the ground reporters, journalists, groups and individuals who write, draw, report, speak, advocate on behalf of justice in India at their own risk.

The Spending & Policy Research Foundation's IndiaSpend, the country's first data journalism initiative, continues to serve as an important hub of data reporting on issues relevant to India, especially as others have been censored and closed down. IndiaSpends contribution, data compilation, charts, statistics, maps and links on cow vigilantism and lynching in India is a one stop shop on the most up to date attacks and reports of cow related violence. Their data has been cited in numerous news articles where they compile data taken from news reports on various cow related cases that occur throughout the nation in an effort to foster better governance, transparency and accountability in the Indian government.[557]

In spite of reporting and censorship difficulties, a first of its kind "statistical perspective" to address a growing phenomenon of religious based violence in India via a 2018 civil society effort entitled Fact Checker in India.[558] The project is multi-organizational and includes Citizen's Religious Hate-Crime Watch, FactChecker.in, NewsClick.in, and Aman Biradari.[559] The website claims that it is a duty of civil society to develop a "robust tracking of hate crime in India," while calling upon the state to officially publish hate crimes.[560] They focus on religious based hate crimes during the period 2009-2018 because they claim that state and others document other forms of violence and crime, therefore Fact Checker have "collated data on crimes motivated partly or wholly by prejudice against the religion of the victim(s)."[561] The website further echoes some of our report findings in that Islamophobia and religious hate crimes are increasing, especially around cow protection and "love jihad," and such crimes "are lost under various sections such as rioting, arson and attempt to murder or murder, which makes it difficult to estimate the scale of violence."[562]

---

554   Scroll Staff, "'Mobocracy Cannot Be Allowed': Supreme Court Recommends New Law against Lynching," Scroll.in - September 12, 2018, https://scroll.in/latest/886846/mobocracy-cannot-be-allowed-supreme-court-recommends-new-law-against-lynching.
555   Ibid.
556   Ibid.
557   Admin, "About," IndiaSpend, archive.indiaspend.com/about. Accessed. October 18, 2018.
558   "Home." FactChecker, May 27, 2018, p.factchecker.in.
559   "About." FactChecker, May 27, 2018, p.factchecker.in/stories/about-1164.html.
560   Ibid.
561   Ibid.
562   Ibid.

In 2018, NDTV conducted a hidden camera investigative report to shed light upon cow vigilantism and the recent wave of lynching. Journalists Saurabh Shukla and cameraperson Ashwini Mehra posed as American field researchers and traveled to the locations of two significant lynchings to find out more. Specifically they wanted to know why these murders continue and why those who kill are released on bail and/or without charges. The report captures the accused on hidden camera "make shocking claims, proudly so, about their roles in brutal assaults, which proved fatal for Qasim Qureishi and Pehlu Khan."[563] One of the accused, Rakesh Sisodia claimed in court that he had no role in the attack and that he was not even present, however on hidden camera he admitted to his participation and stated he was "ready to kill thousands" more, and go to jail thousands of times, proud of his action he said "they were killing cows, I killed him."[564] After his release, he reported returning home to a heroes welcome. Compared to the earlier regime, he said the police are now in favor of vigilantism. One of the accused in the attack on Khan named Vipin was picked up after video identification. He also claimed to authorities that he was not at the site at the time of the lynching of Khan and received bail. Vipin admitted on hidden camera that he actually stopped Khan's truck, pulled him out, put Khan's keys in his pocket, and beat him for over an hour.[565] He reports that the police arrived late and randomly picked up six or seven people.[566] One advocate on the panel discussing the hidden camera footage, found the NDTV report to signal that the police are no longer investigating such crimes, but that the media has taken up their investigative role, and that clearly the guilt of the vigilantes was supported by roadside video evidence. She followed up by stating the police had actually lodged a falsified FIR in the Khan case labeling it 'road rage,' which thus facilitated

the release of one of his lynchers on bail.[567] Other than complicity by the police, panelists asked to comment on the investigative video found it outrageous with this much evidence of a lynching that occurred in broad daylight, how these men were released on bail. Finally, the claims that cow lynchings are simply a law and order problem were crushed.[568]

'Love Jihad', Anti-Conversion Laws and Ghar Vāpasī

Scholarly Resistance

As emphasized by Gupta: "feminist writers and scholars have strongly protested against such attempts at domesticating women in the name of 'love jihad.'"[569]She provides the following examples: Punwani, "Myths and Prejudices about 'love jihad'," Gupta, "The Myth of 'love jihad'," Menon, "'The Meerut Girl.'

Public Protest

In April 2018, students at Jawaharlal Nehru University (JNU) disrupted a film screening on campus, on the issue of 'love jihad'. The screening of the film, titled 'In the name of love - melancholy of God's own country', was organised by the Global Indian Foundation and Vivekanand Vichar Manch of JNU. Members of the Jawaharlal Nehru Students Union (JNUSU) and Gender Sensitisation Committee Against Sexual Harassment (GSCASH) the film focused on religious conversion of girls in Kerala, and the issue of 'love jihad'. These students disrupted the screening, claiming that a hate campaign

563   NDTV, "NDTV Hidden Camera Investigation:Justice Lynched?" YouTube, August 6, 2018, www.youtube.com/watch?v=cL9-7LzBK_8.
564   Ibid.
565   Ibid.
566   Ibid.
567   Ibid.
568   Ibid.
569   Gupta, "Allegories of love Jihad", 209.

was being propagated in the guise of the film screening.[570]

In September 2017 Maharaja's College students organised a protest on Friday in front of the college gate demanding freedom for Hadiya who was under house arrest with her family after her marriage was annulled by the High Court.[571]

Legal Resistance

In March 2018, the Supreme Court overturned the annulment of Hadiya-Akhila's five-month marriage to Jahan allowing the couple to be together.[572]

Journalism and Reporting

Counter-narratives to 'love jihad' are increasingly circulating through journalist research and reporting via a number of alternative media outlets. Such reports detail and publish material that exposes the false claims of 'love jihad'. Such reporting not only brings global awareness to the issue, but also provides a counter-narrative to ultra-right-wing Hindu Nationalist propaganda around 'love jihad'. For example, the *Hinudstan Times* has composed a number of articles on 'love jihad 'including piece on "love jihad': UP's forbidden couples' composed by Appu Esthose Suresh on the 19th October 2016[573], *New Indian Express* reporting of physical violence against an interfaith couples[574] and *The Guardian's* 'long read' on 'Love jihad' in India and one man's quest to prevent it'. Other examples of such news reports were cited throughout the report in the previous section dedicated to 'love jihad'.[575]

A more significant example of such reporting is evident in the Cobrapost and Gulail investigation which was conducted primarily by Cobrapost

correspondent Shishupal Kumar, and Shazia Nigar of Gulail, who met a number of right-wing leaders posing as an M.Phil student from Jawaharlal Nehru University associated with the BJP's student wing ABVP. Titled 'Operation Juliet: Busting the Bogey of 'love jihad", the year-long investigation "reveals how the RSS–VHP–BJP combine and their splinter groups use violence, intimidation, emotional blackmail, duplicity and drugs to split up Hindu–Muslim married couples…the investigation reveals that there is a systematic effort towards using 'love jihad' to polarise communities along communal lines".[576] As reported by The Wire, the investigation by the two web portals captured several important leaders from the Bharatiya Janata Party, Rashtriya Swayamsevak Sangh and Vishwa Hindu Parishad speaking about their role in stoking fears about 'love jihad'. Overall, findings from these secretly recorded conversations and from interviews with the police highlighted that 'love jihad' as a concept it "an invention of the right-wing organisations who use a wide variety of methods – "violence, intimidation, emotional blackmail, duplicity and drugs" – to split up Hindu-Muslim couples. Most alarmingly, the Cobrapost-Gulail investigation has also revealed the widespread misuse of the legal system – including the police and courts – to victimize not only Hindu women who dare to marry out their religion, but also their partners".[577]

---

570   Outlook Web Bureau, "Protests in JNU against Screening of film on Love Jihad", Outlook Magazine, April 28, 2018, https://www.outlookindia.com/website/story/protests-in-jnu-against-screening-of-film-on-love-jihad/311446

571   New Indian Express, "College students stage protest demanding freedom for Hadiya" New Indian Express, September 16, 2017, http://www.newindianexpress.com/states/kerala/2017/sep/16/college-students-stage-protest-demanding-freedom-for-hadiya-1657906.html

572   See previous section on the case of Hadiya-Akhila for a more detailed overview of this case.

573   Suresh, "Love Jihad: UP's forbidden couples".

574   Namita Bajpai, "Meerut: Hindu activists beat up interfaith couple", The New Indian Express. April 12, 2017, http://www.newindianexpress.com/nation/2017/apr/12/meerut-hindu-activists-beat-up-inter-faith-couple-1592826.html

575   Sethi, "Love Jihad in India".

576   Cobrapost, "Operation Juliet".

577   Bhatnagar, "BJP, RSS Leaders Caught Using 'Love Jihad' Bogey".

Spatial Dimensions of Islamophobia

Seeking reparations

Attempts were made to seek compensation from the Gujarat state government for mosques and shrines destroyed during the 2002 pogrom in Gujarat.[578]

Claiming Ownership of Land

Muslims continue claim rights of ownership over the contested land that once housed the Babri masjid, which was destroyed by Hindu fanatics in 1992, claiming it had been built by razing a Hindu temple.[579]

578   The Wire Staff, "Hindutva's 'Love Jihad' Obsession".
579   Gowen, "India's Hindu right intensifies".

Conclusion and Policy Recommendations

International Civil Society

1. Increase the attention of international embassies to issues of religious freedom and related human rights, including to regions who have faced, or are vulnerable to facing politically-stoked violence.[580]

2. Place pressure on the Indian government to ratify the U.N. Convention Against Torture and legislate punishment for the use of torture by government agencies.[581]

3. Demand that state and central police to implement effective measures to prohibit and punish cases of religious violence and protect victims and witnesses.[582]

4. Urge India to boost human rights and religious freedom standards and practices for the police and judiciary, particularly

580   USCIRF, "2017 Annual Report".
581   Alliance for Justice & Accountability, "Minority Rights Violations in India".
582   USCIRF, "2017 Annual Report".

in states and areas with a history or likelihood of religious and communal violence.[583]

5. Hold accountable, outlaw ultra-nationalist Hindu groups, political leaders and members of the RSS-BJP and their affiliates for stoking violence against religious minorities.

6. Strengthen the work of state prosecutors to increase the rate of prosecutions for hate crimes targeting religious minorities.[584]

7. Consistently and accurately monitor politically-stoked violence, with a focus on documenting how this impacts India's diverse religious minorities such as Muslims.[585]

8. Consistently and accurately monitor acts of violence and vigilantism in the name of cow protection and document and collect data on these crimes, their locations, outcomes and impacts.

9. Civil society staff monitoring Islamophobia in India should be trained in culturally and gender-sensitive data collection, ensuring full confidentiality in victim reporting.

10. Pressure the government of India to abide by the U.N Convention on the Prevention and Punishment of the Crime of Genocide.

11. Pressure the government of India to abide by the international norms of non-refoulement and protect the rights of asylum seekers and refugees, as suggested by the United Nations.

12. Provide oversight regarding the rights of Rohingyas and other refugees in India, ensuring that they are protected and that their human needs met. Encourage the government of India to prosecute individuals or groups who commit crimes, including hate crimes, against them.

13. Monitor and document press freedom and journalist safety in India and pressure the government to uphold it.

International Community

1. Spread awareness, education and encourage open discussions around human rights violations against minorities in India, particularly rising Islamophobia

2. Encourage research, documentation and public discussions around Islamophobia in India around the world.

3. Place pressure on the Indian government to ratify the U.N. Convention Against Torture and legislate punishment for the use of torture by government agencies.

Government in India

1. Take prompt and effective legal action against individuals and groups responsible for perpetrating violence against minorities, as well as those facing allegations of complicity. Adopt strong measures to curb the activities of groups including the proliferating and self-proclaimed 'cow-protection units' as well as those involved with anti-'love jihad' and *ghar vāpasī*.[586]

2. Compensate and rehabilitate Muslim victims, and their neighbourhoods, including places of worship of the damages associated with vigilantism and politically-stoked violence.

3. Provide legal freedom for all individuals to practice all religions, and convert to, or marry individuals from their religion of choice.

583   Ibid.
584   USCIRF, "2018 Annual Report".
585   CSSS, "A Narrowing Space".
586   Ibid.

4. Urge the central Indian government to press states that have adopted anti-conversion laws to repeal or amend them to conform with internationally recognized human rights standards.[587]

5. Urge states that have adopted discriminatory beef legislation to repeal them and ensure that cow protection does not come at the cost of human lives.

6. Indian government must publicly rebuke and hold to account, government officials and religious leaders involved in perpetrating or inciting violence against Muslims. Public officials who have been responsible for such incitement of violence for human rights abuses must also be penalized.[588]

7. Provide legislation that protects Muslim communities from communal violence, and provide legal assistance and other support to survivors of such violence in the past.[589]

8. Enact processes that prevent politically-stoked violence that contain effective remedies and reparations for victims e.g. revive the process to adopt the Prevention of Communal Violence (Access to Justice and Reparations) Bill 2013, or similar legislation.[590]

9. Repeal or reform legislation and policies that infringe upon fundamental rights enshrined in the Constitution, and that fuel violence against religious minorities, such as Muslims. For example, India's anti-conversion laws, and recent efforts to expand anti-cow slaughter measures.[591]

10. Introduce more comprehensive anti-discrimination legislation, which includes protections against intersectional discrimination and enables Muslims to access socio-economic opportunities required to overcome this discrimination.[592]

11. Work with advocates and civil society to reform, adopt or utilize existing laws that protect against lynching and ensure their proper application.

12. Provide oversight of law enforcement against corruption and abuse and protect against extra-judicial killing by police.

13. Abide by the U.N Convention on the Prevention and Punishment of the Crime of Genocide.

14. Abide by the international norms of non refoulement and protect the rights of asylum seekers and refugees, as suggested by the United Nations.

15. Ensure that the rights of Rohingyas in India are protected and that their human needs met. Prosecute individuals or groups who commit crimes against them.

16. Ensure press freedom and journalist safety in India.

17. Encourage and support media literacy campaigns.

Social Media Corporations

1. Social media corporations should ensure that terms of service and reporting tools are available in local languages and that they are user friendly.

2. Monitor platforms, collect data, and document reports related to Islamophobia and other forms of hate, abuse and violence.

3. Acknowledge the relationship between online and offline in technology-related abuse and violence.

4. Continue to support academic research on Islamophobia and anti-Muslim rhetoric and hostilities on the internet and social media

587   USCIRF, "2017 Annual Report".
588   Ibid; CSSS, "A Narrowing Space".
589   CSSS, "A Narrowing Space".
590   Ibid.
591   Ibid.
592   Ibid.

Bibliography

"107 Killed in Riots This Year; 66 Muslims, 41 Hindus." *Hindustan Times.* September 24, 2013. www.hindustantimes.com/delhi-news/107-killed-in-riots-this-year-66-muslims-41-hindus/story-uqHMNT093ZqMa0WAsWdIpJ.html

"670 Muslims, 578 Hindus, 6 Christians Arrested for Communal Violence in 2013-17." *Coastaldigest. com.* January 6, 2018. www.coastaldigest.com/news/670-muslims -578-hindus-6-christians-arrested-communal-violence-2013-1.

Aarefa Johari, "Why Has the Rajasthan Police Filed an FIR Against the Victims of the Alwar Lynching?" *Scroll. in.* April 07, 2017. https://scroll.in/article/833929/why-has-The-rajasthan-police-filed-an-fir-against-the-victims-of-the-alwar-lynching

"About." *IndiaSpend.* archive.indiaspend.com/about.

"About." *FactChecker.* May 27, 2018. p.factchecker.in/stories/about-1164.html.

Abraham Delna and Ojaswi Rao. "84% Dead In Cow-Related Violence Since 2010 Are Muslim; 97% Attacks After 2014." *IndiaSpend.* December 8, 2017. www.indiaspend.com/cover-story/86-dead-in-cow-related-violence-since-2010-are-muslim-97-attacks-after-2014-2014.

Adnan, Mir. Twitter Post, July 23, 2018. https://twitter.com/miradnan17/status /1021337951794368512.

AFP. "Butcher Shops Razed amid Crackdown on Beef in India." *Arab News.* March 22, 2017. www.arabnews.com/node/1072471/world.

"After Editor's Exit, Hindustan Times Pulls Down Controversial 'Hate Tracker'." *The Wire.* October 25, 2017. thewire.in/media/hindustan-times-hate-tracker

Ahmad, Salik. "Love Jihad: Muslims of Rajasthan Village Boycotted after Man Elopes with Hindu Woman". *Hindustan Times.* March 22, 2017. https://www.hindustantimes.com/jaipur/love-jihad-muslims-of-rajasthan-village-boycotted-after-man-elopes-with-hindu-woman/story-MOsm6qcSc692GXfiZPBbpl.html

Airbam, Angelica. Twitter Post. July 23 16, 2018. https://twitter.com/AngellicAribam/status/1021347130135506944.

Ali, Mohamad. "Exodus of Nandrauli's Muslims Continues". *The Hindu.* May 20, 2017 http://www.thehindu.com/news/national/exodus-of-nandraulis-mulims-continues/article18516533.ece

Alliance for Justice & Accountability. *Minority Rights Violations in India.* Washington D.C, 2010.https://www.scribd.com/document/349208337/India-Minority-Rights-Violations-Report-2017#from_embed

"All Rohingya Muslim Refugees Are Illegal Immigrants, Will Be Deported despite UN Status, Says Centre." *Scroll.in.* August 14, 2017. scroll.in/latest/847215/all-rohingya-muslim-refugees-are-illegal-immigrants-will-be-deported-despite-un-status-says-centre.

"Alwar District: Census 2011 Data." Jaisalmer District Population Census 2011. Rajasthan Literacy Sex Ratio and Density. http://www.census2011.co.in/census/district/429-alwar.html.

"Alwar Gau Rakshak Attack Did Not Happen: Minister Mukhtar Abbas Naqvi." *The Indian Express.* April 07, 2017. https://indianexpress.com/article/india/alwar-gau-rakshak-attack-did-not-happen-minister-mukhtar-abbas-naqvi-4601726/.

Ameerudheen, TA. "BJP Continues to Fan Communal Tensions in Coastal Karnataka over a Young Man's Mysterious Death." *Scroll.in,* December 18, 2017, scroll.in/article/861774/bjp-continues-to-fan-communal-tensions-in-coastal-karnataka-over-a-young-mans-mysterious-death.

Andrabi, Jalees. "32 Arrested for Lynching of Muslim Man Based on WhatsApp Child Kidnap Rumor." *IndiaAbroad.com.* July 15, 2018. https://www.indiaabroad.com/india/arrested-for-lynching-of-muslim-man-based-on-whatsapp-child/article_aa9e9d46-8860-11e8-bf4e-67ff98f581a6.html.

Angad, Abhishek. "Alwar Attack: Gau Rakshaks Killed a Dairy Farmer, Not Cattle Smuggler." *The Indian Express.* April 07, 2017. https://indianexpress.com/article/india/alwar-gau-rakshaks-killed-a-dairy-farmer-not-cattle-smuggler-4601434/.

Anshuman, Kuman."The Rise of the Communal Hate Soundtrack in India." *The Print.* April 6, 2018.

theprint.in/politics/the-rise-of-the-communal- hate-soundtrack
-in-india/476.

Anwar, Tarique. "Hindu Extremists Attack Mosque, Communal Clashes In 7 Districts In India'S Bihar". *The Dawn News.* March 29, 2018. http://www. thedawn-news.org/2018/03/30/hindu-extremists-attack-mosque-communal-clashes-in-7-districts-in-indias-bihar/

Apparasu, Rao."BJP's Raja Singh Booked for His Threat to Behead Those Opposing Ram Temple." *Hindustan Times.* April 10, 2017. https://www.hindustantimes. com/india-news/bjp-s-raja-singh-booked-for-threatening-to-behead-traitors-who-oppose-ram-temple/story-y7zwpStDdHyFL00NFNKL8I.html.

Aravind, Indulekha. "Social Media Engineering: How Congress & BJP's War Room Are Trying to Woo Voters in Karnataka." *The Economic Times.* March 25, 2018. https://economictimes. indiatimes.com/news/politics-and-nation/ social-media-engineering-how-congress-bjps-war-room-are-trying-to-woo-voters-in-karnataka/ articleshow/63445558.cms.

Arora, Kim. "Facebook post lists inter-faith couples, calls for attacks". *The Times of* India. February 6, 2018. https://timesofindia.indiatimes.com/india/ facebook-post-lists-inter-faith-couples-calls-for-attacks/articleshow/62796340.cms

Australian Human Rights Commission. "Examples of Racist Material on the Internet." December 14, 2012. Accessed October 20, 2018. https://www. humanrights.gov.au/publications/examples-racist-material-internet.

Ayyub, Rana. "Opinion: Bigotry And Islamophobia In Bhansali's "Padmaavat"." *NDTV.com.* February 06, 2018. https://www.ndtv.com/opinion/bigotry-and-Islamophobia-in-bhansalis-padmaavat-by-rana-ayyub-1808938.

Baber, Zaheer. "'Race', Religion and Riots: The 'Racialization' of Communal Identity and Conflict in India." *Sociology*, Volume 38. No. 4: 701-718. https://libproxy.berkeley.edu/ login?qurl=http%3a%2f%2fsearch.ebscohost. com%2flogin.aspx%3fdirect%3dtrue%26db%3dedsj sr%26AN%3dedsjsr.42858189%26site%3deds-live

Bajpai, Namita. "Meerut: Hindu activists beat up inter-faith couple". *The New Indian Express.* April 12, 2017. http://www.newindianexpress.com/nation/2017/

apr/12/meerut-hindu-activists-beat-up-inter-faith-couple-1592826.html

Banerjee, Anuradha, Firdaus Rizvi, Sukhadeo Thorat, and Vinod K Mishra. "Urban Rental Housing Market: Caste & Religion Matters in Access". *Economic & Political Weekly* 50, 26/27 (2015): 47-53. https://www.epw.in/journal/2015/26-27/housing-discrimination/urban-rental-housing-market.html

Basu, Amrita. *Violent Conjunctures in Democratic India.* Cambridge: Cambridge University Press, 2015.

BBC. "India Supreme Court restores 'love jihad' marriage". *BBC*, March 08, 2018. https://www.bbc.com/news/ world-asia-india-43327380

Bengali, Shashank. "Fake News Fuels Nationalism and Islamophobia - Sound Familiar? In This Case, It's in India." *Los Angeles Times*, July 11, 2017. www. latimes.com/world/asia/la-fg-india-fake-news-20170711-story.html

Bhan, Rohit. "'5,000-Strong Crowd Came with Pistols, Weapons': A Gujarat Village, Seared". *NDTV*, March 28, 2017. https://www.ndtv.com/india-news/day-before-riot-gujarat-village-split-sarpanchs-term-for-muslim-hindu-1674486

Bhandari, Aparita. "Review: Padmaavat Perpetuates Stereotypes and Carries a Dangerous Message." *The Globe and Mail.* January 30, 2018. https:// www.theglobeandmail.com/arts/film/film-reviews/ review-padmaavat-perpetuates-stereotypes-and-carries-a-dangerous-message/article37787050/.

Bhatia, Ishita. "Lawyers, Drivers, Students, Waiters, Kiosks in 'Love-jihad' Spy Network." *Times of India*, January 16, 2018. https://timesofindia. indiatimes.com/city/meerut/lawyers-drivers-students-waiters-kiosks-in-love-jihad-spy-network/ articleshow/62514200.cms

Bhatia, Ishita. "Right-Wing Men Assault Youth, Brothers in Court For 'Love Jihad'. *The Times of India.* January 15, 2018. https://timesofindia.indiatimes.com/city/ meerut/right-wing-men-assault-youth-brothers-in-court-for-love-jihad/articleshow/62498624.cms

Bhatia, Rahul. 2017. "The Year Of Love Jihad In India". The New Yorker, 2017. https://www.newyorker. com/culture/2017-in-review/the-year-of-love-jihad-in-india

Bhatia, Sidharth. "Without Punishment, Modi's Advice to BJP Motormouths Is Pointless." *The Wire.* April 23,

2018. https://thewire.in/politics/ Modi-bjp-motormouth-ministers.

Bhatnagar, Guarav V. "BJP, RSS Leaders Caught Using 'Love Jihad' Bogey to Fuel Communal Polarisation". *The Wire.* October 5, 2015. https://thewire.in/ communalism/bjp-rss-leaders-caught-using-love-jihad-bogey-to-fuel-communal-polarisation

Bhattacharya, Snigdhendu and Dipanjan Sinha,"How RSS Plans to Take over West Bengal: Social Media Campaign to New Members," *Hindustan Times.* May 26, 2017. www.hindustantimes. com/india-news/rise-of-rss-In-west-bengal-has-Rocked-mamata-banerjee-s-boat/story-f3zNciQeghSwMgOCsyOrSM.html.

Biswas, Tanima. "BJP Leader Sangeet Som's Links With Meat Export Firms Exposed by Documents." *NDTV. com.* October 10, 2015. https://www.ndtv.com/ india-news/documents-expose-bjp-leader-sangeet-soms-link-with-meat-export-firms-1230567.

"BJP Lawmakers Top List In Hate Speech Related Cases." Association for Democratic Reforms. Accessed June 3, 2018. https://adrindia.org/content/bjp-lawmakers-top-list-hate-speech-related-cases-adr-1

"BJP MLA Says Only Those Muslims Will Stay in India Who Embrace Hindu Culture." *The Indian Express.* January 14, 2018. https://indianexpress.com/ article/india/only-those-muslims-will-stay-in-india-who-assimilate-into-hindu-culture-bjp-mla-5024134/.

"BJP Removes Ghaziabad Unit Head Ajay Sharma over 'love Jihad' clash." *The Financial Express.* December 27, 2017. https://www.financialexpress. com/india-news/bjp-removes-ghaziabad-unit-head-ajay-sharma-over-love-jihad-clash/992122/.

Bose, Meghnad. "Beware: Fake News Fever in Karnataka as Assembly Polls Approach." *The Quint*, May 8, 2018. www.thequint.com/news/webqoof/fake-news-karnataka-assembly-election-2018-jihadi-murder.

"Brand India." IBEF: India Brand Equity Foundation. July 2018. Accessed August 29, 2018. https://www. ibef.org/exports/leather-industry-india.aspx.

Butalia, Urvashi. *The other side of silence: Voices from the partition of India.* India: Duke University Press, 2000.

Center for Study of Society and Secularism (CSSS). "A Narrowing Space: Violence and Discrimination Against India's Religious Minorities." Minority Rights Group International, 2017. http:// minorityrights.org/publications/narrowing-space-violence-discrimination-indias-religious-minorities/.

Chakrabortty, Aditya."Narendra Modi, a Man with a Massacre on His Hands, Is Not the Reasonable Choice for India | Aditya Chakrabortty." *The Guardian.* April 07, 2014. https://www.theguardian. com/commentisfree/2014/apr/07/narendra-modi-massacre-next-prime-minister-india.

Chatterji, Angana P, Shashi Buluswar and Mallika, Kaur eds. *Conflicted Democracies and Gendered Violence: Internal Conflict and Social Upheaval in India.* Berkeley: Zubaan, 2016.

Chatterji, Angana P. "Gendered and sexual violence in and beyond South Asia." *Antyajaa: Indian Journal of Women and Social Change* 1, no. 1 (2016): 19-40 https://doi.org/10.1177/2455632716646278

Chatterji, Angana P. *Violent gods: Hindu nationalism in India's present: Narratives from Orissa.* Gurgaon: Three Essays Collective, 2009.

Citizens for Justice and Peace. *Crime Against Humanity-An Inquiry into the Carnage in Gujarat Findings and Recommendations.* Report. Vol. II. Mumbai: Anil Dharkar, 2002.

"Cobrapost Sting: Big Media Houses Say Yes to Hindutva, Black Money, Paid News." *The Wire.* May 26, 2018. thewire.in/media/cobrapost-sting-big-media-houses -say-yes-To-hindutva-black-money-paid-news.

Cobrapost. "Operation Juliet: Busting the Bogey of "Love Jihad"". *Cobrapost.* 4 October, 2015. https://www. cobrapost.com/blog/operation-juliet-busting-the-bogey-of-love-jihad-2/900

Cunningham, Finian. "Steve Bannon Declares 'War Rooms' to Win European Elections – and That's Not Meddling?" *MintPress News.* September 25, 2018. https://www.mintpressnews.com/steve-bannon-declares-war-rooms-win-european-elections-thats-not-meddling/249823/.

Dabhade, Neha, and Suraj Nair. "Communal Riots: Heads Muslims 'Lose.' Tails They Are the

'Losers.'" *National Herald*. June 28, 2017. www. nationalheraldindia.com/minorities/csss-report-on-communal-violence-2016-muslims-found-to-be-worst-victims-of-both-rioting-and-subsequent-police-action.

Dabhade, Neha, and Suraj Nair. "Govt Data on Communal Violence Also Blacked Out." *National Herald*. June 28, 2017. www.nationalheraldindia.com/minorities/Use-of-social-media-trigger-communal-violence-marked-feature-in-2016-csss-study-government-blacks-out-data-after-may.

Dave, Hiral. "One Killed in Gujarat Village as Students Clash Sparks Communal Riot". *Hindustan Times*. March 26, 2017. https://www.hindustantimes.com/india-news/one-killed-in-gujarat-village-as-students-clash-sparks-communal-riot/story-TyoyOKiMXk2YsCFnfZbN1J.html

Dewan, Saba, Sanjay Kak, and Rahul Roy. "Facebook." Not In My Name. June 28, 2017. Accessed August 29, 2018. https://www.facebook.com/events/832175993606631.

Dhanrajani, Rachna. 2017. "Former Model Accuses Husband Of 'Love Jihad'". *The Hindu*. http://www.thehindu.com/news/cities/mumbai/former-model-accuses-husband-of-love-jihad/article20553502.ece.

Diwakar, Amar. "How "Cow Vigilantes" Launched India's Lynching Epidemic." *The New Republic*. July 26, 2017. https://newrepublic.com/article/144043/cow-vigilantes-launched-indias-lynching-epidemic.

Dixit, Neha. "A Chronicle of the Crime Fiction That Is Adityanath's Encounter Raj." *The Wire*. February 24, 2018. https://thewire.in/rights/chronicle-crime-fiction-adityanaths-encounter-raj.

Dua, Rohan. "VHP a militant religious organization outfit, RSS nationalist: CIA factbook". *Times of India*. June 15, 2018. https://timesofindia.indiatimes.com/india/vhp-a-militant-religious-outfit-rss-nationalist-cia-factbook/articleshow/64594295.cms?from=mdr

Dwarakanath, Nagarjun. "Gauri Lankesh's Murder Was Planned a Year Before: Exclusive Details." *India Today*. August 29, 2018. https://www.indiatoday.in/india/story/gauri-lankesh-s-murder-was-planned-a-year-before-exclusive-details-of-the-killing-1326868-2018-08-29.

Express News Service."Junaid Khan Lynching: 53-year-old Key Accused Granted Bail," *The Indian Express*. March 28, 2018. https://indianexpress.com/article/india/junaid-khan-lynching-53-year-old-key-accused-granted-bail-5115187/.

Express News Service. "Karnataka BJP MP Booked on Charges of Promoting Communal Enmity." *The Indian Express*, December 22, 2017. indianexpress.com/article/india/karnataka-bjp-mp-shobha-karandlaje-booked-on-charges-of-promoting-communal-enmity/.

Feyerick, Deborah. "Muslim DVD Rattles Voters in Key Battleground States." *CNN*. October 15, 2008. http://www.cnn.com/2008/US/10/14/muslim.dvd/index.html.

Financial Express Online. "Rajasthan Government Wants Students, Teachers to Learn About Love Jihad; Here Is How". *The Financial Express*. November, 19 2017. https://www.financialexpress.com/india-news/rajasthan-government-wants-students-teachers-to-learn-about-love-jihad-here-is-how/939167/

Froerer, Peggy. Emphasizing 'Others': The Emergence of Hindu Nationalism in a Central Indian Tribal Community, 2006. *Journal of the Royal Anthropological Institute*. Vol 12. Issue 1:39-59.

Gayer, Laurent, and Christophe Jaffrelot. *Muslims In Indian Cities*. London: Hurst & Company, 2012.

Ghosh, Deepshikha. "BJP Leader Arrested For Spreading Fake News, Says Bengal Police." *NDTV.com*. July 12, 2017. www.ndtv.com/india-news/bjp-leader-arrested-for-spreading-fake-news-says-bengal-police-1723673.

Gopalakrishnan, Raju."Indian Journalists Face Consequences If Critical of Modi's Administration." *The Christian Science Monitor*. April 26, 2018. https://www.csmonitor.com/World/Asia-South-Central/2018/0426/Indian-journalists-face-consequences-if-critical-of-Modi-s-administration.

Gowen, Annie. "India's Hindu right intensifies a religious battle over a demolished mosque". *The Washington Post*. 12 March, 2018. https://www.washingtonpost.com/world/asia_pacific/indias-hindu-right-intensifies-a-religious-battle-over-a-demolished-mosque/2018/03/11/7a35de6a-170b-11e8-930c-45838ad0d77a_story.html?noredirect=on&utm_term=.6aca6c9f69fb

Gupta, Charu. "Hindu women, Muslim men: Love Jihad and conversions." *Economic and Political Weekly* (2009): 13-15. https://www.jstor.org/stable/25663907

Gupta, Charu. "When Society Is Threatened by Love". *The Tribune,* 2014. http://www.academia.edu/10306613/When_Society_is_threatened_by_love

Gupta, Charu. *Allegories of 'love jihad' and ghar wapsi: interlocking the socio-religious with the political"* In *Rise of Saffron Power.* India: Routledge, 2018

Gupta, Nishtha. "The Curious Case of Modi and His Selective Tweets." *India Today.* May 25, 2018. www.indiatoday.in/india/story/the-curious-case-of-modi-and-his-selective-tweets-1241826-2018-05-25.

Halarnkar, Samar. "'Maybe It Is Time to Change My Son's Name': The New Reality of Being Muslim in India." *Scroll.in.* July 08, 2017. https://scroll.in/article/843074/maybe-it-is-time-to-change-my-sons-name-the-new-reality-of-being-muslim-in-india.

Haldevang, Max De. "Trump's Billionaire Backers Funded These Islamophobic Facebook Ads." *Quartz.* April 05, 2018. https://qz.com/1245777/trump-funder-robert-mercer-also-paid-for-islamophobic-facebook-and-google-ads/.

Hansen, Thomas Blom.*The Saffron Wave: Democracy and Hindu Nationalism in Modern India.* New Delhi: Oxford University Press, 2001.

"Hate Crime Laws - A Practical Guide." Women and Political Participation in Malta | OSCE. Accessed August 29, 2018. https://www.osce.orgodihr/36426?download=true%2C.

Hindustan Times. "Hate Tracker:" India's First National Database to Track Hate Crimes." *YouTube,* July 27, 2017. www.youtube.com/watch?time_continue=45&v=go0d8hmNQow.

Hindustan Times. "#LetsTalkAboutHate: Does Inciting Communal Hatred Pay in Politics?" *YouTube.* July 27, 2017. www.youtube.com/watch?v=J2I3bpoQM

Hindustan Times." #LetsTalkAboutHate: The Brutal Lynching of Mohammad Ikhlaq." *YouTube.* July 23, 2017. www.youtube.com/watch?v=0xQpRjTFVgk.

Hiral, Dave, "One Killed in Gujarat Village As Students Clash Sparks Communal Riot." *Hindustan Times.* 2017. https://www.hindustantimes.com/india-news/one-killed-in-gujarat-village-as-students-clash-sparks-communal-riot/story-TyoyOKiMXk2YsCFnfZbN1J.html.

"Home." *FactChecker.* May 27, 2018. p.factchecker.in.

Hossain, Sahel Md Delabul, Ladsaria Seema Kumari, Singh Rajni. "'Love-Jihad'; Protection of Religious Proximity an Indian Situation". *International Journal of Humanities and Cultural Studies* 2, 4 (2016). https://www.ijhcs.com/index.php/ijhcs/article/view/211

Human Rights Watch. "India: Government Critics Jailed and Harassed." *YouTube.* May 23, 2016. https://www.youtube.com/watch?time_continue=101.

Human Rights Watch "World Report 2018: Rights Trends in India". 2018. *Human Rights Watch.* https://www.hrw.org/world-report/2018/country-chapters/india.

Human Rights Watch. 2018. "India". *Human Rights Watch.* https://www.hrw.org/india.

Human Rights Watch. "Impunity in the Aftermath" 2002. July 1 2018. https://www.hrw.org/reports/2002/india/India0402-06.htm

Husain, Yusra. "Men in Lucknow at #Eid Namaz in Solidarity with Those Lynched #StopKillingMuslims #EidWithBlackBand. @TOIIndiaNews, pic. twitter.com/DbSlZvoVUF." *Twitter*, 26 June 2017, twitter.com/yusrahusainTOI/status/879182128726126593.

"India: 'Cow Protection' Spurs Vigilante Violence." *Human Rights Watch.* May 12, 2017. www.hrw.org/news/2017/04/27/india-cow-protection-spurs-vigilante-violence.

Indian Express. "For the Record: 'It Is Absolutely Unsafe to Let (24-Year-Old) Be Free To Do As She Likes.'" *Indian Express*, May 31, 2017. http://indianexpress.com/article/india/for-the-record-it-is-absolutely-unsafe-to-let-24-year-old-be-free-to-do-as-she-likes-4681708/.

Indian Express. "Hindu Yuva Vahini Harasses Interfaith

Couple in Meerut." *Indian Express,* April 12, 2017. https://indianexpress.com/article/india/hindu-yuva-vahini-harassed-a-interfaith-couple-in-meerut-4610464/

"India: Hate Crimes against Muslims and Rising Islamophobia Must Be Condemned." *Amnesty International.* June 28, 2017. www.amnesty.org/en/latest/news/2017/06/india-hate-crimes-against-muslims-and-rising-islamophobia-must-be-condemned/.

IndiaSpend. *Hate-Crime Database.* data.indiaspend.com/hate

India Today. 2018. "Hadiya's Marriage Restored, Supreme Court Says No Love Jihad". *India Today,* March 8, 2018. https://www.indiatoday.in/india/story/hadiya-s-marriage-to-shefin-stays-supreme-court-overturns-kerala-high-court-order-1184561-2018-03-08.

Jaffrelot, Christophe.*The Hindu Nationalist Movement and Indian Politics: 1925 to the 1990s: Strategies of Identity-Building, Implantation and Mobilisation.* London: Viking Penguin in Association with C. Hurst & Co.,1996.

Jain, Bharti. "Government Releases Data of Riot Victims Identifying Religion - Times of India." *The Times of India.* September 24, 2013. https://timesofindia.indiatimes.com/india/Government-releases-data-of-riot-victims-identifying-religion/articleshow/22998550.cms.

James, Luke. "EXCLUSIVE: EU Told to Scrap 'Islamophobic' Election Advert by British MEP." *Yahoo! Finance.* September 28, 2018. https://finance.yahoo.com/news/exclusive-eu-told-drop-islamophobic-election-advert-british-mep-113911379.html?_fsig=jMHhroSnCtExIt6Wfp0YIQ--

Jeelani, Gulam. "From Love Jihad, Conversion To SRK: 10 Controversial Comments by UP'S New CM Yogi Adityanath". *Hindustan Times.* April 6, 2017. https://www.hindustantimes.com/assembly-elections/from-love-jihad-conversion-to-srk-10-controversial-comments-by-up-s-new-cm-yogi-adityanath/story-5JW2ZFGZzAdIZeIcjcZCNM.html.

Jha, Dhirendra. "Attack on Mosque in India Ignites Fears of a Larger Communal Design". *Dawn,* August 20, 2015. https://www.dawn.com/news/1201687.

Khalid, Saif. "Taj Mahal Dropped from Tourism Booklet of Uttar Pradesh". *Aljazeera,* October 9, 2018. https://www.aljazeera.com/news/2017/10/taj-mahal-dropped-tourism-booklet-uttar-pradesh-171008161648332.html

Khalid, Saif. "The Hadiya Case and The Myth Of 'Love Jihad' In India". *Aljazeera.* August 24, 2017 https://www.aljazeera.com/indepth/features/2017/08/hadiya-case-myth-love-jihad-india-170823181612279.html

Khan, Yasmin. *The Great Partition: The Making of India and Pakistan.* North Yorkshire: Yale University Press, 2007.

Krishnan, Kavita. "SC Should Defend Women's Privacy, Autonomy, Not Perpetuate 'Love Jihad' Myth." *The Wire,* August 20, 2017. https://thewire.in/communalism/love-jihad-nia-probe-kerala-court.

Johari, Aarefa. "Why Has the Rajasthan Police Filed an FIR Against the Victims of the Alwar Lynching?" *Scroll.in.* April 07, 2017. https://scroll.in/article/833929/why-has-the-rajasthan-police-filed-an-fir-against-the-victims-of-the-alwar-lynching.

Juggernaut Books Blog. "#NotinOurName: Why You Should Support the #NotinMyName Protests." *The Lowdown.* June 28, 2017. http://blog.juggernaut.in/not-in-my-name/.

"Junaid Khan Lynching: 53-year-old Key Accused Granted Bail." *The Indian Express.* March 28, 2018. https://indianexpress.com/article/india/junaid-khan-lynching-53-year-old-key-accused-granted-bail-5115187/.

Kathuria, Charvi."Indian Female Journalists Battle Threats for Having Opinions." *SheThePeople TV.* June 15, 2018. https://www.shethepeople.tv/news/indian-Female-journalists-facing-online-threats.

Khalid, Saif. 2018. "Taj Mahal Dropped from Tourism Booklet of Uttar Pradesh". *Aljazeera.* https://www.aljazeera.com/news/2017/10/taj-mahal-dropped-tourism-booklet-uttar-pradesh-171008161648332.html.

Khalid, Saif. "The Hadiya Case and The Myth Of

'Love Jihad' In India". *Aljazeera*. August 24, 2017 https://www.aljazeera.com/indepth/features/2017/08/hadiya-case-myth-love-jihad-india-170823181612279.html

Khalid, Saif. "What is 'triple talaq' or instant divorce?" *Al Jazeera,* August 22, 2017. https://www.aljazeera.com/indepth/features/2017/05/tripple-talaq-triple-divorce-170511160557346.html

Khan, Mehz. Twitter Post, July 17, 2018. https://twitter.com/mehzkhan/status/1022067694953267202.

Khanna, Anahita. "Bill Seeking Death Penalty For Cow Slaughter Introduced In RS By Subramanian Swamy." *HuffPost India*. March 25 2017. www.huffingtonpost.in/2017/03/25/bill-seeking-death-penalty-for-cow-slaughter-introduced-in-rs-by_a_22011334/.

Krishnan, Kavita. 2017. "SC Should Defend Women's Privacy, Autonomy, Not Perpetuate 'Love Jihad' Myth." *The Wire*, August 20. https://thewire.in/communalism/love-jihad-nia-probe-kerala-court.

Krishnan, Murali. "Undeclared War: India's Muslims 'in Constant Fear' as Vigilante Murders Increase." *ABC News*. July 29, 2017. http://www.abc.net.au/news/2017-07-30/fear-growing-among-muslims-in-india/8751380.

Kumar, Chandna. "More Trouble for Shah Rukh Khan: Shia Community Offended by Raees Scene." *Hindustan Times*. December 15, 2016. https://www.hindustantimes.com/bollywood/more-trouble-for-shah-rukh-khan-shia-community-offended-by-raees-scene/story-noJIL997hd4udticwqCrnM.html.

Kumar, Nagothu Naresh. "Dissecting Hindutva: A Conversation with Jyotirmaya Sharma." Toynbee Prize Foundation. June 30, 2017. http://toynbeeprize.org/interviews/jyotirmaya-sharma/.

Kumar, Rahul. "Beef Exports From India Doubled Under Modi Government." Asian Independent. July 27, 2018. https://www.theasianindependent.co.uk/beef-exports-from-india-doubled-under-modi-government/.

Kumar, Sanjeev H.M. Metonymies of Fear: Islamophobia and the Making of Muslim Identity in Hindi Cinema, *Society and Culture in South Asia*, Volume 2, Issue:

2, July 1, 2016: 233-255.

Larkin, Barbara. Annual Report on International Religious Freedom 2000. Washington DC: Department of State, 2000 https://www.gpo.gov/fdsys/pkg/CPRT-106JPRT66723/pdf/CPRT-106JPRT66723.pdf

"Let's Talk about Hate: In Indian Politics, Candidates Who Stoke Communal Hatred Thrive." *Hindustan Times*. July 27, 2017. http://www.hindustantimes.com/india-news/let-s-talk-about-hate-does-stoking-communal-hatred-guarantee-electoral-victory-for-politicians-yes-says-data/story-VVmK9r6hG2xeoWQxlySUbP.html.

"Let's Talk About Hate: Kashmiri Students Face Verbal and Physical Abuse." *Hindustan Times*. July 2017.www.hindustantimes.com/videos/india-news/let-s-talk-about-hate-kashmiri-students-face-verbal-and-physical-abuse/video-NbRBhGvSfmPgZQg9vxLrmL.html.

Lumb, David. "Fake News on WhatsApp Is Inciting Lynchings in India." *Engadget*. July 03, 2018. https://www.engadget.com/2018/07/02/india-fake-news-whatsapp-groups/.

Mahanta, Siddhartha. 2014. "India's Fake 'Love Jihad'". *Foreign Policy*. https://foreignpolicy.com/2014/09/04/indias-fake-love-jihad/.

Mander, Harsh. "Pehlu Khan, One Year Later." *The Indian Express*. April 21, 2018. https://indianexpress.com/article/opinion/columns/pehlu-khan-rajasthan-cow-lynching-5145631/.

Mannathukkaren, Nissim. "The Fast Disappearing Muslim in the Indian Republic." *The Indian Express*. January 22, 2018, indianexpress.com/article/opinion/the-fast-disappearing-muslim-in-the-indian-republic-bjp-mla-hindu-saffron-religion-5034205/.

Mashkoor, Muhammed. "The Number Question: Muslim Demography and Islamophobia in India". *Islam And Muslim Societies: A Social Science Journal* 11, 11 (2018) 32-39.

Masih, Niha. "HT Hate Tracker: A National Database on Crimes in the Name of Religion, Caste,

Race." *Hindustan Times*. July 28, 2017. www.hindustantimes.com/india-news/ht-hate- tracker-a-national-database-on-crimes-in-the-name-of-religion-caste-race/story-xj2o03dKF9PsW4IYIEvdgI.html.

Menon, Kalyani D. "'Security', Home, And Belonging in Contemporary India: Old Delhi As A Muslim Place". *Etnofoor* 27, 2 (2015): 113-131. https://www.jstor.org/stable/43656022

Menon, Shruti. "Behind Rajasthan Killing, Mistaken Identity, 'Love Jihad' Lie, Hate Clips." *NDTV*, December 26, 2017. https://www.ndtv.com/india-news/behind-rajasthan-killing-mistaken-identity-love-jihad-lie-hate-videos-1792369.

Ministry of Home Affairs. "Revised Guidelines of 'Central Scheme for Assistance to Civilians Victims/Family of Victims of Terrorist, Communal and Naxal Violence'. (n.d). July 1, 2018 https://mha.gov.in/sites/default/files/T-Guide141008_0.pdf

Ministry of Home Affairs. "RGI releases Census 2011 data on population by religious communities". 2015. http://pib.nic.in/newsite/PrintRelease.aspx?relid=126326

Minority Rights Group. "Muslims - India". 2018 http://minorityrights.org/minorities/muslims-2/.

Minority Rights Group. Oral Statement Minority Rights Group Human Rights Council. 36th session. "MRG, Citizens Against Hate and People's Watch Reacts to the UPR of India." September 21, 2017. minorityrights.org/advocacy-statements/mrg-citizens-hate-peoples-watch-reacts-upr-india/.

Mirchandani, Maya, Ojasvi Goel, and Dhananjay Sahai. "Encouraging Counter-Speech by Mapping the Contours of Hate Speech on Social Media in India." *Observer Research Foundation*. August 29, 2018. https://www.orfonline.org/wp-content/uploads/2018/03/ORF_Report_Counter_Speech.pdf.

Mishra, Gourav. "Love Jihad Incidents In 2017 Which Went Beyond Religion to Alleged Terrorist Links". *International Business Times India Edition*. December 30, 2017. https://www.ibtimes.co.in/love-jihad-incidents-2017-which-went-beyond-religion-alleged-terrorist-links-754996

Mishra, Ishita. "Pro-BJP or Anti-BJP: Inside the Modi-Shah Media Tracking 'War Rooms'." *The Wire*. August 11, 2018. https://thewire.in/politics/narendra-modi-amit-shah-bjp-india-media.

Mishra, Ishita. "VHP Sacks Man Behind 'Beti Bachao, Bahu Lao' Campaign" *The Times of India*. 2015. https://timesofindia.indiatimes.com/india/VHP-sacks-man-behind-Beti-bachao-Bahu-Lao-campaign/articleshow/48181480.cms.

'Muslims Should Not Live in This Country,' Says BJP MP Vinay Katiyar." *Scroll.in*. February 7, 2018. scroll.in/latest/867827/muslims-should-not-live-in-this-country-says-bjp-mp-vinay-katiyar

"Narendra Modi's Image Factory." *The Economist*, August 09, 2018, www.economist.com/asia/2018/08/09/narendra-modis-image-factory.

Nazir, Hishma Tanseema. "Raising a Unified Voice against Hate." *The Hindu*. November 20, 2017. https://www.thehindu.com/todays-paper/tp-national/tp-newdelhi/raising-a-unified-voice-against-hate/article20608003.ece.

NDTV. "3D Avatar of Modi to Campaign in Delhi's Streets." *YouTube*. November 14, 2013. https://www.youtube.com/watch?v=6cSREmEMOX0.

NDTV. "BJP's Yogi Adityanath Praises Trump Ban, Compares Western UP To Kashmir." *YouTube*. January 31, 2017. www.youtube.com/watch?v=UPZ4QIX0Yb0.

NDTV. "'Black Eid' In Junaid's Village: India Shifting To 'Mobocracy?" *YouTube*. June 26, 2017. https://www.youtube.com/watch?v=W7mxH2vwBo4.

NDTV. "Government's 'Pink Revolution' Destroying Cattle, Says Narendra Modi." *YouTube*. April 02, 2014. https://www.youtube.com/watch?v=1ElnjqtBbuc.

NDTV. "NDTV Hidden Camera Investigation: Justice Lynched?" *YouTube*. August 6, 2018. www.youtube.com/watch?v=cL9-7LzBK_8.

NDTV. "'Love Jihad' And Religious Conversions in Uttar Pradesh". 2014. https://www.ndtv.com/india-news/love-jihad-and-religious-conversions-in-uttar-pradesh-659439.

Nelson, Dean."'Magic' Modi Uses Hologram to Address

Dozens of Rallies at Once." *The Telegraph.* May 02, 2014. https://www.telegraph.co.uk/news/worldnews/asia/india/10803961/Magic-Modi-uses-hologram-to-address-dozens-of-rallies-at-once.html.

NewsClickin. "A Year On, Pehlu Khan's Murderers Still Not Convicted." *YouTube.* April 04, 2018. https://www.youtube.com/watch?time_continue=250&v=ErOz-LQEvu8.

New Indian Express. "College students stage protest demanding freedom for Hadiya" *New Indian Express,* September 16, 2017. http://www.newindianexpress.com/states/kerala/2017/sep/16/college-students-stage-protest-demanding-freedom-for-hadiya-1657906.html

Oboler, Andre. *Islamophobia in Cyberspace: Hate Crimes Go Viral.* By Imran Awan. Surrey:Ashgate, 2016. 41-63.

Om Prakash v. State of Jharkhand (2012) 12 SCC 72. http://www.supremecourtcases.com/index2.php?option=com_content&itemid=99999999&do_pdf=1&id=43052.

OSCE and ODIHR. *Hate Crimes A Practical Guide.* 2009. https://www.osce.org/odihr/36426?download=true.

Outlook Magazine. "Hindu Sena Protests against Rohingya Muslims at Jantar Mantar." *YouTube.* September 11, 2017. https://www.youtube.com/watch?v=J3A7bqAr0Io.

Outlook Web Bureau. "Protests in JNU against Screening of film on Love Jihad". *Outlook Magazine,* April 28, 2018. https://www.outlookindia.com/website/story/protests-in-jnu-against-screening-of-film-on-love-jihad/311446

"Outrage over Slaughter of a Cow vs a Human – an Analysis of 100 BJP Leaders Active on Social Media." *Alt News.* May 31, 2017. https://www.altnews.in/outrage-slaughter-cow-vs-human-analysis-100-bjp-leaders-active-social-media/.

"Padmaavat: Why a Bollywood Epic Has Sparked Fierce Protests." *BBC News.* January 25, 2018. https://www.bbc.com/news/world-asia-india-42048512.

Pandey, Sidharth. "UP Elections 2017: BJP Promised Anti-Romeo Squads to Stop Love Jihad, says Its Meerut Leader". *NDTV.* February 05, 2017. https://www.ndtv.com/india-news/up-elections-2017-bjp-promised-anti-romeo-squads-to-stop-love-jihad-says-its-meerut-leader-1656250

Pepper Smoker. Twitter Post, July 23, 2018. https://twitter.com/pepper_smoker/status/1021336758468964352.

"PM Modi Hits Back at Aiyar's 'neech' Remark, Says This Is Mughlai Mindset." *The Times of India.* December 07, 2017. https://timesofindia.indiatimes.com/india/pm-modi-hits-back-at-aiyars-neech-remark-says-this-is-mughlai-mindset/articleshow/61963820.cms?utm_source=contentofinterest&utm_medium=text&utm_campaign=cppst.

Poovana, Sharan. "Right-Wing Outfits Campaign in Karnataka Against 'Love Jihad'". *Livemint.* January 04, 2018. https://www.livemint.com/Politics/T4DS9yZjZVOIDSH4xHTc1M/Rightwing-outfits-campaign-in-Karnataka-against-love-jihad.html..

"Population Census 2011." Religion Data - Population of Hindu / Muslim / Sikh / Christian. March 31, 2011. http://www.census2011.co.in/.

Post-Sachar Evaluation Committee. "Post-Sachar Evaluation Committee Report". September. 2014 http://iosworld.org/download/Post_Sachar_Evaluation_Committee.pdf

Press Trust of India."BJP Legislator Sees Muslim Conspiracy To Take Over India By 2030." *NDTV. com.* January 01, 2018. https://www.ndtv.com/india-news/muslim-population-growth-puts-existence-of-hindus-in-danger-bjp-mla-1794559.

Press Trust of India. "Delhi BJP Leader Shared Gujarat Riots Photo As From Bengal." *NDTV.com.* July 10, 2017. www.ndtv.com/delhi-news/delhi-bjp-leader-denounced-on-twitter-for-sharing-gujarat-riots-photo-as-bengals-1722698.

Press Trust of India. "Expecting 30-35% From Minorities Will Vote For BJP In 2019": Minister." *NDTV.com.* July 08, 2018. https://www.ndtv.com/india-news/mukhtar-abbas-naqvi-says-oppositions-fear-mongering-campaign-has-been-demolished-by-modi-government-1879754.

Press Trust of India."Rohingyas a Security Threat, Deport

Them: RSS." *The Indian Express*. May 03, 2018. indianexpress.com/article/india/rohingyas -a-security-threat-deport-them-rss-5101212/.

Press Trust of India. "Uttar Pradesh Tops the List of Communal Violence Hit States in 2017, Says Government." *The Indian Express*. March 14, 2018. indianexpress.com/article/india/uttar-pradesh-tops-the-list-of-communal-violence-hit-states-in-2017-says-government-5097651/.

Puniyani, Ram. "India and Hindu Muslim Unity." TEDxTalks. *YouTube*, 22 May 2018, www.youtube.com/watch?v=_nj7x5N5pA8.

Rachna Dhanrajani, "Former Model Accuses Husband Of 'Love Jihad'", *The Hindu*. November 18, 2017, http://www.thehindu.com/news/cities/mumbai/former-model-accuses-husband-of-love-jihad/article20553502.ece.

Rai, Arpan. "No Namaz, No Salaam: Muslims in Modern India Forced to Self-Censor." *The Quint*. July 27, 2018. https://www.thequint.com/videos/indian-muslims -twitter-on-lynchings-bigotry-and-hate.

Rajamani, Rajesh. "The Savarna Redemption: Why 'Not In My Name' Campaign Is a Part of the Problem." *The News Minute*. June 28, 2017. https://www.thenewsminute.com/article/savarna-redemption-why-not-my-name-campaign-part-problem-64288

"Rajasthan Police Deliberately Weakened Pehlu Khan Lynching Case, Says Independent Fact-finding Team." *Scroll.in*. October 27, 2017. https://scroll.in/latest/855578/rajasthan-police-deliberately-weakened-pehlu-khan-lynching-case-says-independent-fact-finding-team.

Raj, Suhasini, and Najar, Nida. "Hindu Group Claims Christians Tried Forced Conversions in India." *New York Times*, April 8, 2017. https://www.nytimes.com/2017/04/08/world/asia/india-uttar-pradesh-hindu-christian-church-conversions.html.

Rao, Hitender. "Immigrants from India Increasing at US-Mexico Border." *VOA*. August 20, 2018. https://www.voanews.com/a/immigrants-india-Us-mexico-border/4533007.html.

Rao, Mohan. "Love Jihad and demographic fears." *Indian Journal of Gender Studies* 18, 3 (2011): 425-430. https://doi.org/10.1177%2F097152151101800307

Rao, Smitha."Saffronisation of the Holy Cow: Unearthing Silent Communalism." *Economic and Political Weekly*. Vol. 46, No. 15, 2011: 80–87. JSTOR. www.jstor.org/stable/41152321.

Reuters. "Aggressive Variant Of McCarthyism vs Media, Says Prannoy Roy." *NDTV.com*. April 26, 2018. https://www.ndtv.com/india-news/india-falls-in-world-press-freedom-index-prannoy-roy-says-aggressive-variant-of-mccarthyism-vs-media-1843406

Riin. Twitter Post, July 23, 2018. https://twitter.com/hiei900/status/1021434569726148608.

Ritesh, Mishra. "40,000 cows saved since 2009 in Madhya Pradesh, claims VHP." *Hindustan Times*, July 28, 2016. EBSCO*host* (accessed March 30, 2018).

RSF. "Our Activities | Reporters without Borders." April 05, 2018. Accessed September 14, 2018. https://rsf.org/en/our-activities.

"RSF Index 2018: Hatred of Journalism Threatens Democracies." April 26, 2018. rsf.org/en/rsf-index-2018-hatred-journalism-threatens-democracies.

"RSF Issues Warning to India in First World Press Freedom Index Incident Report." *Reporters Without Borders For Freedom of Information*, July 4, 2018. https://rsf.org/en/news/rsf-issues-warning-india-first-world-press-freedom-index-incident-report

Saberin, Zeenat."The Perils of Being a Journalist in Modi's India." *Al Jazeera*. June 14, 2018. https://www.aljazeera.com/indepth/features/perils-journalist-modis-india-180614103115577.html.

Sachar, Rajindar. "Report on Social, Economic and Educational Status of The Muslim Community Of India." Ministry of Minority Affairs. 2006. http://minorityaffairs.gov.in/reports/sachar-committee-report

Safi, Michael. "Cow Slaughter to Be Punishable by Life Sentence in Gujarat." *The Guardian*. March 2017. www.theguardian.com/world/2017/mar/14/indian-State-government-life-sentence-cow-slaughter.

Said, Edward W. *Covering Islam*. Random House, 1997.

Said, Edward W. *Orientalism*. Vintage Books, 2003.

Saldanha, Alison. "99.38% Indians Now Live In Areas

Under Cow-Protection Laws." *IndiaSpend*. April 15, 2017. http://www.indiaspend.com/cover-story/99-38-indians-now-live-in-areas-under-cow-protection-laws-42787.

Sarkar, Sumit. "Indian Nationalism and the Politics of Hindutva," In Contesting the Nation: Religion, Community and the Politics of Democracy in India. Edited by Steve E. Ludden. Pennsylvania: University of Pennsylvania Press, 1996.

Saxena, Anmol. "India: more than half of undertrials are Dalits, Muslims and tribals", *Al-Jazeera*. November 1 2016, https://www.aljazeera.com/blogs/asia/2016/11/trial-india-dalits-muslims-tribals-161101150136542.html

Sayyid, S. "A Measure of Islamophobia."*Islamophobia Studies Journal*. Vol. 2. No. 1. 2014. doi:10.18411/d-2016-154.

Scroll Staff. "Beed: Storm over Video Purporting to Show Police Officer Saying She Files False Cases against Dalits." *Scroll.in*. December 2, 2018. scroll.in/latest/904259/beed-video-of-police-officer-saying-she-targets-dalits-muslims-with-false-cases-goes-viral.

Scroll Staff. "'Mobocracy Cannot Be Allowed': Supreme Court Recommends New Law against Lynching," *Scroll.in*. September 12, 2018. https://scroll.in/latest/886846/mobocracy-cannot-be-allowed-supreme-court-recommends-new-law-against-lynching.

Sethi, Aman. "'Love Jihad' in India and One Man's Quest to Prevent It". *The Guardian*. January 29, 2015. https://www.theguardian.com/world/2015/jan/29/love-jihad-india-one-man-quest-prevent-it

Shaheen, Jack G. "Reel Bad Arabs: How Hollywood Vilifies a People." *The Annals of the American Academy of Political and Social Science*. Vol 588. 2003:171-93. http://www.jstor.org.libproxy.berkeley.edu/stable/1049860.

Shamshir_Gaya. Twitter Post, July 23, 2018. https://twitter.com/shamshir_gaya/status/1021339625779023872,

Shamshir_Gaya. Twitter Post. July 23, 2018. https://twitter.com/shamshir_gaya/status/1021343424530837504,

Shamshir_Gaya. Twitter Post. July 23, 2018. https://twitter.com/shamshir_gaya/status/1021339080343375873,

Sharma, Betwa. "Meet The UP Businessman Giving Lok Sabha Tickets To Hindus Who Have Lynched Muslims." *HuffPost India*. October 2, 2018, www.huffingtonpost.in/2018/09/30/meet-the-up-businessman-giving-lok-sabha-tickets-to-hindus-who-have-lynched-muslims_a_23546403/.

Sharma, Jyotirmaya. *Hindutva: exploring the idea of Hindu nationalism*. New Delhi: Penguin Books India, 2011

Sharma Saurabh. 2018. "A Year After Lynching Of Man In Bulandshahr Over 'Love Jihad' Issue, Victim's Family Members Live Like Refugees." *Firstpost*, June 7. https://www.firstpost.com/india/a-year-after-lynching-of-man-in-bulandshahr-over-love-jihad-issue-victims-family-members-live-like-refugees-4501227.html.

Shukla, Nelanshu."Muslim Community Should Abstain from Touching Cows, Provoking Hindus: BJP Leader on Alwar Lynching." *India Today*. July 23, 2018. https://www.indiatoday.in/india/story/muslim-community-should-abstain-from-touching-cows-provoking-hindus-bjp-leader-on-alwar-lynching-1294041-2018-07-23.

Siasat Hyderabad."Was Lord Ram Born on Babri Masjid Land? Prof Ram Puniyani Explains Conspiracy."*YouTube*, December 6, 2017. www.youtube.com/watch?v=kCuzRbrm_6k

Siddique, Mohammad. "Five Accused in India Mosque Blast Acquitted". *Gulfnews*. April 16, 2018. https://gulfnews.com/news/asia/india/five-accused-in-india-mosque-blast-acquitted-1.2206499

Silva, Chantal Da."Nearly Half of All Immigrants Detained in Federal Prison Are Indian Asylum Seekers." *Newsweek*. August 14, 2018. https://www.newsweek.com/growing-number-asylum-seekers-india-showing-us-mexico-border-1072329.

Singh, Giriraj. "Muslims Threat to Social Harmony, Development: Union Minister Giriraj Singh." *DNA*. January 03, 2018. https://www.dnaindia.com/india/report-muslims-threat-to-social-harmony-development-union-minister-giriraj-singh-2572543.

Singh, Vijaita. "No conversion money seen in 'love jihad' cases: NIA". *The Hindu.* November 2, 2017. https://www.thehindu.com/news/national/no-conversion-for-money-seen-in-love-jihad-cases-nia/article19966254.ece

Siyedh, Mohammed Sinan. "India's Rohingya Terror Problem: Real or Imagined?" *South Asian Voices.* February, 9, 2018. http://southasianvoices.org/indias-rohingya-terror-problem-real-imag.

Smith Candace and Liz Kreutz. "Hillary Clinton's and Donald Trump's Campaigns by the Numbers." *ABC News.* November 07, 2016. https://abcnews.go.com/Politics/hillary-clinton-donald-trumps-campaigns-numbers/story?id=43356783.

Special Report. "In Modi's India, Cow Vigilantes Deny Muslim Farmers Their Livelihood." *Reuters.* November 6, 2017. www.reuters.com/investigates/special-report/india-Politics-Religion-cows/.

"Special Squad. Police Patrolling Every 24 Hours To Prevent Slaughter: Uttarakhand HC Issues Directions For "Welfare" of Cows & Other Stray Cattle." *Live Law.* August 14, 2018. https://www.livelaw.in/special-squad-police-patrolling-every-24-hours-to-prevent-slaughter-uttarakhand-hc-issues-directions-for-welfare-of-cows-other-stray-cattle-read-judgment/.

Sreenivasan Jain, et al. "Rohingyas A Terror Threat? NDTV Finds Little Evidence Of Government Claim." *NDTV.* September 16, 2017. www.ndtv.com/india-news/rohingyas-a-terror-threat-ndtv-finds-little-evidence-of-government-claim-1751114.

Srivastava, Piyush. "Dharm Jagran Samiti Leader Vows to Create Hindu Rashtra by 2021". *India Today.* December 19, 2014. https://www.indiatoday.in/india/story/dharm-jagran-samiti-leader-vows-to-create-hindu-rashtra-by-2021-231854-2014-12-19

"States Where Cow Slaughter Is Banned So Far, and States Where It Isn't." *News18.* May 26, 2017. www.news18.com/news/india/states-where-cow-slaughter-is-banned-so-far-And-states-where-it-isnt-1413425.html.

Stevens, Harr. "Let's Talk about Hate: In Indian Politics, Candidates Who Stoke Communal Hatred Thrive." *Hindustan Times.* July 2017. www.hindustantimes.com/india-news/let-s-talk-about-hate-does-stoking-communal-hatred-guarantee-electoral-victory-for-politicians-yes-says-data/story-

VVmK9r6hG2xeoWQxlySUbP.html.

Suraiya, Jug. "The Meaning of the Silence of Prime Minister Modi." *Times of India Blog*, April 14, 2018 blogs.timesofindia.indiatimes.com/jugglebandhi/the-meaning-of-the-silence-of-prime-minister-modi/.

Suresh, Appu E. "Love Jihad: UP's forbidden couples". *Hindustan Times.* October 19 2016. https://www.hindustantimes.com/static/uttar-pradesh-communal-riot/love-jihad-uttar-pradesh/

Susewind, Raphael. "Muslims in Indian cities: Degrees of segregation and the elusive ghetto." *Environment and Planning A* 49, 6 (2017): 1286-1307. https://doi.org/10.1177/0308518X17696071

Swain, Ashok. "Rohingya Refugees: India Should Not Pass The Buck To Muslim World By Adopting A False And Blinkered Narrative." *OutlookIndia.com.* September 9. 2017.www.outlookindia.com/website/story/rohingya-refugees-india-should-not-pass-the-Buck-to-muslim-world-by-adopting-a-f/301498

Talbot, Ian; Singh, Gurharpal. *The Partition of India.* Cambridge University Press: United Kingdom, 2009.

Teitelbaum, Benjamin R. Saga's Sorrow: Femininities in Despair in the Music of Radical Nationalism. *Ethnomusicology*, Vol. 58, No. 3, Fall 2014. 405-430.

"The Constitution Of India 1949." *Article 15(4) in The Constitution Of India 1949*, indiankanoon.org/doc/237570/.

The Financial Express, "Rajasthan Government Wants Students, Teachers To Learn About Love Jihad; Here Is How". 2017. The Financial Express. https://www.financialexpress.com/india-news/rajasthan-government-wants-students-teachers-to-learn-about-love-jihad-here-is-how/939167/.

The Hindu. "VHP's social service activities". *The Hindu,* December 18, 2011. https://www.thehindu.com/todays-paper/tp-national/tp-kerala/vhps-social-service-activities/article2725683.ece

The Quint. "BJP MLA Sangeet Som Calls Taj Mahal 'a Blot on History.' *YouTube.* October 16, 2017. www.youtube.com/watch?=NHOJ-MPP5Jo.

The Quint. "Communal Violence Spikes in 2017. UP

Records Most Number of Riots." February 7, 2018. www.thequint.com/news /india/communal-violence-spikes-in-.

The Quint. "Junaid's Last Moments - The Train Journey That Killed Him." *YouTube*. July 13, 2017. https://www.youtube.com/watch?v=g3zC4kZ614U.

The Quint. "Silence on Mob Lynchings Broken at #NotInMyName Protest." *YouTube*. June 28, 2017. https://www.youtube.com/watch?v=ywQBloQAxWQ.

The Quint. "Three Muslim Clerics Allegedly Attacked on a Moving Train in U.P.," *YouTube*. November 24, 2017. https://www.youtube.com/watch?v=VBLME8z1N6U.

The Quint. "We Are Scared & Angry": Khandawli Villagers After Junaid's Death." *YouTube*, June 28, 2017. https://www.youtube.com/watch?v=PnqLLEvRAKM

The Representation of the People Act, 1951. http://www.legislative.gov.in/sites/default/files/04_representation%20of%20the%20people%20act%2C%201951.pdf

The Telegraph. "SC Refuses Damages for Shrines." *The Telegraph*, August 30, 2017. https://www.telegraphindia.com/1170830/jsp/nation/story_169903.jsp.

The Wire Staff. "Hindutva's 'Love Jihad' Obsession Leads to Murder of Muslim Man in UP". *The Wire*. May 3, 2017. https://thewire.in/politics/hindutvas-love-jihad-obsession-leads-to-murder-of-muslim-man-in-up

"The World Factbook." Central Intelligence Agency. November 30, 2010. http://www.cia.gov/library/publications/resources/the-world-factbook/geos/in.html.

The World Bank Group. "The World Bank in India Overview". 2018 https://www.worldbank.org/en/country/india/overview

Times of India. "'Love Jihad' Case: SC Sets Aside Kerala High Court Order That Annulled Hadiya's Marriage."*Times of India*, March 8, 2018. https://timesofindia.indiatimes.com/india/kerala-love-jihad-case-sc-sets-aside-kerala-hc-order-that-annulled-hadiyas-marriage/articleshow/63215330.cms.

Times of India. "In Numbers: The Rise of BJP and decline of Congress". *Times of India*. May 19, 2016. https://timesofindia.indiatimes.com/india/In-Numbers-The-Rise-of-BJP-and-decline-of-Congress/articleshow/52341190.cms?

Times Now Digital. "Rajasthan Hacking: Accused Made 'Love Jihad' Claim to Cover His Affair With 'Hindu Sister', Say Police". Jan 15, 2018. *Times Now News*. http://www.timesnownews.com/india/article/rajsamand-hate-crime-accused-shambhu-lal-regar-killed-afrazul-khan-love-jihad-claims-to-hide-illicit-relationship-rajasthan/189165

TNN & Agencies. "Union Minister Jayant Sinha Garlands 8 Lynching Convicts, Faces Opposition Flak India." *The Times of India*. July 07, 2018. https://timesofindia.indiatimes.com/india/union-minister-jayant-sinha-garlands-8-lynching-convicts-faces-opposition-flak/articleshow/64901863.cms.

Törnberg Anton and Petter."Muslims in Social Media Discourse: Combining Topic Modeling and Critical Discourse Analysis." *Discourse, Context and Media*. Vol 13. 2016: 132–142.

Tripathi, R., 'Faith accompli', IndiaToday, 18 December 2014.

United States Commission on International Religious Freedom. 2016. "2016 Annual Report". Washington DC: United States Commission on International Religious Freedom. http://www.uscirf.gov/reports-briefs/annual-report/2016-annual-report

"Union Minister Jayant Sinha Garlands 8 Convicted for Ramgarh Mob Lynching." *India Today*. https://www.indiatoday.in/india/story/union-minister-jayant-sinha-garlands-8-convicted-for-ramgarh-mob-lynching-1279601-2018-07-06.

United States Commission on International Religious Freedom. "2018 Annual Report". Washington DC: United States Commission on International Religious Freedom. 2018. http://www.uscirf.gov/sites/default/files/2018USCIRFAR.pdf

United States Commission on International Religious Freedom. "2017 Annual Report". Washington DC: United States Commission on International Religious Freedom, 2017. http://www.uscirf.gov/

sites/default/files/2017.USCIRFAnnualReport.pdf

United States Commission on International Religious Freedom. "2016 Annual Report". Washington DC: United States Commission on International Religious Freedom. 2016. http://www.uscirf.gov/reports-briefs/annual-report/2016-annual-report

United States Commission on International Religious Freedom. "2015 Annual Report". Washington DC: United States Commission on International Religious Freedom. 2015. http://www.uscirf.gov/sites/default/files/India%202015.pdf.

United States Department of State. "International Religious Freedom Report for 2014 – India". Bureau of Democracy, Human Rights and Labor. 2014. http://www.state.gov/j/drl/rls/irf/religiousfreedom/index.htm?year=2014&dlid=238494

Unstarred Question 534."Stand of Government on Rohingyas." Government of India Ministry of Home Affairs. December 20, 2017. https://mha.gov.in/MHA1/Par2017/pdfs/par2017-pdfs/rs-20122017/534.pdf.

"U.P: BJP MLA Sangeet Som Booked For Showing Anti-Muslim Documentary." Telugu Global. www.bing.comcr?IG=C80218B76E474AD7BD3B851CA1508AB6&CID=2E15FC2213726494383FF022128F65BD&rd=1&h=PqvGLt8h1iDPewqloTUH1yfEhURDODnK2Dq8_5XCl-E&v=1&r=https%3a%2f%2fwww.teluguglobal.in%2fu-p-bjp-mla-sangeet-som-booked-for-showing-anti-muslim-documentary%2f&p=DevEx.LB.1,5311.1

"US Court Dismisses Lawsuit against India's Narendra Modi." BBC News, BBC, 15 Jan. 2015, www.bbc.com/news/world-asia-india-30826044.

Vaishnav, Milan. "Understanding the Indian Voter." Carnegie Endowment for International Peace, 23 June 2015,carnegieendowment.org/2015/06/23/understanding-indian-voter-pub-60416.

Venkataramakrishnan, Rohan. 2014. "A Brief History of Love Jihad, From Jodhaa Akbar to the Meerut Gang-Rape". Scroll.In. https://scroll.in/article/674314/a-brief-history-of-love-jihad-from-jodhaa-akbar-to-the-meerut-gang-rape.

VHP. "Swagatam". 2010. 1 August 2018. http://vhp.org/swagatam/.

Wacquant, Loïc. Urban Outcasts: A Comparative Sociology of Advanced Marginality. Oxford: Wiley, 2008.

Waikar, Prashant. "Reading Islamophobia In Hindutva: An Analysis Of Narendra Modi's Political Discourse". Islamophobia Studies Journal 4 no. 2 (2018) Forthcoming.

"We Are Scared & Angry": Khandawli Villagers After Junaid's Death." YouTube. June 28, 2017. https://www.youtube.com/watch?v=PnqLLEvRAKM.

"Why Has the Rajasthan Police Filed an FIR Against the Victims of the Alwar Lynching?" Scroll.in, April 07, 2017. https://scroll.in/article/833929/why-has-the-rajasthan-police-filed-an-fir-against-the-victims-of-the-alwar-lynching.

World Population Review. "India Population 2018". 2018. http://worldpopulationreview.com/countries/india-population/

Wu, Huizhong. "Indian Muslims Are Hashtagging This Holiday #BlackEid." CNN. June 28, 2017. https://www.cnn.com/2017/06/26/asia/black-eid-india-muslim/index.html.

Younus. "Kerala: NIA finds only 11 out of 89 'love-jihad' cases to be true". The Siasat Daily. 9 March, 2018. https://www.siasat.com/news/kerala-nia-finds-only-11-out-89-love-jihad-cases-be-true-1327711/